Tableau®

2nd Edition

by Jack Hyman

Tableau® For Dummies®, 2nd Edition

Published by: **John Wiley & Sons, Inc.,** 111 River Street, Hoboken, NJ 07030-5774, www.wiley.com

Copyright © 2023 by John Wiley & Sons, Inc., Hoboken, New Jersey

Published simultaneously in Canada

Library of Congress Control Number: 2023937361

ISBN: 978-1-119-68458-9 (pbk)

ISBN 978-1-119-68462-6 (ebk); ISBN 978-1-119-68459-6 (ebk)

SKY10071174_032924

Contents at a Glance

Table of Contents

Introduction

Maybe you've picked up this book because you want to know about business intelligence and data analytics from the perspective of an enterprise vendor. Or perhaps you want to get into the proverbial weeds of learning how to use an enterprise-class business intelligence platform to tell stories using data visualization techniques. As you read *Tableau For Dummies,* 2nd Edition, you may just develop a zest for both.

Tableau is a French word that means to present a graphic description or a representation, which may include artistic groupings, arrangements, or scenes. Translating this idea into the technology platform, the Tableau platform allows users to take their datasets and create competing data visualizations, reports, and key performance indicators (KPIs) to help tell a story.

Tableau For Dummies, 2nd Edition, offers a look at all the versions of Tableau, but the central focus is on working with Tableau Desktop, Tableau Prep, and Tableau Cloud. Whether you are a novice learning how to create robust data solutions, an analyst looking to explore your datasets, or an end user wanting to consume a story told by Tableau through data visualizations, this book will give you a great start on working with Tableau.

About This Book

If you purchased this book from an online website such as Amazon or Barnes & Noble, it may interest you to know that these retailers use data analytics tools, including Tableau, to evaluate user behavior and customer purchasing patterns. Deciding to buy this book instead of the 250+ other books and counting on Tableau authored over the past five years may be the result of a pervasive pattern. Or perhaps it comes down to what retail market you live in when searching for this book. Ah, the beauty of big data!

In this Tableau primer, you find out how to use Tableau to delve into various questions and scenarios. Examples in this book use publicly accessible datasets found on the website Kaggle.com, an open-source data science community owned by Google, and usaspending.gov, the official source for all spending records in the United States Government.

Tableau For Dummies, 2nd Edition, has been completely revamped since the first edition of 2015. Since the acquisition of Tableau by Salesforce in 2019, many new application features have been added to the product family. Remember that what you see and read in this book reflects the 2022 edition of Tableau, not older versions.

This book doesn't get deep into the programmatic weeds, nor does it show you everything about all the product offerings of Tableau. Instead, this book focuses on understanding and using Tableau Desktop, Tableau Prep, and Tableau Cloud — what I call the foundation for all things Tableau.

If you've used other best-in-breed business intelligence and data analytics solutions, you'll see that Tableau keeps in line with commonly desired features available industry wide. However, Tableau offers many unique nuances that this book helps you uncover. Some concepts are easy to grasp, whereas others take time and patience, even for the most experienced data scientist.

As you read the book, I point to the specific websites for those areas that get a bit hairy. If vendors such as Tableau change the URL to the website, don't fret! Run a Google search for using the heading of whatever section of the book you're currently reading as a guide to finding the latest resources. I'm confident that you'll often find the updated link on the first page of the results.

Also, the many step-by-step exercises in the book use easily obtained, existing datasets to demonstrate the concepts. And you don't have to start at Chapter 1 and work your way through each chapter to move on to the next (most of the time).

Now, I have some good and bad news for you. Getting a free copy of Tableau is easy for a short while. Tableau offers a free trial of the foundational solutions we cover in this book for 14 days. If you need to take a spin for a few more days, don't hesitate to ask for a trial extension. Instructions are abundantly available online to achieve this. Be warned that you won't get all the bells and whistles needed to complete this book until you purchase an actual license, though.

To get a handle on everything covered in *Tableau For Dummies,* 2nd Edition, you'll need access to (a minimum) one Tableau Creator license, which costs about $900 per year. Yes, there are cheaper options, such as a Tableau Explorer or Tableau Viewer license. The only way you'll get access to all the tools covered in the book (especially Desktop and Prep) is by acquiring a Creator subscription.

Tableau offers a free edition for students and educators in K-12 or those active in the college classroom reading this book and wanting to get through most of the exercises. The catch: You must have a valid institutional email address and credentials to back the claim. To get your hands on the academic edition, search for the Academic Programs link under the Resources menu at www.tableau.com.

Foolish Assumptions

I've written this book with a few assumptions about you in mind:

>> **You want to learn about data analytics and business intelligence.** For readers new to business intelligence and data analytics, this book introduces a cornucopia of terminology and high-level concepts in the context of a leading industry tool. By the time you finish this book, I hope you'll feel comfortable enough to consider yourself no longer a newbie.

>> **You hope to learn a new enterprise business intelligence and data analytics platform.** In this book, I walk you through the core features you need to know to get Tableau up and running in an enterprise-scale business intelligence operation. I also help you identify those features so that you can grab the crowd's attention.

>> **You need a one-stop shop and hands-on Tableau reference:** If you are overwhelmed by Tableau's online documentation or the litany of online training offered, you are not alone. This book synthesizes the key messages across the foundational products into a single reference.

Regardless of your situation, I hope that by acquiring this book, you'll gain tremendous knowledge to help accelerate your professional and personal goals as a data and analytics expert.

Icons Used in This Book

If you've read a *For Dummies* book before, you're probably familiar with the icons, but here's what I've used them for:

TIP

The Tip icon offers a few pieces of advice as you work diligently through the book.

REMEMBER

This icon points to those "must know" concepts. If you see one of these icons, take a gander because it provides sage advice on dealing with a significant product, feature, or concept.

TECHNICAL STUFF

If you're looking to dig a bit further into the rabbit hole, I point out exactly what to look for and often how to get to the finish line. Take or leave these bits as you see fit.

WARNING

The Warning icon is the equivalent of an "uh-oh; watch out!" Heed the sound advice in these paragraphs; their goal is to keep you from getting stuck in the Tableau trenches.

ON THE WEB

If you are curious and want to learn well beyond the book, the On The Web icon points to detailed references and solutions, often directly on Tableau.com.

Beyond the Book

Every *For Dummies* book has an associated cheat sheet available online, and *Tableau For Dummies*, 2nd Edition, is no different. The cheat sheet offers you essential tips, tricks, and shortcuts to achieve mastery in Tableau quickly. You can locate the cheat sheet by visiting `https://www.dummies.com` and typing **Tableau For Dummies** in the Search box.

Where to Go from Here

Many folks, including myself, tend to focus on a few critical areas when reading a *For Dummies* book. Although the flow of the book makes sense if you read each chapter sequentially, I anticipate that you'll dance around a bit between chapters. And you indeed can, because all the chapters stand on their own. With that, let's rock and roll!

1

Tackling Tableau Basics

IN THIS PART . . .

Grasp the key concepts necessary to become proficient as a data analyst using Tableau.

Learn how to build the appropriate Tableau solution based on the modular approach to delivery for you and your organization.

Understand the full data life cycle and how it fits into various data modeling and visualization approaches.

Chapter **1**

Learning Tableau Lingo

There is much hype about data, and the use of business intelligence, data analytics, and data visualization tooling gets plenty of hype as well. Although there are many enterprise business intelligence tools on the market, Tableau stands out among the leaders for being bundled as a single platform for business intelligence, analytics, and visualization.

In this chapter, you start exploring the Tableau landscape by discovering the main Tableau terminology you need to familiarize yourself with regarding business intelligence, data analytics, and data visualization functionality. In addition, you can dip your toes into what it takes to install Tableau applications and the various file-based output types produced depending on the Tableau product.

What Is Tableau?

Tableau is a business intelligence platform that helps users see and understand their data using highly visual representations. Unlike other enterprise business intelligence platforms, Tableau incorporates business intelligence, data analytics, data science, data mining, and data visualization into a single solution. As a result, its capabilities are considered the broadest and deepest for data evaluation on the market.

In 2019, Salesforce acquired Tableau. At the time, Tableau's focus on data was big but not all-encompassing. It included enterprise data applications, data management and governance, visual analytics, and end-to-end storytelling. As with every other platform on the market, machine learning (ML) and artificial intelligence (AI) have become entrenched in the platform. Salesforce's Einstein AI engine is built into Tableau to help accelerate data analytics predictions, provide a strong recommendation engine, and afford an advanced workflow while touting a low-code development environment.

Tableau is not a single product but is rather a suite of products that includes Tableau Desktop, Tableau Prep, and Tableau Server or Tableau Cloud. Chapter 2 describes the purpose of each in more detail, but in brief, people use Tableau Desktop to create their data models. In contrast, Tableau Prep facilitates data preparation. And when users are ready to collaborate with others, they must publish their outputs from Desktop and Prep to Tableau Server or Tableau Cloud.

Tableau and Business Intelligence

The term *business intelligence* refers to taking in the big picture of an organization's activities and goals, from the collection and analysis of data to the presentation and dissemination of the data using a single platform. A look at the big picture is precisely what you get with Tableau. This best-in-breed platform allows users like yourself to customize views of their data to make data-driven decisions at speed and scale.

Why do folks like you and me need an enterprise business intelligence (BI) solution to organize data? The more data you have, the more difficult it is to dig in and get the information quickly. Making informed decisions requires various capabilities, from data mining to visualizations and analytics. With business intelligence solutions, you get everything under a single umbrella. The key benefits of business intelligence are plentiful, but here are the main ones:

REMEMBER

>> **Provide a platform for faster analysis:** BI platforms perform heavy-duty data processing, leading to quick calculations and the creation of stunning visualizations. Assuming that you've connected to your data source and you have already gone about prepping the data with a robust data model, Tableau can accelerate the visualization and analysis process by as much as 100 times as conducting data analysis and business intelligence activities manually, especially when integrating many data sources into a single repository.

>> **Create business efficiency and driving decisions:** Leaders can benchmark results with speed and agility when a business intelligence platform offers a holistic view of operations. It's easy to spot opportunities and find those

needle-in-a-haystack moments. Instead of spending hours poring through datasets, users can filter, aggregate, and forecast using Tableau data analytics and visualization options, thereby cutting down the time to make decisions from months, weeks, or days to perhaps even minutes. Talk about saving time!

>> **Drive customer and employee experience satisfaction:** What is the worst possible thing for an organization to experience? Sure, most say financial loss. But financial loss results from two factors: lack of customer satisfaction and low employee morale. A primary culprit is the inability of customers and employees to access data quickly; it impacts their entire experience of interacting with the organization, internally and externally. Investing in business intelligence solutions that present a 360-degree view from all data sources can lead to less time worrying about analysis paralysis and more time innovating. The opportunity costs are often measurable in loyalty and, yes, financial rewards.

>> **Have data you trust:** When you have many data sources, organizations try to figure out ways to control the disorganized chaos. When you have thousands of Excel or CSV files, a good tactic is to centralize them in a single data repository. But wait a moment: How do you connect the dots — that is, discover the relationships between the data in those files? The answer is to use a business intelligence solution. Relationships exist if the data is like-kind, and you can create potential single-point data sources, hence the use of governed data repositories in a business intelligence platform such as Tableau. Trusted data is not limited to the one-off files; engagement rules apply to relational and nonrelational database stores with tens of millions of records.

Connecting Big Data with Business Intelligence

Make no mistake: The term *big data* is undoubtedly a catch–all buzzword. It pops up a lot in this book. It's meant to encompass five aspects of a business intelligence activity: data volume, data velocity, data veracity, data value, and data variety. Big data brings together *unstructured data* (data with no organized convention), *semi-structured data* (data that has some logical order but isn't necessarily formalized), and *structured data* (data that is formalized or organized). Each of these data types maintains some level of these five attributes:

>> **Volume:** The amount of data that exists

>> **Velocity:** The speed at which data is generated and moves

>> **Veracity:** The quality and accuracy of data available

>> **Value:** The credibility, in monetary and nonmonetary terms, that the data provides

>> **Variety:** The diversity of data types available within the dataset

Big data is paramount for business intelligence solutions such as Tableau because businesses constantly create more data, practically by the minute. These businesses must keep up with the data deluge. A good business intelligence platform such as Tableau grows with the increasing demands; however, if the data is not maintained, your ability to handle data visualizations and the associated data sources also becomes impaired. Therefore, it's essential to implement good data hygiene and maintenance practices.

Analyzing Data with Tableau

Don't get business intelligence confused with data analytics. Business intelligence platforms use data analytics as a building block to tell the complete story. A data analyst or scientist evaluates the data using the treasure trove of tools built into Tableau, from advanced statistics to predictive analytics or machine learning solutions to identify patterns and trends.

Tableau offers that end-to-end data analytics experience so that the analyst, scientist, and collaborator can complete the entire data life cycle, from gathering, prepping, analyzing, collaborating, and sharing data insights. The big difference between Tableau and its competitors is the self-service nature of the offering, allowing users to ask questions or predict the kind of visualizations the user may require without manually completing the work, thanks to the predictive Einstein AI engine.

Like the three-year-old child asking "Why?" all the time, as you ask more questions and the platform learns, Tableau builds an analysis output while simultaneously learning from the output. The result is an opportunity for the system to understand why something happens and what can happen next. Business intelligence platforms take the resulting models and algorithms and break these results into actionable language insights for data mining, predictive analytics, and statistics. The final product is data analytics, the byproduct of answering a specific question (or set of questions). The collection of questions helps the organization move forward with its business agenda.

Visualizing Data

Raw data that is transformed into useful information can only go so far. Assume for a moment that you were able to aggregate ten data sources whose total record count exceeded 5 million records. As a data analyst, your job was to try to explain to your target audience what the demographics study dataset incorporates among the 5 million records. How easy would that be? It's not simple to articulate unless you can summarize the data cohesively using some data visualization.

Data visualizations are graphical representations of information and data. Suppose you can access visual elements such as charts, graphs, maps, and tables that can concisely synthesize what those millions of records include. In that case, you are effectively using data visualization tools to provide an accessible platform to address trends, patterns, and outliers within data.

TIP

For those who are enamored with big data, the use of data visualization tools helps users analyze massive amounts of data quickly by applying data-driven decisions using graphical representations rather than requiring users to parse through lines of text one by one.

Understanding Key Tableau Terms

Before you begin drinking from the terminology firehose, I want to set the record straight on a few things. Tableau has its own product-specific terminology, but there are also terms you can't escape no matter what business intelligence and data analysis tool you use, whether it's Microsoft Excel, Microsoft Power BI, IBM Cognos, or others. In this section, I review the most critical Tableau-specific terminology, not the entire business intelligence dictionary.

Data source

A *data source* in Tableau comes from anywhere that Tableau can extract, transport, and load relational and nonrelational data. Sources of data used by Tableau are often divided into the four classifications, with some examples of several:

» **Files:** `.csv`, `.txt`, Excel

» **Relational databases:** Oracle, SQL Server, DB2

>> **Cloud databases and virtualization platforms:** Microsoft Azure SQL, Google Big Query, Amazon Aurora, Denodo

>> **ODBC datastores:** Datastores using ODBC-related connections

Figure 1-1 shows an overview of the abundant number of data sources you can connect to in Tableau Desktop.

A Tableau data source may contain multiple data connections to different databases or files, as described previously. The connection information includes where the data is located, such as the filename and path of the network location, or perhaps details on connecting to the data source, such as the database server name and the authentication credentials. Regardless, many data sources can connect in a single instance of Tableau. Still, categorically, they connect to some file or server connection, whether local or cloud based.

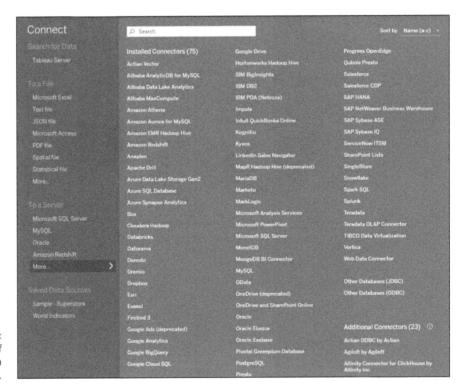

FIGURE 1-1: A sampling of Tableau data sources.

Data type

Going down the data path a bit more, a data field, which is part of a data source (see more details in the next section), must always have a data type. A *data type* reflects whether the field is a number, a type of date, or a string. For example, every area code is an integer (703); a date of birth represents a date (01/01/23); and a state on the U.S map ("Virginia") is a string. Users can identify the data type they are looking for as part of the data field in the Data pane. Each data type also includes one of several icons, including those represented in Figure 1-2. Although the examples are not exhaustive, you see a few common examples of data type icons mapped against their respective data types. The complete list of Tableau data types includes

>> Text (string) value

>> Date value

>> Date & Time value

>> Numerical value

>> Boolean value (relational data only)

>> Geographic value (map data)

>> Cluster groups

FIGURE 1-2:
Examples of data types icons.

⊕	City
Abc	First Name
Abc	Gender
Abc	Last Name
⊕	State
⊕	Zip Code

Data fields

Every time you connect a data source to Tableau, the connection presents the users with one or more tables from said source. A table includes many data fields composed of a collection of several data types.

As shown in Figure 1-3, data fields are explicitly defined as dimensions or measures as the Tableau database is created. Based on data integrity and quality, Tableau automatically organized the data fields. All data fields containing text date or Boolean values are dimensions by default. On the other hand, fields containing numerical values are measures. The next section talks about how Tableau deals with dimensions and measures.

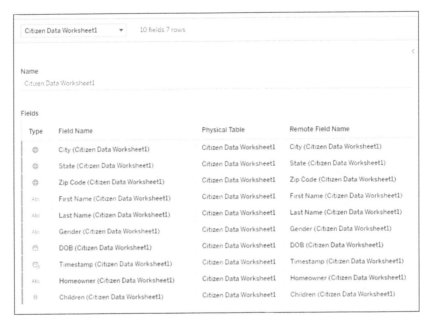

FIGURE 1-3:
Examples of
data fields.

Dimensions and measures

In Tableau, dimensions and measures are both data field types. If the field type contains non-numeric data, Tableau references the field as a dimension. Examples include the day of the week, a product category, or geographic data. These variable types don't allow you to complete mathematical equations. Here's an example of an equation with variable types:

State + City / Country = Invalid

All these items are strings because you can't add a state plus a city and divide it by a country to get some magical answer, right?

In Tableau, you can drag each of these fields into a view, which is the part of the Tableau canvas where a visualization is created. Tableau creates headers for each data field. That means you can think of each field as a category, or a dimension of data. If the dimension of data is placed in a row, the header label is vertically placed. The label is horizontally placed if the dimension is placed in a column. An example of data placed in both rows and columns is displayed in Figure 1-4.

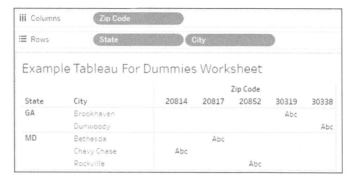

FIGURE 1-4: Rows and column data for dimensions in Tableau.

Measures are numerical data field types. Tableau assumes that these field types are continuous and tags these values by default. Examples of measures include temperature and financial instruments. Unlike independent dimensions, or values that do not rely on other data fields, measures are dependent because they allow you to do the math, as in the following example:

Age (20) + Age (1) / Age (3) = Age (7)

As with dimensions, if you drag a measure into a view, Tableau creates a continuous axis. If a measure is placed in a row, the axis is vertical, whereas a column is horizontal.

In Figure 1-5, you can see that each row (dimension) contains a state, city, and zip code. The column data looks at each value individually and then aggregates the data in the data setup. For example, three individual records in Bethesda, MD 20817 contain children identified. Aggregated, the measure is SUM (3).

FIGURE 1-5: Rows and column data for measures in Tableau.

Continuous versus discrete

As you'll quickly realize, Tableau separates many concepts based on mathematical reasoning. If a field is based on mathematical representation, Tableau refers to this data as *continuous*. On the other hand, if the data is non-numeric, the data is known as *discrete*.

When it comes to continuous data, you are looking for data that is unbroken, whole, or without interruption. That means data that contains a range of values such as temperature, time, or monetary values. If the data can be added, averaged, or aggregated, and appear as a measure in Tableau, you can almost certainly assume that the value is continuous.

Discrete data is almost always individualized, separate, and unique data. You can have only a particular value. For example, do you have more than one shoe size at a time? Can you be at more than one place at a given location? How many distinct individuals can you claim on a personal tax return? The number 2.39 is not possible; 1, 2, or 3 is more like it.

With discrete data, you have no way to add, average, or aggregate the data points because the values will always be unique by default.

TECHNICAL STUFF

When dragged onto the Tableau View area, discrete data appears as a *blue pill* to form a discrete axis on a chart. Continuous data, on the other hand, appears as a *green pill* to form a continuous axis on a chart.

Filter

The capability for filtering data is one of the essential features of any business intelligence solution associated with big data. Tableau lets a user filter data, whether an individual view contains a few records or an entire data source with millions of records based on dimensions, measures, or values.

As with databases, filtering helps a user see only the data they need based on targeted criteria. When using Tableau filters, you can visualize the data in a readable, actionable format. The real benefit of filtering is to streamline data to limit the number of records for improved performance. An example filter would be to filter all the U.S. states with the word *New*. The result set would return a response of New Hampshire, New Jersey, New Mexico, and New York.

Various filter types are available in Tableau, including the extract, data source, context, dimension, measure, and user filters. You dive into filters a bit more in Chapter 7.

Aggregation

Combining data, also known as *aggregation*, is not uncommon in a business intelligence platform. In Tableau, aggregating measures or dimensions is pervasive. However, aggregation is often numerically focused, meaning focused on the use of measures. Suppose you add a measure to a view. In that case, the aggregation is applied to the specific measure by default, which varies based on context. Read on for an example.

Pretend for a moment that you're the CEO of a Fortune 100 company (think Walmart, Coca-Cola, or Exxon). One of your data analysts prepares a report for you that presents the minimum, maximum, summary, and average number of sales opportunities for a specific product in each region. The scenario would appear as follows (with the bold signifying each data field that is aggregated).

> **Opportunity Value** = 20,000 **products sold** in five **varieties** across 4 **regions** with a customer population of 1,000,000 **households**.

You've now calculated the opportunity value by utilizing the aggregation functions, a way to calculate a set of values and derive a single value.

WARNING

There are limits to what you can aggregate. You can only limit data found in relational data sources. Multidimensional data sources contain data that has already been aggregated, which is impossible to complete. Furthermore, at this time, multidimensional data source aggregation is supported only in the Windows edition of Tableau Desktop.

Workbook and worksheet

Tableau hasn't deviated much from other industry-leading products when it comes to the name of file and formatting conventions. There is a Tableau *workbook*, the main Tableau file, which contains a collection of sheets. The collection of sheets represents the workbook much like that in Microsoft Excel or Microsoft Power BI. In Tableau, a *worksheet* is a single file within a workbook. A worksheet is an element within a dashboard or story.

Although the workbook represents the proverbial catalog of dashboards or stories, the worksheet is a single element or a view. Figure 1-6 represents an example of a single worksheet contained within a Tableau workbook.

FIGURE 1-6:
A Tableau
worksheet.

REMEMBER

Here are points to consider when thinking about the use of workbooks and worksheets:

>> A Tableau worksheet may contain a single view with many shelves, cards, legends, and analytics panes, which are included as part of a single sidebar on a single page to tell a story.

>> When you add many worksheet pages to a workbook, you can generate a *dashboard*, which is a collection of views from many worksheets.

>> As you create many worksheets within a workbook, you are compiling a *story*, which is a sequence of worksheets that paint a picture to fuse information.

>> Most notably in Tableau Desktop, but also in Tableau Cloud, you can combine views of data by dragging and dropping fields onto the Tableau *shelves*, which are part of a worksheet and which help you create presentations.

In Chapter 7, you take a tour of a worksheet and workbook to see how to collect, organize, and extract data.

Gearing Up for the Tableau Journey

Now that you know the basic Tableau terminology, you can dance your way into installing Tableau. You may be scratching your head, asking "Aren't some instances of Tableau in the cloud?" The answer is yes. Tableau is not a single application; it's a suite of applications. Some Tableau applications still sit on your desktop such as Tableau Desktop and Tableau Prep Builder, which are available for both Windows and Mac OS. Then, users have a choice to publish the data produced to either Tableau Cloud or Tableau Server. So, without further ado, you can start tiptoeing around the Tableau environments before you explore the entire Tableau portfolio in Chapter 2.

Understanding installation prerequisites

Most users assume that Tableau is cloud-based because its owner, Salesforce, is a software-as-a-service (SaaS) platform. Although Tableau Cloud is indeed where users' Tableau files ultimately wind up, folks still need to do things on their desktops because cloud computing capacity can't necessarily handle the speed and scale of some data activities in Tableau. Take, for example, the creation of the data model or data preparation process. You can do these activities over the web, but the computing capacity required is expensive and labor intensive. The cost to perform the same activities on the desktop or a server is pennies on the dollar. That's why almost all vendors with a business intelligence product like Tableau have a desktop product for data modeling, data prep, and the first stage of reporting, visualizing, and dashboarding.

In this book, I cover three products: Tableau Desktop, Tableau Prep, and Tableau Cloud. Table 1-1 shows the prerequisites for working with Tableau in Windows or Macintosh OS. These are the absolute minimum. Suppose you want to blaze through your datasets without slipping and sliding with some long wait times while the numbers are crunching. In that case, I strongly recommend increasing your RAM and CPU capacity, commonly referred to as compute and memory utilization in business intelligence and cloud computing.

TABLE 1-1 Installation Prerequisites for Tableau Desktop, Tableau Prep, and Tableau Cloud

	Windows OS	Macintosh OS
Tableau Desktop	**OS Version:** Microsoft Windows 8/8.1 or higher (64-bit)	**OS Version:** macOS Mojave 10.14, macOS Catalina 10.15, and Big Sur 11.4+
	CPU: Intel Core i3 or AMD Ryzen 3 (Dual Core) Processor, including CPU support that integrates SSE 4.2 and POPCNT instruction sets	**CPU:** Intel processors, Core i3 (Dual Core) or newer, in which the CPU must support SSE4.2 and POPCNT instruction sets; another option is M1 processors under Rosetta 2 emulation mode
	RAM: 2GB or larger	**RAM:** 2GB or larger
	Disk Space: 2GB HDD or larger hard drive	Disk Space: 1.5GB minimum free disk space

(continued)

TABLE 1-1 *(continued)*

	Windows OS	Macintosh OS
Tableau Prep	**OS Version:** Microsoft Windows 8/8.1 (64-bit)	**Operating System:** macOS Mojave 10.14, macOS Catalina 10.15, and Big Sur 11.4+
	CPU: Intel Core i3 or AMD Ryzen 3 (Dual Core), including CPUs; must support SSE4.2 and POPCNT instruction sets	**CPU:** Intel processors, Core i3 (Dual Core) or newer, in which the CPU must support SSE4.2 and POPCNT instruction sets; another option is M1 processors under Rosetta 2 emulation mode
	RAM: 4GB memory or larger	**RAM:** 4GB memory or larger
	Disk Space: 2GB HDD free or larger	**Disk Space:** 2GB HDD free or larger
Tableau Cloud	**Web Browsers**	
	Chrome on Windows, Mac, and Android	
	Microsoft Edge on Windows	
	Mozilla Firefox and Firefox ESR on Windows and Mac	
	Apple Safari on Mac and iOS	
	Data Sources	
	Extracts of all data sources must have a compatible version of Tableau Desktop.	
	Live connections must allow for a connection to many data sources hosted in the cloud and on-premises using the Tableau Bridge client. This requires meeting the minimum prerequisites of Tableau Desktop.	
	Storage	
	All plans require a minimum of 100GB (standard offering).	
	Internationalization	
	Tableau's products are Unicode enabled and compatible with data stored in most spoken languages.	

Getting familiar with Tableau file types and sources

Unless you are 100 percent responsible for the data creation process, you likely have limited control over data quality and the destiny of your data sources. As you embark on a data selection journey with Tableau, you need to consider numerous factors, from data type and source variety to suitable instrumentation and collection methodology. Selecting data is both an art and a science, as you'll realize over time.

TIP

Don't be blind to the fact that the data selection process is, first and foremost, determining what data types, sources, and instruments are appropriate to answer your research questions. You need to know what each field should contain, the data type the field must adhere to, and the output structure you need or want.

WARNING

Despite what Tableau and every other business intelligence vendor touts as intelligent data connections, the connectors are not all *that* smart. The quality and breadth of your data dictate the accuracy of the data connection. After you've connected to a data source, you'll need to create a data connection, but that's when the fun begins. Why? Because you'll still need to do a bit of cleanup to ensure that data sources accurately reflect the data types, the columns map, and even that the data translates appropriately. Integrity issues are not uncommon, so do not let your guard down and trust Tableau just because it advertises its data connectors as being the most intelligent on the market.

As a closing note to this chapter, the rest of this section helps you become familiar with the various data file and source types that you'll get your hands on as you work with Tableau Desktop, Tableau Prep, and Tableau Cloud. The following list provides the spectrum of the most common options, also shown in Figure 1-7.

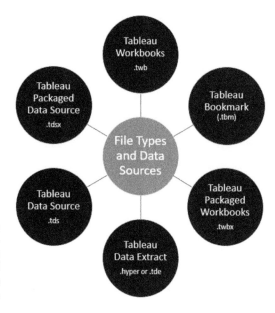

FIGURE 1-7: The most common Tableau file type and data source options.

- » **Tableau workbooks** (.twb): The workbook is the most popular file format you'll get your hands on and is the default for most users. Workbooks contain worksheets, dashboards, stories, and other components.

- » **Tableau bookmarks** (.tbm): A Tableau bookmark contains a single worksheet (not a workbook). You can easily share your work products, such as a single dashboard, story, report, or another component.

- » **Tableau packaged workbooks** (.twbx): This file type contains the metadata about a workbook's constituents and data derived from a data source. Initially, a .tde file (see the next item in this list) includes the data extracted from the start. The output is the extension .twbx, which is used for Tableau packaged workbooks. Suppose you need to share a workbook with a user who does not have access to a live data connection. You can use the .twbx file instead of the traditional .twb file to connect to the data for easy connectivity.

TIP

A Tableau packaged workbook is also a great option if you must include information about images or geocoding.

- » **Tableau extracts** (.hyper or .tde): The .tde is used only for data extract files, whereas there are other use cases for the .hyper extension. Local copies of a complete or a subset of data from a source get stored in this Tableau file type. This file type is location agnostic, meaning that nothing is tied to the data source, workbooks, dashboard, or other data assets. Because every asset is highly compressed, you often use these files when the goal is to help expedite connectivity for slow connections or those working in offline mode.

- » **Tableau data source** (.tds): These files contain all the data-connection instructions, not the actual files themselves. Say you want to connect to a relational database like Oracle. The Tableau data source stores all the connection strings to the Oracle database, not to all the data inside the Oracle database. Undoubtedly, the Tableau data source is a bit more sophisticated than just a connection to the source; it also allows for the metadata and any user customizations to be stored, such as custom fields and table joins across systems.

- » **Tableau packaged data source** (.tdsx): In contrast to a Tableau data source, a packaged data source contains information about a data source and the data. The extracted data is saved by applying for the .tde file extension; the source information is kept in a .tds file. You can shift the data around using a local file structure such as a text file or perhaps a .hyper file. You may also want to utilize a Microsoft-based file such as an Excel file to shuffle the data to and from the source. Here's the catch: The Tableau Packaged Data source has a unique extension, .tdsx. When you need to share data about a specific data source, but the user does not have access to said source or the data, your best option is to use a packaged data source because it brings the connection and data together in one fell swoop.

REMEMBER

The subtle but significant difference between a .tds and .tdsx file type is that the information about the data, not the data itself, is held in the .tds file. Data is also available in the Tableau packaged data source file type, .tdsx.

Regardless of the file type or data source type used, you can save Tableau files in an associated folder in any Tableau Repository directory, which is automatically created in your My Documents folder on a Windows or Macintosh OS computer. You can save work files in other locations. Still, best practice is to save to a central location versus randomly saving to locations such as your desktop or an ad hoc network directory.

Chapter **2**

Venturing into Tableau Versions

As I mention in Chapter 1, the Tableau product family isn't just one or two applications but a collection of solutions that come together to support an organization's end-to-end business intelligence needs. From its inception in the scrappy halls of the Department of Computer Science at Standard University in the late 1990s, the founders of Tableau had a single mission: to help folks like you and me see and understand big data visually. Today, Salesforce maintains this goal because they know that delivering a successful data experience is essential for everyone, from the workforce to students in our classrooms.

In this chapter, you figure out what parts of the Tableau portfolio are appropriate for your business needs based on user type and business use case.

Getting to Know the Tableau Product Line

Tableau is a business intelligence platform that provides tools for users to engage and interact with data across all phases of the analytics life cycle. Such tools and techniques include data management and governance functionality, visual analytics and storytelling, collaboration and communication, and deep learning that leverages artificial intelligence–powered capabilities.

The Tableau platform brings together all user types at the interaction layer. It offers various analytic and data management options (discussed in upcoming sections), and the connections to all data sources are either cloud based, database ready, or file based. You can deploy all Tableau solutions either in Tableau Cloud, which is a public cloud infrastructure, or by hosting them in an on-premises environment. Every layer of the Tableau platform allows for tight integration with industry-standard APIs, and a core tenet of the platform is the application of governance, security, and compliance. Figure 2-1 shows the core platform architecture of Tableau, and the following sections offer an overview of each of the Tableau products. The interaction layer contains each of the end-user connection types. Data connections can be with the cloud, a database, or a file. The deployment options with Tableau include Tableau Cloud, Tableau Server, or Tableau Public. It's the two middle layers, the analytic and data management options, that this book heavily focuses on. Each organization has its own approach, and as you review your data, you figure out what the best choice is for your organization. At any time, as shown on the left side of Figure 2-1, all facets of the model should incorporate security, governance, and compliance. On the right side, APIs, also known as Application Programmable Interfaces, can be integrated to handle one or more of the layers in the Tableau architecture.

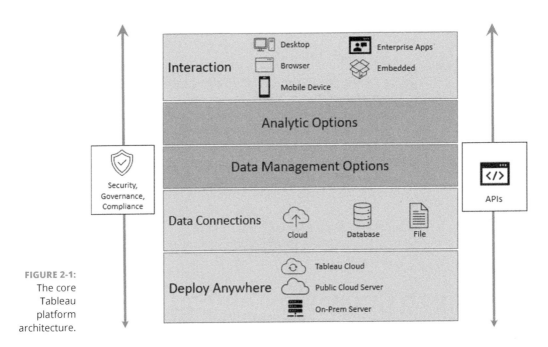

FIGURE 2-1:
The core
Tableau
platform
architecture.

A BRIEF HISTORY OF TABLEAU

Tableau was founded in 2003 by three Stanford University Department of Computer Science researchers, Pat Hanrahan, Christian Chabot, and Chris Stolte. As budding researchers, the dynamic trio specialized in visualization technologies using relational databases, particularly with the use of data cubes and data warehousing technology.

The trio realized that there was a commercial market void for such technologies because none of the legacy IT vendors offered a broad-based solution for enterprise-scale data visualization. Eventually the research lab experiment at Stanford became the company called Tableau. By 2010, the company was offering cloud computing with Tableau Public, followed by Tableau Online in 2013 (now Tableau Cloud), driven by their belief in data democratization, or the idea that everyone should have access to a way to analyze and understand data.

In 2019, Salesforce acquired Tableau because they wanted to provide a 360-degree view of customers' data. Salesforce enriched the Tableau by expanding it with exceptional artificial intelligence, machine learning, advanced data management, and data visualization functionality.

To see a chart on all the Tableau features and when they were released from Tableau from the day the company started, go to `https://public.tableau.com/app/profile/jmackinlay/viz/TableauInnovation/History`.

Tableau Desktop

Every dataset doesn't just jump from the data source location to Tableau Cloud or Tableau Server instantly. You follow a process to explore the data and turn it into a meaningful model for consumption. Next, a transformation process must occur to support data visualization, and then you need a mechanism by which to publish the data. Tableau Desktop is where the entire process begins.

Tableau Desktop is, first and foremost, the platform people use to independently complete data exploration and visualization activities before collaborating with others. Users complete these activities by using an intuitive drag-and-drop interface. Anyone looking to independently evaluate their data and make decisions without cleansing or publishing their data for collaboration can stop at Tableau Desktop. Collaboration requires other tools described in this chapter.

Figure 2-2 depicts the process by which data is consumed and utilized across Tableau, most notably between Tableau Desktop, Tableau Prep, and Tableau Server or Cloud.

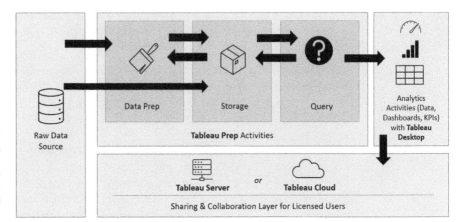

FIGURE 2-2:
How you work
with data
across Tableau
Desktop, Prep,
Server, and
Cloud.

As you read the upcoming chapters, you'll recognize that there is a consistent process to handle data ingestion, manipulation, and visualization using Tableau Desktop. Here is a high-level overview of the steps you may take from data ingestion to visualization, starting with Tableau Desktop:

1. **Connect to your data source in Tableau Desktop (raw data source).**

   Remember that there are a few data connection types, some of which allow real-time updates whereas others require manual updating over time.

2. **After Tableau Desktop recognizes the data source, manipulate the data for data models and visualizations.**

   If you must cleanse and transform data, you need to head to Tableau Prep to complete those activities.

   After the data sources go through the cleansing process (also referred to as Extract, Transform, and Load [ETL]; see Chapter 4), Tableau stores that data in its memory.

   You can now create one or more visualizations by querying the dataset in Tableau Desktop, as shown in Figure 2-3.

3. **Having readied your data for prime time, publish it using one of the following three options, depending on what type of Desktop client you have:**

   - **Tableau Server** licensing requires Tableau Desktop to save the workbook to a private, on-premises environment, or to a private, cloud-hosted environment. Either option requires a paid subscription.

   - **Tableau Cloud** licensing requires Tableau Desktop to save the workbook to the Salesforce software-as-a-service (SaaS)–hosted environment, which requires a paid subscription.

REMEMBER

TECHNICAL STUFF

- **Tableau Public** limits your ability to save files anywhere but the Tableau Public Cloud.

You don't have data-sharing limits if you are licensed for Tableau Desktop Personal or Professional. If you choose not to procure a Tableau license and instead opt for using Tableau Public for free, you can only share your data with others openly, which limits your ability to protect your sensitive data.

Tableau Desktop and Tableau Prep work together. Some users bypass the process of cleansing their data using Tableau Prep and jump straight to Desktop. I'll do that in some examples, so don't panic if you think I am skipping a few steps.

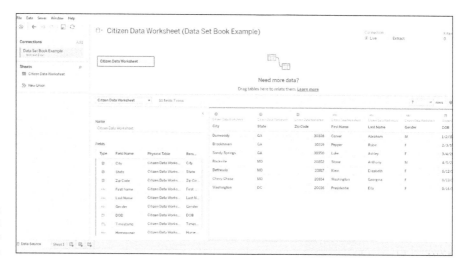

FIGURE 2-3:
The Tableau Desktop interface.

Tableau Prep

Unlike other enterprise business intelligence platforms, the extract, transport, load (ETL), and cleanse process occurs in a separate application within the solution suite, Tableau Prep. When users need to combine data sources, shape and manipulate sources to behave a certain way, clean data that may contain a specific attribution, or analyze a massive dataset at scale before data visualization, they use Tableau Prep. The data prep environment offers users three different views of their data:

>> Row-level profiles

>> Column-level profiles

>> The entire dataset

Depending on the task at hand, a user can fine-tune the data, including by making real-time changes within Prep using the same drag-and-drop experience available in Tableau Desktop. Figure 2-4 shows the Tableau Prep Builder interface.

Tableau Prep is often the glue that combines raw data and the final product because raw data often needs some TLC. The more data sources you introduce within Tableau Prep, the more the Tableau artificial intelligence engine works to reconcile the proper business operations given a source's data types and fields. After the data is cleansed, it can go to two possible destinations: Tableau Desktop, to continue with the data visualization and analysis journey; and Tableau Server (on-premises) or Tableau Cloud (online), for storage, with the intent of sharing and collaborating with other end users later.

TECHNICAL STUFF

Data cleansing is a complex process requiring users to evaluate their data for formatting errors, duplicates, incomplete values, inconsistencies, and a host of other potential issues. When you have a bit of data cleansing to do, use Tableau Prep. If you know that your data is sound and the problem is a one-off, updating your work using Tableau Desktop will be just fine.

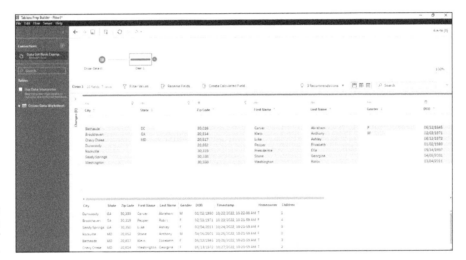

FIGURE 2-4:
The Tableau Prep Builder interface.

Tableau Server and Tableau Cloud

There are a few differences between Tableau Server and Tableau Cloud. Still, at the core, their purposes are precisely the same. Tableau Server requires the enterprise user to host the environment. In contrast, Tableau Cloud is a SaaS-hosted infrastructure managed by Salesforce. From a licensing perspective, there are some caveats to using each of these Tableau environments, as noted in Table 2-1.

Server and Cloud are purpose built to distribute, share, and collaborate user and organizational datasets, visualizations, dashboards, and reports across the Tableau enterprise, most notably between Tableau Desktop and Tableau Prep.

TABLE 2-1 **Licensing Differences between Tableau Server and Tableau Cloud**

	Tableau Server	Tableau Cloud
License Structure	Core-based or role-based.	Role-based.
Administration	Hardware is required. A server can be virtualized. All updates are the end user's responsibility, including backups and data recovery.	Fully managed by Salesforce in the Tableau Cloud SaaS environment.
Capacity	No specific limits beyond environmental resource constraints.	Site-wide limits exist based on feature type, role-based license type, and utilization of back-end resources.
Sites	Can have an infinite number of sites on the same Tableau Server. A distributed architecture is not allowed.	Multiple sites are charged additional fees, but cross-region support is provided.
Identity Management	Allows identity-management platform support, such as Microsoft Active Directory domain integration for syncing users and groups.	Must use a Tableau Account to log in.
Monitoring	Can only use Server logs and analyze the PostgreSQL repository.	Prebuilt monitoring tools are available through Tableau. No server log access.

Figure 2-5 shows an example of what the Tableau Cloud user experience provides.

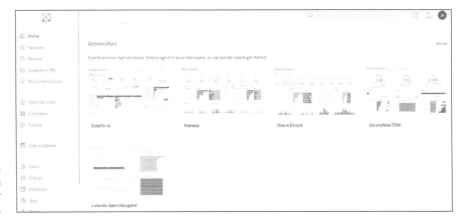

FIGURE 2-5: The Tableau Cloud user experience.

Organizations requiring tighter security, especially in regulated settings, or perhaps wanting to create custom applications with embedded analytics functionality should consider Tableau Server over Tableau Cloud because SaaS platforms come with obvious shared infrastructure limitations.

Tableau Public

In the "A brief history of Tableau" sidebar, earlier in the chapter, I indicate that the folks at Tableau had a mission to make data accessible to everyone and anyone for free. Tableau Public is that free forum for sharing your datasets and data visualizations with the world. Users can explore, create, and publicly share those data models that become data visualizations online using a combination of Tableau Desktop Public (which is a watered-down version of Tableau Desktop Personal) and what is essentially Tableau Cloud for the public.

What makes Tableau Desktop Public watered down? Tableau Desktop Public is a free online platform that allows users to learn data skills, create and distribute their data or visualizations to the public (not with select users in mind), discover, access new datasets, and share your knowledge of business intelligence. It's a great option for those who have incidental business intelligence requirements that can be shared without security controls or team collaboration.

So, you might be asking, why would someone want to spend hundreds of dollars per license if Tableau offers a free product? The answer boils down to the features and capabilities listed in Table 2-2.

Free use comes with limitations. Tableau Public limits users on how many rows of data per workbook can be consumed, with the limit currently at 15 million. You also can't connect to servers other than Tableau Public. And you know that copy of Tableau Desktop Public that Salesforce gives you for free? You can save your files to a hard drive only if you have a paid license. Also, you have only one online location where you can save the files: Tableau Public.

You use Tableau Public if you want to share your data with the world — as a blogger, journalist, student, or research scientist, for example. You share the data in the form of *vizzes* (short for data visualizations; see Figure 2-6 for an example). These are the kinds of data visualizations you see on Top 10 websites with all the bells and whistles. When is Tableau Public not appropriate for use? Suppose you are in business and trying to publish a financial statement. Tableau Public is not for you because the dataset likely contains confidential data. The public service announcement here is to be aware that after you expose a data viz to the world, it is genuinely public to the world. Always ask yourself: Is the data meant for the world to see?

TABLE 2-2 Comparing Tableau Versions

	Tableau Public	Tableau Desktop	Tableau Cloud	Tableau Server
Access	A massive, public, noncommercial Tableau Server on which everything is free to view.	A development client that sits on the user's computer. Some versions have access only to Tableau Public (Desktop Public), some have limited data-source scope (Desktop Personal Edition); and complete data-source capabilities are offered with the Professional Edition.	Brings everything from the Tableau Server edition to the cloud, which Salesforce hosts in its SaaS environment.	Tableau software is installed in the privately managed, served environment for enterprise usage. Users can host Tableau Server in their cloud infrastructure or within their data centers.
Publication Limits	You must publish your data to the public cloud.	Users with the paid subscription can publish to Tableau Cloud or Tableau Server, depending on how they've set up their licensing.	A user controls access to data sharing based on personal or organizational requirements.	A user controls access to data sharing based on personal or organizational requirements.
Desktop Client	A free desktop client called Tableau Desktop Public with limited features is available.	Two paid editions are available: a personal edition and a professional edition for developer consumption.	Not applicable	Not applicable

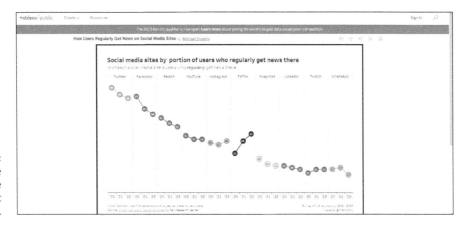

FIGURE 2-6:
An example of a viz on the Tableau Public website.

Tableau Reader

Users of Tableau Desktop and organizations who deploy Tableau Server may want to share and distribute packaged workbooks with a limited number of individuals. With a *packaged workbook,* the end user receives a package that contains the extracted data source, created explicitly in Tableau Desktop. In other words, a packaged workbook contains copies of a data source referenced by Tableau Reader to avoid accessing the data source using an online connection.

Another important caveat is that although Tableau Reader is a free download, you must still purchase, at a minimum, a fully licensed copy of Tableau Desktop, Tableau Server, or Tableau Cloud to use the Reader download.

WARNING

Tableau Reader is not compatible with those using Tableau Public because all data resides in the Tableau Public cloud one hundred percent of the time.

Tableau CRM Analytics

Salesforce acquired Tableau because it needed an analytics platform far more robust than its own in 2019. What Salesforce did was take the best of its own Einstein Analytics platform and then merge the data management, visualization, and preparation functionality into a single solution that was native Tableau. The result is a rebranded product, Tableau CRM Analytics.

Tableau CRM Analytics is, first and foremost, for the mobile user or those requiring flexible customer-driven analytics from CRM-specific applications. Although Tableau CRM works with virtually any data source, including virtually any CRM, it is optimized for the Salesforce ecosystem.

Think of Tableau CRM, not as a CRM-specific analytics tool but more of a question-and-answer agent. Suppose you work at a bookstore with a CRM containing 50,000 customer records. You keep track of every customer and the most recent transaction in the CRM. When a user connects via their mobile device and enters a query, such as, "Find me all customers who purchased books with a title including Tableau," the result is only those customers who purchased books that include Tableau in the title name.

The example illustrates that if your analytics data is deeply integrated into the CRM, particularly the Salesforce CRM, the platform can provide AI-driven insights with little effort. It is not meant to be an end-all-be-all visualization platform like the core Tableau platform. For those looking to augment their CRM footprint with a feature set that provides targeted and even workflow-driven insights based on questions and answers, Tableau CRM is the appropriate product for your organization.

WARNING

Salesforce claims they don't discriminate against data sources with Tableau CRM, but they do. So long as the data comes from a structured CRM in Salesforce, a financial system such as SAP, or an inventory-based system such as Oracle Fusion, you can use Tableau without many limitations. Check whether the integration from a third-party application is housed in Salesforce. If that is the case, the integration likely requires separate enterprise licensing to handle the data exchange outside the Salesforce ecosystem, leveraging Tableau's Data Management feature set.

TIP

The field is narrow if you are not leveraging Salesforce technologies for CRM with Tableau, so consider the traditional Tableau platform setup for most CRM analytics to get the best bang for your buck.

Tableau Data Management

Assume for a moment that your organization has hundreds of offices. Here's the catch: the Tableau Server sits in one location — maybe New York or Los Angeles. Across the enterprise, there is content sprawl whereby hundreds of data sources exist; the data must feed into that single Tableau instance.

Lifting and shifting the data from locations so that it can reside in the single data center of the Tableau Server is no longer a necessary task thanks to data virtualization. With Tableau's Data Management platform, an administrator can create a virtual connection for shared central access to point to those hundreds of disparate data sources. It's a better alternative than creating a one-off connection for each data instance.

Users can curate the relevant tables for analysis in a single location while simplifying their data management into a single graphical user interface experience. The process of extracting, transporting, and loading is minimized to optimize queries for the data warehouse and Tableau environment. You gain numerous benefits by leveraging virtual connectivity using the Data Management platform because it

TIP

» Offers a way to strengthen data governance across disparate datasets

» Helps to better define data lineage and quality issues in support of consistency

» Streamlines the extract, transport, and load process into a tightly coupled process

Tableau Advanced Management

After your organization deals with massive datasets and requires enterprise-scale security to manage its mission-critical analytics, you likely need to use Tableau Advanced Management to round out the solution platform.

The use case for Tableau Advanced Management is for organizations with many data sources — think hundreds or thousands. Those organizations need a way to manage the sources using an additional layer of security, and to scale the data when running in a mission-critical environment. What defines mission critical? Organizations involved in national security, financial exchanges, and health care all have mission-critical operations.

To use Tableau Advanced Management, you need, for starters, an enterprise license for either Tableau Cloud or Tableau Server because this is not a product for the lightweight Tableau Desktop client. The reason is that you are creating configurable profiles to administer and regulate data for specific user scenarios based on the content available in a server setting, not for a single user.

Choosing the Right Version

If you've read this entire chapter, you've probably realized by now that purchasing the right Tableau product may require you to purchase more than just one product. That's not to say that Salesforce won't sell users a single license; they will, of course, sell parts of the engine. But getting the whole experience requires buying Tableau as a bundle.

Tableau has come up with product bundles based on user activity type. The bundles are known as Viewer, Explorer, and Creator.

>> **Viewer:** Allows users to access existing dashboards. This option is available only to teams and organizations. The licenses start at $15.00 per user as of this writing.

>> **Explorer:** Allows users to edit existing dashboards. This option is available only to teams and organizations, and the licenses start at $42.00 per user as of this writing.

>> **Creator:** Allows users to connect to data, create vizzes (visualizations), and publish dashboards. Every Tableau subscription requires a minimum of one Tableau Creator license. These licenses start at $70.00 per user as of this writing.

Each Creator license entitlement provides an organization with a single copy of Tableau Desktop and Tableau Prep. The catch is that the Creator license provides an initial single-user license to Tableau Server or Tableau Cloud. Additional Creator licenses are then tied to the original Creator license entitlement of Tableau Server or Tableau Cloud.

TIP

When you purchase the Creator license, it's best to decide early on what server architecture best suits your organization because once you're hooked, it's hard to go back. Your choice is an on-premises server or the cloud.

REMEMBER

If you decide to go with the Explorer or Viewer user type, you must have a minimum of a single Creator license. The license is tied to an organization, hence the team or group requirement noted previously. So, for example, Data Inc. may have one Creator doing all the development work but can have many Explorers and Viewers completing limited activities inside Tableau Desktop. Depending on your license type, features are enabled or disabled upon purchase based on the procured license type.

Chapter **3**

Mapping Out the Data Journey

Finding answers to data questions is often a complex process of data manipulation, and with a business intelligence solution such as Tableau, you have many levers to pull to get to the exact spot you want. After you do that, though, you are well on your way to the races.

Imagine someone sending you a 2GB file with more than 1 million rows of data. A typical scenario may be to find the median of a single data column. Sounds simple, right?

Well, it's a bit more complicated because if you assume that the data is pure but it's not, you've encountered a significant roadblock. Now you need to clean the data. After the data is clean, you go back to the drawing board to complete a cursory analysis. You can decide what data column should be evaluated and charted if everything is ready to go. And then, of course, you take the last part of the journey: deriving the answer. After the answer is ready, you might need to publish it to the world.

With Tableau, the process described requires three separate applications: Tableau Desktop, Tableau Prep, and Tableau Server (on-premises) or Tableau Cloud. This book focuses on Desktop, Prep, and Cloud to map the journey. Throughout this chapter, I introduce you to the framework you need to familiarize yourself with each time you begin a new data analytics engagement, noting key concepts and interfaces along the way.

Cycling Down the Tableau Highway

Most successful enterprises follow a structured process that gets the data from discovery to destination. If you are remotely familiar with any enterprise IT project, you've probably heard of two types of life cycle processes used by data management types: waterfall and agile. These processes involve multiple steps, and like them, Tableau projects seldom get completed in one or two steps. In Figure 3-1, the Tableau cycle consists of six steps.

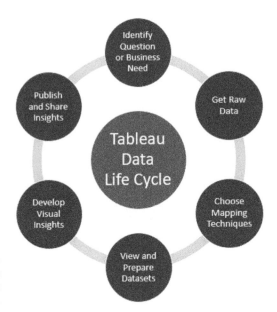

FIGURE 3-1: The six stages of the Tableau data life cycle.

REMEMBER

The Tableau data life cycle, which includes getting to the visual analysis stage, is a nonlinear process. The process involves a bit of trial and error when data transformation is required during the viewing and preparation of the dataset phase, after which you shift to developing insights. You may have an initial question in mind only to discover that your question isn't appropriate. In essence, you'll keep asking questions by leveraging your dataset until you realize you've honed in on the right question and found the right set of answers.

Identifying the right question or business need

If you hold the proverbial keys to your organization's data, you may have plenty of questions about your data and its reliability. So, your first task isn't necessarily jumping straight into the technology but answering these business questions: What is my problem? How many questions am I trying to solve with my available data?

TIP

I always tell anybody embarking on the Tableau journey not to try to boil the ocean. That is, don't try to analyze a dataset that is too difficult to digest. Look for discrete patterns that are meaningful but substantive. The dataset shouldn't be so narrow that it can't be analyzed. For example, say that you're responsible for a corporate help desk. Here are some of the questions a manager might want you to research, assuming there are multiple call centers:

>> How many calls did the help desk receive monthly?

>> What locations did calls from the help desk come to most often?

>> Did any particular applications cause the majority of the help desk calls?

>> Which location answered the most help desk calls during business hours?

You should understand the underlying business questions if you are responsible for the data. Otherwise, it can be hard to determine the business needs that should be addressed. Therefore, building the questions and then identifying where those datasets reside (and to be clear, there may be many locations) is quite the activity that won't require a single Tableau solution. The activity merely requires you to find your data sources to be consumed later by Tableau Desktop and Tableau Prep.

Getting raw data

Ah, you've narrowed your question set and think you may have found the shiny source of data that holds all the keys to the kingdom! Now comes the data glut (or rut).

All kidding aside, finding the right data from data sources can be hit or miss. It can sometimes feel like you are throwing spaghetti at the wall because you may feel you have found the ideal source, only to be forced to keep digging. When you try to connect the dots, you sometimes just can't. Failing to find the answer to your question happens, and it is perfectly normal. You already know that data sources come in structured, semi-structured, and unstructured forms, meaning that no two data silos are the same. The most significant challenge is to get the correct data for visualization analysis and data transformation.

TECHNICAL STUFF

Tableau Prep is the first step you take in tinkering with raw data. You might have ten different data sources, with each one being evaluated individually or in aggregate. The end objective is to find the data model that answers the question you need to answer.

Figure 3-2, explained in the following bullets, offers an example of how two separate datasets appear after being imported in into Tableau Prep. (These datasets are from usaspending.gov.)

Flow pane

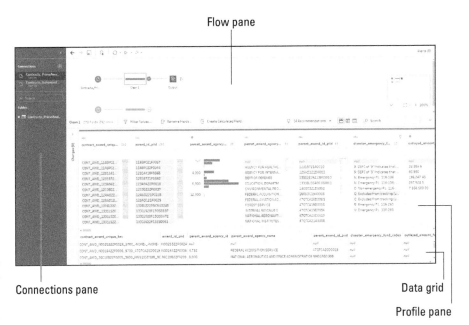

FIGURE 3-2:
Key interface panes for data evaluation in Tableau Prep.

Connections pane

Data grid

Profile pane

>> **Load the data (Connections pane):** In Figure 3-2, two datasets are loaded into the Connections pane in Tableau Prep: Prime Contract Awards and Subcontract Awards Connections pane. (You'll find all the active databases, files, and online source connections in the Connections pane.) To integrate a new data source, you first want to add the source via the Connections pane. Then you drag the table you desire into the Flow pane.

>> **Evaluate the data source (Flow pane):** The Flow pane is a visual presentation of all the steps Tableau must complete to ensure that your data is reliable, and each source requires a new flow. Because there are two data sources in this example, two independent evaluations are being conducted: one for the Prime Contractor data source and another for the Subcontractor data source. Each flow has a rule or a series of procedures it must go through

before it can run at the output step. The rule presented states that should a data source be approved, Tableau Prep can run the source and create a .hyper file, which is the output produced at the end of each flow.

>> **Evaluate the data structure (Profile pane):** The underlying attribute for each data column, such as the column name and data type, are characteristics you must evaluate as part of the evaluation process. You'll want to evaluate the data for quality parameters; however, the objective is to present a best-in-class data profile. That's why users look to the Profile pane, which shows the structure of the data during the data life cycle, given the use of a flow. How the data is represented may differ based on the type of operation needed to be performed.

>> **Look at the details (Data Grid):** You want to skip to the Data Grid to get into the weeds. Here's where you find the low-level details, such as the data columns and data types. Although the values displayed in the Data Grid map to the operations in the Profile pane, the secret sauce of the Data Grid is the ability to conduct cleansing and transformation operations, as you can in the Profile pane, but at a finer-grained level.

Choosing mapping techniques

Selecting the datasets and initially running them through Tableau Prep Builder can be enlightening because you may find interesting nuggets of information. But understanding the visualization possibilities of raw data is a different matter. The data creator should explore how to add measures and dimensions to the Views. Views are a way to graphically visualize a dataset using conventions such as tables, bar charts, circle charts, and scatter plots. The list of ways to render visuals can go on; the point here is that when your data is mature enough and can be visualized, you may want to create a View after you import the data from Tableau Prep Builder into Tableau Desktop. I say *may* want to for a reason.

As you start contemplating how to present your visualization as a story in Tableau, your options fall into five broad areas:

>> Comparing data using bars

>> Spatial data using maps

>> Temporal data using one or more lines

>> Comparative measures using scatterplots

>> Precise numerical values using a tabular format

Figure 3-3 presents a scatterplot. The trend noted in the figure is that conducting more evaluations often leads to a higher score, assuming that the number of evaluations applies to a SUM measure. On the other hand, if you change the measure from SUM to AVERAGE and add a filter (see Figure 3-4), you see a drastically different dataset from what appears in Figure 3-3. The filter applied in Figure 3-4 is a Quality Score of at least 50.

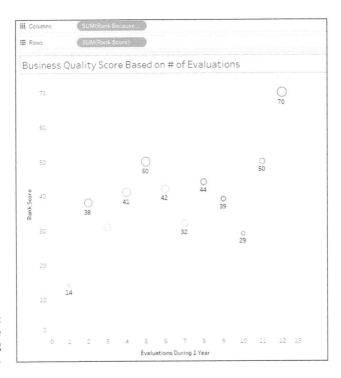

Viewing and preparing datasets

In the last stage of the data prep life cycle, finding an unusual relationship, an outlier, or a trend is not uncommon. Surprises may lead to reshaping the initial question or stimulating a deeper dive, requiring you to find even more data.

REMEMBER

Tableau instantly updates itself based on any changes you make to your approach. For example, if you create a filter and add a condition, that change instantly results in a new result set.

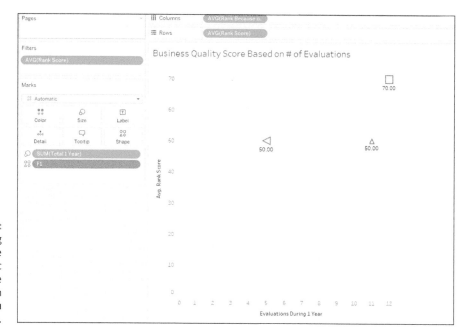

FIGURE 3-4: Changing a measure has a drastic effect on the visualization in Tableau Desktop.

You may wonder why incremental change is essential to viewing and preparing data. Isn't it better to keep data static? The answer is no, no way, for the simple reason that if you can't see the changes (no matter how finite or broad the change is in real time), you can't know what additional modifications are required. You need to constantly keep your data fresh through cleansing and preparation. If your data isn't clean and accurate, your visualizations won't be valuable because they will be deemed erroneous.

TECHNICAL STUFF

Tableau Desktop's interface metaphor is built for users looking to refine their questions into answers incrementally. Every Tableau user can derive meaningful information from data based on their ability to review data points individually or in aggregate to produce reports, dashboards, and stories.

TIP

You may shuffle between Tableau Desktop and Tableau Prep during the view-and-prepare-data stage. If you must introduce new datasets into the mix or you find obscure data, you should consider revising your hypothesis and reviewing the data in Tableau Prep — an extract, transport, and load tool — instead of a data visualization tool such as Tableau Desktop.

Developing visual insights

Many of the enterprise business intelligence applications back in the day were used to separate the data analysis and data visualization aspects of a business intelligence solution across a catalog of solutions. Your data analyst would have to run queries and craft long-winded calculations in one application, pointing to a targeted data source only to reference back to another application to create the visualization. This wasn't a particularly time-efficient process.

When you bring the analysis, visualization, and programmatic nature of data visualization under a single umbrella, you can explore data in a more meaningful, context-rich way. As the data changes, Tableau also concurrently updates the data sources and the visualizations produced.

Developing visual insights requires a tool for data manipulation after the data has been cleansed and adequately formatted. The final dataset is then utilized to create visualization outputs, whether in the form of reports, dashboards, KPIs, or a collection of visualizations, leading to the authoring of a story. Only one application in the Tableau solution, Tableau Desktop, can accomplish all the above.

Figure 3-5 presents an example of a dataset and various model types in the form of a *tree map*.

Using this map, a user can select from a variety of data visualization types from the Show Me section. A user can also change the visualization reflected in the largest area of Tableau Desktop, the workspace.

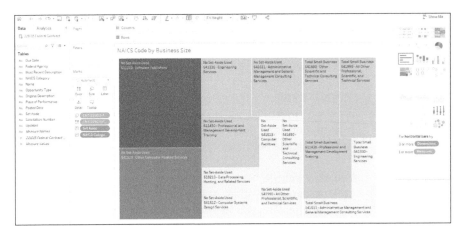

FIGURE 3-5:
A tree map in Tableau Desktop.

Publishing and sharing insights

When users move outside Tableau Desktop, they ultimately choose to publish and share their insights, which may include the datasets. Sharing findings is the last stage in the life cycle, although it may trigger more investigations by the consumers of the data. Users can do only so much when the data resides on their desktop. After a user publishes to either Tableau Server or Tableau Cloud, the ability to complete real-time activities among a team becomes possible. For example, the team can

>> Build new workbooks

>> Establish data sources built from a direct (or live) connection

>> Create data sources that are built on a predefined schedule

>> Prepare flows using automated routines

>> Craft personalized data capabilities inside workbooks containing views, dashboards, stories, and data connections

>> Administer the data at scale by applying data governance standards

Sharing and collaborating with others is the thread that brings users together no matter what license type is purchased. And as you'll see in the following sections, publishing and sharing occur throughout user interactions within the Tableau ecosystem.

Knowing What Tools You Need in Each Stage of the Data Life Cycle

As mentioned in Chapter 2, the Tableau portfolio isn't a one-and-done solution platform but rather a collection of business intelligence solutions. Undoubtedly, every tool mentioned in the last chapter has a place in the Tableau data life cycle. This book focuses on three solutions to bring the life cycle together.

>> **Tableau Desktop:** The solution that helps users create reports, dashboards, stories, and graphs from a workbook containing datasheets. The data can be shared locally or publicly.

>> **Tableau Prep:** The solution within the suite of Tableau products meant to help users prepare data, including combining, shaping, extracting, transforming, and cleansing for analysis in Tableau Desktop.

>> **Tableau Cloud:** The solution that allows users to share, collaborate, and manipulate visualizations and datasets created in Tableau Desktop and Tableau Prep.

Keep in mind that some of the stages in the Tableau Data Life cycle are one hundred percent based on human intervention, meaning that no tool can answer every business intelligence problem. For example, can a tool craft a business hypothesis? I am sure some artificial intelligence agent can propose a question or two for you. Still, it doesn't know the dataset's context, hence the need to combine, shape, and transform the data to its destination among the data life cycle stages. Table 3-1 shows which tools you apply to the life cycle stages described in "Cycling Down the Tableau Highway," earlier in this chapter.

TABLE 3-1:   **Tools to Utilize For the Tableau Data Life Cycle**

Life Cycle Stage	Tableau Desktop	Tableau Prep	Tableau Cloud
Identify the question or business need	N/A	N/A	N/A
Get raw data	No	Yes	No
Choose mapping techniques	Yes	No	No
View and prepare datasets	Yes	Yes	No
Develop visual insights	Yes	No	No
Publish and share insights	No	No	Yes

As Table 3-1 reveals, the only stage that requires more than one tool is viewing and preparing data. The cleansed data moves between Tableau Desktop and Tableau Prep when data is extracted, transformed, and loaded during the cleansing and querying process. First Tableau Prep readies the data. After the data is cleansed, Tableau Prep allows for the data to once again be shared with Tableau Desktop for visualization. To summarize, most of the work in this stage is completed in Tableau Prep because there is cleansing and organization going on, not visualization.

Understanding User Types and Their Capabilities

Chapter 2 provides a brief look at the three user classifications (Viewer, Explorer, and Creator) for the sole purpose of helping you understand what license you need to procure. This chapter helps you better understand how Tableau is not a one-trick pony but rather a solution-based platform, and in this section, you take a deep dive into what each user type can accomplish.

There are two licensing models: user based and core based. Both Tableau Cloud and Tableau Server require at least one Creator license, which comes as a user-based license. For on-premises users, though, Tableau Server is available on a core (server-based) consumption model. To purchase a Viewer or Explorer license, a Creator license is necessary.

Viewer

The Viewer is by far the most restricted user. Viewers are often the team members who need data gathering and viewing activities, not the data creation tasks. Viewers can interact with the data, dashboards, and visualizations by being informed reviewers of the sources. These users can collaborate within their assigned Tableau environment with other users through commenting, downloading, and creating custom views of existing published data. But that is where their involvement stops. The ability to create new assets is prohibited for the Viewer.

Viewers who want to learn more about Tableau Cloud's capabilities, because most of your interaction occurs when data is published, should read Chapters 11 and 12.

Explorer

As a power user, the Explorer has far more ability to act upon published data, including workbooks. The Explorer can create calculations, change chart types, and craft new filters. Unlike the Viewer, who can only review the data and comment, the Explorer can save the files they modify as separate workbooks or over-write the original file with the necessary site permissions. The Explorer has a sliver of developer capacity. They can build their workbook from scratch directly on either Tableau Server or Tableau Cloud. However, the entire publishing life cycle is by no means comprehensive like that of the Creator, who has the most access rights.

Explorers may find the chapters on Tableau Desktop and Tableau Cloud the most helpful, particularly when making changes to work already completed by Creators in Tableau. I suggest you focus your attention on Chapters 7–12.

Creator

The world is your oyster if you are a Creator because you have all the tools to master the entire Tableau data life cycle. Suppose you have a single Creator license. In that case, by default, you are the system administrator for your Tableau Cloud or Tableau Server instance. However, when many parties are involved, including those with Explorer and Viewer licenses, the Creator must assign roles and responsibilities to each licensed Viewer and Explorer. Creators in larger organizations have a varying degree of system administrative privileges, which means that some may be able to provide users with licenses. In contrast, others may have project-level access.

Creators are granted a single license of Tableau Prep to support data acrobatics from cleansing to extracting and loading activities across multiple data sources. In addition, a user is granted access to a full version of Tableau Desktop (not one with reduced functionality), which allows for developing robust data visualization solutions. Finally, at the onset of a user contract, you get to pick between Server or Cloud for publishing and managing your user across all Tableau solutions.

TIP

As a Creator, you'll probably want to read the entire book because all topics are applicable. Still, pay special attention to the Tableau Prep chapters found in Chapters 4–6.

WARNING

There are many caveats to be aware of for the Creator user and what activities one might need to engage in, so look carefully before you leap into your licensing selection choice. First, a Server license is often far more expensive in the long run than a Cloud consumption license, especially if you procure based on cores consumed. (*Cores consumed* refers to how many CPUs are on a given server.) Second, after you lock in your adoption of the Server or Cloud model, it's hard to transition from one to another. To learn more about the process of migrating from Server to Cloud or vice versa, head over to `https://help.tableau.com/current/blueprint/en-gb/bp_move_to_cloud.htm`.

ON THE
WEB

To get into the weeds of each licensing model, go to `https://help.tableau.com/current/server/en-us/license_product_keys.htm`.

Engaging Users Based on User Type

Themes you encounter throughout the remainder of this book relate mainly to how users access, author, prepare, interact, collaborate, and govern their data across Tableau Desktop, Tableau Prep, and Tableau Cloud based on their user type. The reality is that the data life cycle is not a perfectly cyclical process.

Most users cannot make the Tableau data life cycle constant. Deviations occur because datasets offer unpredictability, primarily as users interact and collaborate with Tableau. Then again, you may hit the bull's eye on the first try after authoring and preparing the perfect data solution.

Moving forward, I don't call out the license type in the remaining text. Instead, I focus on the functionality and the application that completes the activities being described. My goal for this last section is to provide a quick reference for you to return to if you need to know a user's limitations when it comes to access, authoring, preparing the data, and so on.

Access

It should come as no surprise that Tableau wants the world to gain access to data, so to be sure that all users have access, all license types are fully supported across all key capabilities, whether external or embedded in the content-based user experience. Tableau recognizes two discriminating access types, as shown in Table 3-2.

TABLE 3-2: **Key Access Capabilities**

	Creator	Explorer	Viewer
Web and mobile	✓	✓	✓
Embedded content	✓	✓	✓

Author

Authors in Tableau focus more on their own needs than others. They leverage the Tableau platform to make decisions by digging into the available data sources to create visualizations for themselves or manage those for others in a power-user capacity, as noted in Table 3-3.

The author does have the capacity to create and use existing data sources so that they create modified views, dashboards, and analytic outputs for others. Fundamentally though, authoring focuses on personal consumption rather than collaboration and interaction. An author eventually transitions collaboration and interaction after preparing, collaborating, and interacting with Tableau solutions over time.

Prepare

Data preparation is one area that stands out for those requiring the development functionality found in Tableau Desktop. Unless you are merely the orchestrator of data, which includes scheduling the data for dissemination, all data preparation actions fall under the Creator user type (see "Understanding User Types and Their Capabilities," earlier in this chapter). The key capabilities for data preparation that you should acclimate to are included in Table 3-4.

TABLE 3-3

Key Author Capabilities Offered in Tableau

	Creator	Explorer	Viewer
Edit existing workbooks and visualizations	✓	✓	
Create and publish new workbooks from existing published data sources only	✓	✓	
Explore existing published data sources with Ask Data, a natural language engine for analytics analysis	✓	✓	
Create and publish new workbooks with one or more new data sources	✓		
Create and publish new data sources	✓		
Create new workbooks based on Dashboard Starters, a way to integrate with other enterprise software applications such as Salesforce CRM or SAP ERP (Tableau Cloud only)	✓		

TABLE 3-4

Key Preparation Capabilities Offered In Tableau

	Creator	Explorer	Viewer
Create new data flow files (`.tfl`) or `.hypher` file	✓		
Edit and modify data flow files	✓		
Export data files (`.tde`, `.hyper`, `.csv`)	✓		
Publish and run flows	✓		
Schedule flows	✓	✓	

Interact

Interaction is a big part of the sales pitch with the Tableau brand, so it's not surprising that all license types include a bevy of interaction options. The noticeable difference is the ability to download summaries as opposed to full data, as shown in Table 3-5. For some, this difference may be trivial, but the feature can be helpful if you need to know finite details about a selection within a data source. If you need to dig into the weeds on a data source, the Creator license is non-negotiable.

TABLE 3-5   ## Key Interaction Capabilities Offered in Tableau

	Creator	Explorer	Viewer
Interact with data using a variety of visualization types	✓	✓	✓
Create and share views	✓	✓	✓
Download visualizations as static images (`.pdf`, `.png`, `.jpg`)	✓	✓	✓
Download summary data	✓	✓	✓
Download full data	✓	✓	

Collaborate

Except for allowing one or more parties to share, a Viewer has all the same collaboration features as a Creator and Explorer. As shown in Table 3-6, the various collaboration features enable subscriptions and alerts for others as part of the programmatic process, which a developer or power user often completes.

TABLE 3-6   ## Key Collaboration Capabilities Offered in Tableau

	Creator	Explorer	Viewer
Comment on any visualization, including dashboards, reports, KPIs, and stories	✓	✓	✓
Create subscriptions for yourself	✓	✓	✓
Receive alert notifications	✓	✓	✓
Create subscriptions for others	✓	✓	
Create alert notifications for others	✓	✓	

Govern

Govern is the fancy term for system administration. Viewers have no administrative capabilities, whereas an Explorer, the "power user," can limit user access. But when it comes to managing enterprise security for data sources and integrating with security tenants, a way to isolate privileged and secure organizational data using an identity management platform such as Microsoft Azure Directory, you must be a Creator, as noted in Table 3-7.

TABLE 3-7   **Key Governance Capabilities Offered in Tableau**

	Creator	Explorer	Viewer
Manage users and permissions	✓	✓	
Manage content and certify data sources	✓	✓	
Perform server administration	✓		
Conduct fine-grained security management	✓		

2
Prepping Data in Tableau

IN THIS CHAPTER

» Learn data connectivity
fundamentals across all Tableau
solutions

» Explore the different ways
to create meaningful data
relationships in Tableau

» Get hands-on experience in joining
and blending data sources

» Build ad-hoc data connectors
in Tableau Desktop using
clipboard data

Chapter **4**

Connecting Your Data

S tarting up any Tableau product is like turning on a car for the first time. You need a set of keys, some fuel in the car to operate, and a basic understanding of how to operate the vehicle. As previous chapters show, the data source is the holy grail to running the Tableau engine. If you have no data source, the application won't go very far. More data provides better insights, but if you have a small set, it is still better than nothing.

In this chapter, you explore the various data source options at your fingertips. After showing you how to figure out which option is suitable for your need, I walk you through how to plan the configuration and customization of the data source. Sometimes the process is fluid because only one person needs to access the data, whereas in other situations, thousands, if not millions, of users, may access the data, and this chapter looks at these considerations in this chapter. The last half of the chapter talks about data source construction before you dig deep into the cleansing and prep stage of your data.

Many people want to jump straight to analysis and skip this part, and you may find doing so to be adequate. But if the data impacts a broader audience, the step-by-step process I take you through in this chapter should undoubtedly make you a strong data analyst using Tableau Desktop, Tableau Prep, and Tableau Cloud.

Understanding Data Source Options

Whether you are using Tableau Prep or Desktop, the first activity you must complete is to connect to data. Otherwise, guess what? You'll get nothing out of using Tableau. That's right: zip!

Looking for the Connect button, shown where the arrows point in Figures 4-1 and 4-2, is your golden ticket no matter which Tableau solution you intend to use.

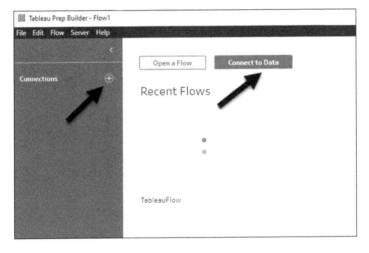

A few flavors of data sources are available across Tableau Desktop, Tableau Prep, Tableau Server, and Tableau Cloud. Tableau has conveniently broken down your search for options into a few classifications. Users can search for data in the following places

>> Directly from Tableau Server, in Tableau Server and Tableau Cloud

>> From files such as text, JSON, Access, PDF, and XLS

>> From a server such as Microsoft SQL, MySQL, Oracle, and Amazon Redshift

As you'll notice, within these categories, you have many options to choose from in Tableau. The list is lengthy, with 100+ connector types and counting across enterprise applications if you have the Professional Edition of Tableau Prep and Desktop. Among the data sources, it's essential to know that Tableau is not married to fixed data structures; it can handle semi-structured and unstructured data for analysis. (See the "Data structure differences" sidebar to understand how these types differ from one another.)

WARNING

Some data sources require more steps than others to connect Tableau. For example, with the Microsoft applications in Tableau, multifactor authentication is required to connect to your Azure Active Directory account. On the other hand, validating your account credentials, which may include the account password, is all that is necessary to use Google Analytics. Figure 4-3 offers an example of a user authenticating outside Tableau using their Box credentials. Finally, any enterprise database, virtualization platform, or enterprise resource planning (ERP) software requires the server name, port, service type, username, password, and one-off credential options. Oracle Databases (Figure 4-4) represent an example of a more complicated data source.

DATA STRUCTURE DIFFERENCES

Here's a very brief primer on the difference between structured, semi-structured, and unstructured data among data source types:

- **Structured data:** This type of data can be easily scanned and analyzed because it has a defined structure with repetition and consistency. An example is a spreadsheet or a relational database table.

- **Semi-structured data:** This type of data falls somewhere between structured and unstructured because it doesn't have a rigid format and is considered semi-structured. It doesn't conform to a data table, but it does have classifying characteristics associated with the dataset. Examples may include semantic tagging or metadata markup, as well as XML or JSON files.

- **Unstructured data:** This type of data is found in file formats that analysts cannot easily extract answers from because the format is not well defined. A PDF or a multimedia- based file such as a PPT, MOV, or WMV file are all fine examples of unstructured data.

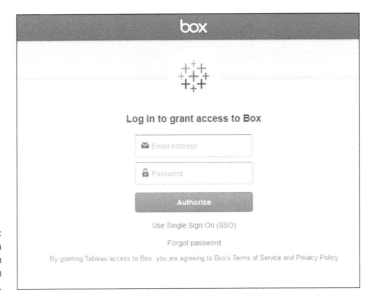

FIGURE 4-3:
A simple data
source login
for users with
Box accounts.

Connect to Data

Oracle   ×

Oracle

Server: | Port: Option

Service: Optional

Enter information to sign in to the server

○ Integrated Authentication
◉ Username and Password

Username:

Password:

☐ Require SSL (recommended)

Show Initial SQL

Sign In

FIGURE 4-4:
A complex data
source con-
figuration for
users needing
to connect to
Oracle.

Connecting to Data

To connect to a data source in Tableau, you must first enter the necessary credentials. You usually complete the connection on a single screen unless the application
has two-factor authentication (which is becoming more common these days). Tableau then provides a prompt indicating that you are now connected (see Figure 4-5).

But then what? Is connecting to a data source that simple? The answer is yes! You
can start playing with your data at this point. Figure 4-6 shows that I connected
to a SharePoint list, which is a Microsoft data source. Now I can start importing
the data from one or more of the available SharePoint lists.

Making the Desktop or Prep connection

Whether you launch Tableau Desktop or Tableau Prep, you make a data connection
by using the Connect pane. As described earlier in the chapter, each application
has the Connect pane in a slightly different location. Your best bet is always to
locate the left panel and find either the Tableau logo (Desktop) or the connection
with the plus symbol (Prep) to initiate the connection without fussing around the
respective applications. Table 4-1 describes the different data source connection
types accessible for Desktop-client users.

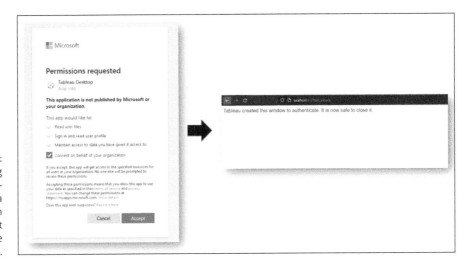

FIGURE 4-5:
Connecting to a Microsoft data source, with the prompt confirming the source active.

FIGURE 4-6:
Accessing a OneDrive + SharePoint data source using the Microsoft Data Source Connection.

TABLE 4-1 ## Connection Types in Tableau Desktop and Prep

Source Type	Description
Tableau Server or Tableau Cloud	Users connect to the on-premises Tableau Server address or the URL-provided Tableau Cloud address.
File	Users obtain a file by pointing to it on their desktop. There are 25+ file types currently supported. File types can contain structured, semi-structured, and unstructured data.
Server application	Most enterprise applications and enterprise database sources fall into this category. Examples include Oracle, SAP, IBM, Salesforce, and Microsoft applications. You can also integrate with data virtualization platforms such as Denodo and Snowflake.
Other database (JDBC)	Users can create a connection to a Java Database Connectivity (JDBC) API-based data source.
Other database (ODBC)	Users can create a connection to a Microsoft Open Database Connectivity (ODBC) interface data source.

REMEMBER

In the Tableau documentation, the term "Connect pane" is specific to Tableau Desktop whereas "Connections pane" is specific to Tableau Prep. Both terms refer to the same element, however.

Tableau provides the native connectors to the most common file and database types under the respective Connect menus. Assuming that you cannot find your enterprise data source, you have a few options. If a JDBC or ODBC connection can consume your application, quickly utilize these options to create a data source.

TECHNICAL STUFF

Suppose you can't find what you're looking for? In that case, consider creating your own web data connector or even a connector plug-in using the Tableau Connector SDK. Tableau provides limited support for connection to these options, and details for building such functionality is well beyond the scope of this book.

REMEMBER

Tableau adds new data connector types to its platform all the time. If you have the 2018 edition of Tableau Desktop and Tableau Prep, I can guarantee that you have far fewer data connections available than the version this book is based on (the 2022 edition). To keep up with the latest data connectors, go to `https://help.tableau.com/current/pro/desktop/en-us/exampleconnections_overview.htm`.

Locating the Server and Online connections

Connecting to a data source inside the Tableau ecosystem is easier than connecting to another vendor's product. However, you may expect the process within Tableau to be a bit more descriptive than it is, given that Tableau offers two publishing-oriented products. Still, when you know where to go to get started, connecting within Tableau should go pretty smoothly.

You can find all connections under a single menu, the Server menu. In that menu, you go to the menu option Sign-In and enter the URL of the Tableau Server into the Server field, and then press the Connect button. Or you can connect to Tableau Online using Quick Connect by pressing the link to Tableau Online, as seen in Figure 4-7. Tableau then prompts the user to log in to their Tableau Cloud account, as shown in Figure 4-8.

FIGURE 4-7:
The Tableau Server and Tableau Cloud data connection.

FIGURE 4-8: Log in to Tableau Online using the Quick Access link.

Setting Up and Planning the Data Source

Connecting to a data source doesn't mean you're done with the data source management's planning and design stage. Not even close, in fact. Setting up the data source is step one; bending it to your liking such that it can produce exemplary result sets is a different activity. This and the following sections in this chapter describe how to go about analyzing and preparing the data before data analysis, visualization, and publishing.

Although this is not a self-help book, it's time to ask yourself some critical questions about your wants and needs on data! Is your goal to quickly explore your dataset? If so, you may want to attach your data source to Tableau Desktop or Tableau Prep and take a quick tour of what's under the hood. Perhaps build a few visualizations and see whether you can discern anything of use. You'll get a good sense from your first pass of how good (or bad) the data quality is. And yes, you can figure out how much data cleanup is required. The most significant step is to consider whether the data meets the business needs. Another more pivotal question as you plan is whether the data source meets your needs in terms of source location, cleanliness, customizability, security, and performance maturity. Table 4-2 explores these questions.

TABLE 4-2   **Data Source Planning Categories and Questions**

Category	Description	Question
Location	Identify where the data source resides.	Is the data source on-premises or cloud-based?
		Is the data source a file or part of an application?
		Is the data source a database?
		Does Tableau offer a data connector? If not, will a data connector need to be created to support the database source, such as an ODBC or JDBC connection?
Access	Identify the specific functionality needed to operate in the location, including authentication and authorization credentials.	Who should have access to the Tableau data source?
		What level of access should the users have based on the data source location?
		What type of user filtering and row-level security may be utilized in accessing the data source?
Cleanliness	Identify how well structured and formatted the data may be, leading to a range of extract, transport, and load (ETL) processes that might be completed using Tableau Prep Builder.	How well structured is the data source?
		Is Tableau Data Prep required to clean and automate prep flows?
		Are there any calculations and manipulations that may best be done natively in Tableau?
		Should data be removed to improve speed and performance or enhance data cleanliness?
Customization	Identify ways that require unique naming conventions or formatting requirements that allow the data to align with Tableau's native capabilities.	Is the data source adequate, or will add-on capabilities be required, such as calculations?
		Will the tables and fields within the data source require modification to be understood to explore dimensions and measures better?
Scale	Identify the pervasiveness of the data source and how it should be utilized within Tableau. Scaling data includes model maturity and combining of data.	Should data be spread among several systems or centrally contained in a single environment?
		Does it make sense to combine data from each table into a single source of truth?

(continued)

TABLE 4-2 *(continued)*

Category	Description	Question
Security	Identify where the data source is created and utilized, such as the native workbook or perhaps an embedded data source published to Tableau Server or Tableau Online.	Can the data source remain independent, or does it need to be embedded in another data source?
		Where will the public data source be published?
		Who owns the data source, ultimately?
		What authentication and authorization schema is required for the dataset?
Performance	Identify the type of connection required to support the data source throughout its entire life cycle.	Does the data source require a live connection, or is a data extract adequate?
		If a data extract is adequate, is a refresh schedule planned using Tableau Server or Tableau Cloud?
		If Tableau Cloud is being used, will Tableau Bridge also be used?

TECHNICAL STUFF

On the subject of data connections, be aware that Tableau Bridge (referenced in the Performance category of Table 4-2) is a unique connection type. Tableau Bridge is a lightweight client software application that sits on the desktop or local server within your computer network (think on-premises). The client software interacts with Tableau Cloud to ensure that the data source on the local machine, which connects to a private network data source that Tableau Cloud can't reach ordinarily, always remains up to date.

Relating and Combining Data Sources

No two data sources come in the same shape and size. The typical scenario with Tableau is to have Tableau from a table in one source, with a second source having another like-kind table. You connect both sources in the same workbook and then drag the two tables onto the canvas to build a single view. But building a single view may be easier said than done, assuming that your data can be combined across multiple databases.

ON THE WEB

For some of the steps in this chapter, I use a dataset about Worldwide University rankings found on Kaggle.com which you can download at `https://www.kaggle.com/datasets/aneesayoub/world-universities-ranking-2022`. The download contains four csv files, which you use to extract data into Tableau to complete the following and later steps in this chapter.

To connect to the data sources you've downloaded, follow these steps:

1. **Connect to the data source.**

2. **Drag a table or sheet of data to the canvas, which then releases the table or sheet onto the canvas for manipulation.**

3. **To add another table from the same data source (in this example, that is; see Step 7 to use a different source), drag that second table or sheet to the canvas and release it.**

   One of two things might happen:

   - A "noodle," or a line between two items in the Flow pane, forms indicating that an automatic relationship is created after you map the three like-kind fields. (See Figure 4-9.)

   - The Edit Relationship dialog pops up, prompting you to provide Tableau with the fields that must be mapped, depending on the warning symbol's message. (See Figure 4-10.)

   For Step 3, you want to map the Acceptance Rate for all tables against the Top 300 Universities of the World, resulting in the noodle shown in Figure 4-9. Otherwise, you'll continue to get a result like Figure 4-10.

4. **Continue adding tables to the canvas as needed, assuming that the tables come from the same data source under these conditions.**

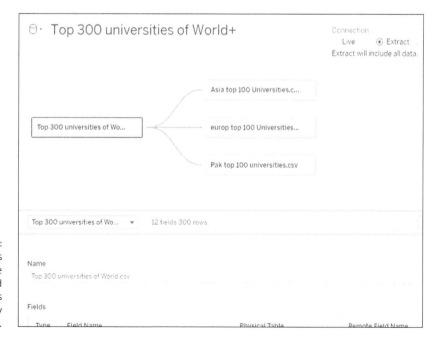

FIGURE 4-9:
Four tables connect due to data field similarities, as indicated by the noodle.

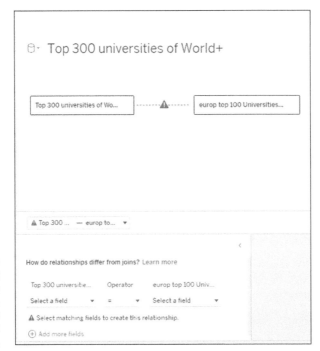

Top 300 universities of World+

Top 300 universities of Wo... ------▲------ europ top 100 Universities...

▲ Top 300 ... — europ to... ▾

How do relationships differ from joins? Learn more

Top 300 universitie...   Operator   europ top 100 Univ...
Select a field   ▾   =   ▾   Select a field   ▾
▲ Select matching fields to create this relationship.
⊕ Add more fields

FIGURE 4-10:
An edit
relationship
dialog appears,
prompting the
user to select
the fields.

There is a slight modification to the preceding steps if you require multiple data connections.

5. **To connect to a different data source, switch to one of the other available data connections in the left pane by dragging the desired table to the canvas and releasing it.**

Multiple data sources appear the same way as a single data source does; the only difference is that two data sources now form a connection.

6. **Complete the activity by following Steps 2–4, except you should switch between data connections when needed.**

TECHNICAL STUFF

Relationships are the most practical way to combine data in Tableau because they are flexible and allow users to combine data across multiple sources, especially if you have many tables to analyze. You can also join and blend tables, as described in "Joining Data" and "Blending data from multiple sources," later in this chapter.

Working with Data Relationships

Creating relationships is the cleanest and most simplistic approach a user can use to combine data across the Tableau platform. Another benefit is that a relationship limits your need to join and blend data — activities that can compromise data quality and reliability. Relationships have numerous advantages, especially when dealing with multitable data sources. Of course, they have a few disadvantages as well. The following sections offer more details on the advantages and disadvantages of using relationships.

Knowing the advantages of relationships

Here are the main advantages of creating relationships:

» Users do not need to configure a join type between tables. You need to select only the fields that relate to the tables.

» Tables remain distinct; no comingling of data occurs because there is no data merging.

» Relationships automate joins on your behalf to support the appropriate visualization type, hence no guessing. As the user conducts analysis, the relationship join is flexible, and changes are made to the data.

» Unmatched measures don't get dropped; they remain preserved, ensuring that no data loss occurs.

» Relationships help to avoid data duplication and filtering issues, which often arise with joins.

» Relationships generate the correct aggregations and join types so that during analysis, you have little concern regarding the data types associated with a field in use within a worksheet.

Seeing the disadvantages of relationships

And now for some of the downsides of relationships:

» Poorly formatted data, especially multi-table data, can make analysis very complex.

» Using any data filter can limit Tableau's ability to utilize *join culling,* which involves simplifying queries by eliminating unnecessary join statements.

>> Unmatched values across relationships can be left in limbo.

>> Attempting to mix and match multiple fact tables with multiple-dimension tables, thereby resulting in modeling shared or conformed dimensions, does not yield fruitful results.

WARNING

Using a join can be tricky to manipulate, so use joins cautiously. Furthermore, if you are trying to use a join with published data, doing so is not supported using any version of Tableau.

WARNING

There is one more use case when relationships may not yield the results you want that I want to bring your attention to: limited support of relational connections. Tableau has many prebuilt connectors. Some offer exceptional data interoperability, including the use of many logical tables. A few of those connectors limit you to a single logical table, however. You won't be imagining things if you attempt to use sources such as Cubes, SAP HANA, JSON files, or Google Analytics and can pull only a single table, not an infinite number. Other examples of limited support include adding a stored procedure to a connection that commits the connection to a single logical table and publishing data to Tableau Cloud or Tableau Server, where data sources cannot be interrelated.

Creating relationships

To get a grasp of relationship building, it's a good idea to try your data in Tableau Desktop before putting it through Tableau Prep Builder. Doing so lets you see how the fields are labeled and whether any meaningful relationships can be built in the logical layer of the data sources based on the default view of the canvas. Taking the same previous dataset from Kaggle.com (see "Relating and Combining Data Sources," earlier in this chapter), follow these steps to run your data through Tableau Desktop:

1. **Open Tableau Desktop.**

2. **Connect all four csv files into Tableau Desktop as provided in the zip package you've downloaded from Kaggle.com (assuming that you've extracted them all).**

3. **Drag the table derived from the data source Top 300 Universities of World.csv to the canvas (see Fig 4-11).**

4. **Locate the table from the data source Asia Top 100 Universities.csv and drop the table onto the canvas when you see the noodle form between the two tables.**

   A connection forms (see Fig 4-12).

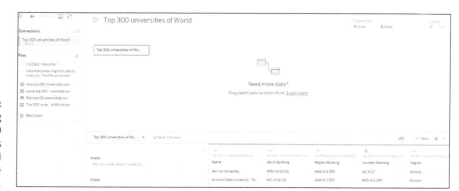

FIGURE 4-11:
Dragging
the Top 300
Universities
of the World
table onto the
canvas.

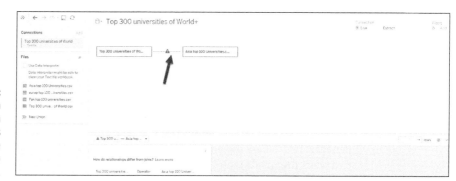

FIGURE 4-12:
A connection
forms between
two tables
when they're
dragged onto
the canvas.

Editing relationships

Although Tableau attempts to create a relationship between existing data types (for example, string to string or integer to integer) and field names, it may not always find a perfect match. You should anticipate that you'll need to come up with meaningful relationships based on the data types matching appropriately.

To edit the relationships in Tableau Prep Builder, you'll need to identify which columns require editing. After you've identified the specific columns in Tableau Prep Builder, follow these steps:

1. **To change the fields, select the field pairs between the two tables.**

2. **Select the field's name from the two drop-down lists to create a pair of matching fields.**

3. **Repeat Steps 1 and 2 to create multiple field pairs for relationships.**

TECHNICAL STUFF

Sometimes, Tableau doesn't detect constraints, which happens when data has been labeled poorly. Poor labeling is the case with the dataset shown in this chapter, which is why you have had to do a bit of data acrobatics to map fields like *Name* to *name* even though the field names are identical. Tableau isn't perfect. The field names must be identical, including the capitalizations (not kidding here). When these situations occur, you'll have a many-to-many relationship form, leading to referential integrity being set to some record match. Tableau's settings accommodate safe choices, offering flexibility to your data sources. That means your data should accommodate full outer joins (which you find out more about in the next section). Users optimize queries by aggregating table data way before forming joins for the data. The change results in all column and row data becoming available for analysis.

Moving tables to create different relationships

The example using the Top 300 Universities in the World+ dataset in this chapter contains four tables (which you can download from `https://www.kaggle.com/datasets/aneesayoub/world-universities-ranking-2022`, as mentioned in "Relating and Combining Data Sources," earlier in this chapter.) The primary table, Top 300 Universities in the World.csv, connects with Asia Top 100 Universities.csv, Europe Top 100 Universities.csv, and Pak Top 100 Universities.csv. Say you wanted to move one of the tables because there may be a better relationship between two tables instead of the primary table, Top 300 Universities. Here are two ways to move a table:

>> Drag the table requiring the change to the new table with which you intend to establish the relationship. In this example, you move the PAK Top 100 Universities next to Asia Top 100 Universities (see Figure 4-13).

>> Alternatively, you can hover over the table and click the arrow. Then select Move To and select your preferred alternative table location (see Figure 4-14).

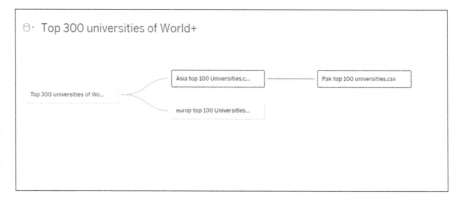

FIGURE 4-13: Dragging a relationship on the canvas to a new table.

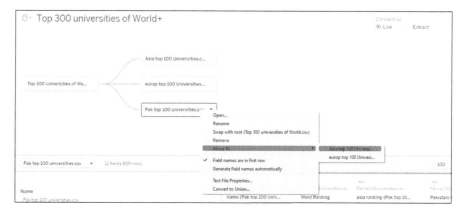

FIGURE 4-14:
Hovering over
a table to
select an alter-
native table
location.

Changing the root table of a relationship

The root table is considered the primary data table within a Tableau data model. When a model integrates several like-kind tables, but one table offers a superior set of fields, you may want to switch the primary table with one of the connecting tables. For example, as shown in Figure 4-15, I decided that the Asia Top 100 Universities.csv is a superior fit compared to the Top 300 Universities of World+. To swap the root table with another, right-click the logical table that should become the primary table in the model. Then select Swap with Root.

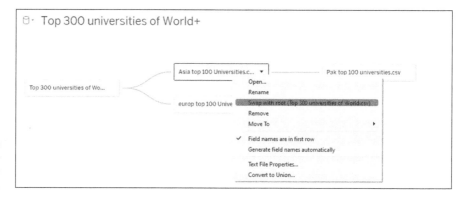

FIGURE 4-15:
Changing the
root table of a
relationship.

Removing tables from a relationship

As you review the data across one or more tables, you may find a table that's not helpful, and removing it from the relationship on the canvas would make sense. To remove a table, follow these steps:

1. **Hover your cursor over the table on the canvas.**

2. **Right-click the table and then select Remove.**

3. **Release the mouse to make the table disappear.**

   Deleting a table on a canvas also automatically deletes all related relationships to the primary descendant table.

In the example shown in Figure 4-16, the table Europe Top 100 Universities.csv is selected for removal.

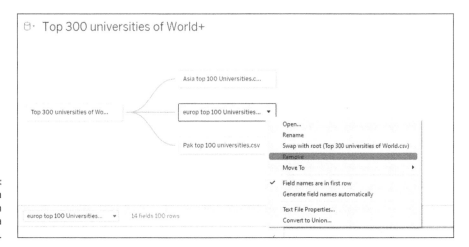

FIGURE 4-16: Removing a table from an existing data relationship.

TIP

Before you remove a table from a relationship, hover your cursor over a noodle to view the relationship status. Check for three things: the relationship between the tables; the cardinality of the relationship; and the fields mapped between the relationship.

Joining Data

Creating relationships is generally the preferred approach to establishing a data source. You may sometimes want to use a join to control data, however. Whether you want to ensure specific types of filtering or reduce filtering deliberately, the join is the technique a data analyst must use to extend the relationship.

A *join* allows the merging of data from two or more tables into a single table. Under ordinary circumstances, if you merge data from many tables into one, you find lots of redundant data, and filtering can be quite cumbersome. Sometimes the values are even returned null or empty. For these reasons, you need to select the correct type of join to determine how Tableau handles your data.

REMEMBER

In Tableau, joins and the more simplistic relationship act differently because they are defined in different data model layers. Relationships are defined at the logical layer of the data source. In contrast, joins are defined at the physical layer of the data source.

TECHNICAL STUFF

Depending on your data-shaping requirements, the Tableau tool you'll use varies. Tableau Desktop is more than adequate when you're looking to complete basic shaping and create standard joins. If you need to create multiple joins or do a bit of data cleanup from modifying field names, changing data types, and establishing filters or sorts, head over to Tableau Prep Builder.

Understanding join types

Most users stick with one of four join types: left, right, inner, and full outer. The other option is union, depicted along with the other types in Figure 4-17. In the following sections, you can see how to create a join, handle various clause types, and deal with null values generated during join creation.

Inner		When using an inner join, the result is a table that contains values that match from both tables only.
Left		When using a left join, the result is a table that contains all values from the left table and only those corresponding matches from the right table. If the table on the left table doesn't contain a corresponding match in the right table, a null value appears.
Right		When using a right join, the result is a table that contains all values from the right table and only those corresponding matches from the left table. If the table on the right table doesn't contain a corresponding match in the left table, a null value appears.
Full outer		When using a full outer join to combine tables, the result is a table that contains all values from both tables. If one or more tables don't contain a match with another table, you see a null value in the data grid.
Union		The union, although not a type of join, is a method to combine two or more tables by appending rows of a table from one table to another. Tables that you attempt to union should have the same types of attribution, such as field names and data types.

FIGURE 4-17: The most commonly used join types.

Setting up join clauses

You perform a join by setting up one or more join clauses. The *join clause* tells Tableau which fields are shared between the tables, including how to match the corresponding rows. For example, rows should be equal when the same identifiers are aligned in the results table using the equal (=) operator. Similarly, you can search for values such as less than, greater than, less than, or equal to, greater than, or equal to, and does not equal, as shown in the drop-down menu in Figure 4-18.

FIGURE 4-18:
Operator types
supported in
forming joins.

Joins are not limited to a single clause, either. They can contain multiple clauses. For example, you may have multiple parameters, such as "Name = Name" and "State = State", as indicated in the .csv files evaluated in this chapter. The conditions must be considered valid for both rows to be joined. Other conditions may include when the Name is shared but the State is not. The join clause may appear as "Name = Name" and "State <> State".

Unlike other business intelligence platforms, Tableau supports join clauses containing calculations. You can concatenate fields "[City] + [State] = [City]+[State]." That said, only certain data sources support calculations with join clauses. Most file and relational sources are supported, whereas enterprise applications are hit or miss.

Creating a join

To create a join, you need to identify at least one data source, preferably two. You may have a single source, or there may be multiple tables in a database or worksheets in an Excel spreadsheet representing different sources. You may also want to use completely different data sources, which is the case with the example throughout this chapter that uses the four CSV files from Kaggle.com (see "Relating and Combining Data Sources," earlier in this chapter). If you intend to combine tables using a cross-database join, Tableau applies a color scheme to the canvas.

WARNING

Color coding is at the heart of many features within Tableau. Although Tableau offers the user many opportunities to configure dashboards, worksheets, and stories so that they're accessible for public distribution of work, discriminating colors for dimensions and measures inside applications such as Tableau Desktop and Tableau Prep do not support American Disability Act (ADA) Section 508 Compliant standards for its interfaces. As for visualizations, it is up to you to ensure that outputs meet accessibility requirements.

Follow these steps to create a join:

1. **To create a join, drag one table to the canvas; then drag a second table to the canvas.**

   A Join dialog box appears, enabling you to create a data join. Select the join type.

   A relationship forms, as shown in Figure 4-19.

FIGURE 4-19:
A relationship forms when you drag two additional tables to the canvas.

2. **Double-click the first table to open the join canvas.**

   A separate window opens, showing a join canvas on the right with all the tables listed in the left pane (see Figure 4-20).

3. **Select one or more of the tables to create joins.**

   Drag one or more tables onto the first table you've created from the Connections pane and place it on top of the first table. You'll be asked to create a union or join. Select the join, not a union. At this point, you'll want to select the join type to create after the new relationship has been formed on the canvas.

4. **Repeat this process as many times as you need to by double-clicking another table from the Data Source pane and dragging it to the canvas as needed to build additional join clauses as desired.**

5. **When you have all the desired tables on the canvas, click the join relationship icon to select the join type desired.**

   You need to configure the field mappings based on the join type. In the example shown in Figure 4-20, all fields are tied to the Name or Country.

6. **When you're done, close the Join dialog box, and the join canvas is saved.**

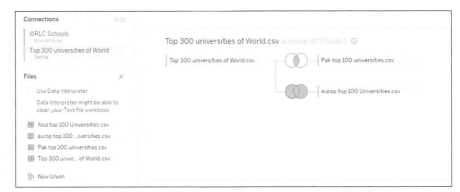

FIGURE 4-20:
Creating a
join table.

For this example, I selected three tables. I connected the Top 300 Universities of World.csv with Pak Top 100 Universities.csv to form an *inner join,* which results in a table containing only matching values from both tables. I've also formed a *full outer join* (which results in a table containing all values from both tables) between the Top 300 Universities of World.csv with Europe Top 100 Universities.csv.

Joining fields that contain null values

It goes without saying that if you use joins and constrain data in a table, some fields will have null values. If fields used to join tables do not contain any values, the system returns rows with null values. Null values may not be returned with single-connection data sources, however, and believe it or not, such sources are very popular with Tableau users. That's why Tableau provides various options to allow users to join fields containing null values with other values, which also contain null values. To handle these conditions, follow these steps:

1. **Go to the Data Source page in Tableau Desktop.**

2. **Select the Data menu option; then locate Join Null Values to Null Values on the menu that appears.**

   If this option is grayed out, as it is in Figure 4-21, that means it's not available to your data source. This can happen if, for example, you added a second data source connection. In that case, the join reverts to the default behavior, meaning that it has decided to eliminate rows with null values.

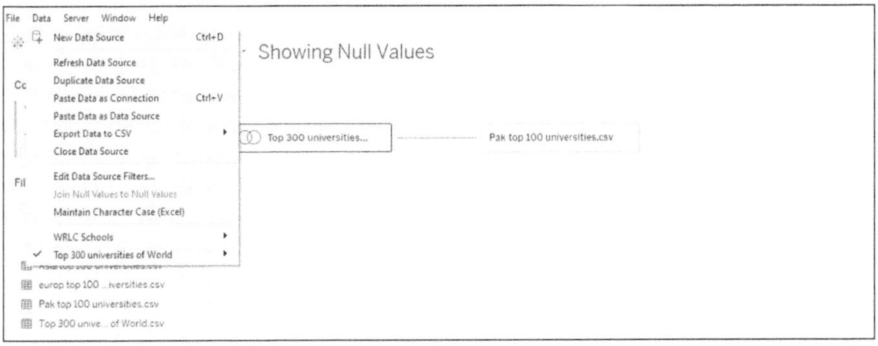

FIGURE 4-21:
Tableau has
eliminated
rows with
null values in
this case, as
indicated by
the greyed-out
option.

Blending data from multiple sources

Suppose you want to combine data from multiple sources. In that case, you need to blend your data to bring in additional information across many data sources so that it can be displayed with the primary data source within the same view.

Whereas blends and relationships can combine data from multiple data sources, queries don't combine data; they query each source independently. Results are aggregated and presented visually in a single view. Blends, in contrast to queries, can handle different details and work with different published data sources. You should consider using blending, especially when the goal is to link fields across many data sources on a sheet-by-sheet basis when combining data sources.

To blend data, follow these steps:

1. **Connect to your primary data source. Then, in the Data pane, select the sheet that contains the data you want to blend.**

   The first data source becomes the primary.

2. **Click the Data Blending icon in the top-right corner of the screen, which means you can then select the secondary data source you want to blend with the primary data source.**

   This source then becomes the secondary data source.

   Drag a field from the secondary data source to the Filters or Columns/Rows shelf.

   For the example, I've added the workbook used in Chapters 2 and 3, which includes Citizen Data and a new data source containing universities in Washington, D.C. The data fields (those in Sheet1) show the potential blending opportunities in Figure 4-22. The blended opportunity, as described in the relationship, is depicted by the noodle in Figure 4-23.

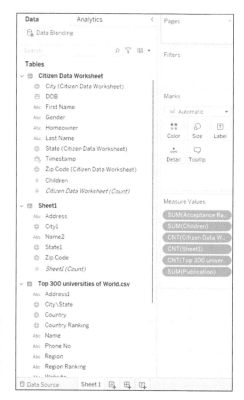

FIGURE 4-22:
Blending data
within the
Data pane
using Tableau
Desktop.

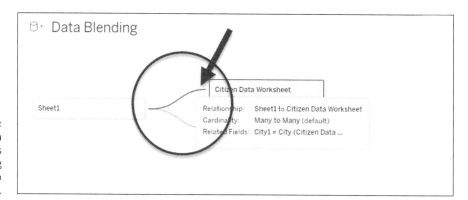

FIGURE 4-23:
How a data
model reflects
blending
between two
data sources.

Watch how Tableau automatically creates a relationship between the two data sources based on the fields you've dragged using the orange noodle, as shown in Figure 4-23.

If the line is grey, that often means there is a broken link icon. To remedy this situation, click the icon next to the field that links the two data sources. Find a field that is appropriate to match both sides of the match. Then the blended relationships turn orange, representing an active link.

TECHNICAL STUFF

You can't get away with a single data source when blending. There is a mandatory requirement for a primary and secondary data source. The first data source becomes the primary, which defines the view. The secondary source is restricting, helping only to keep values that have corresponding matches to the primary data source. For all purposes, you should consider a blend like a left join.

REMEMBER

Joins and blending have subtle differences. Data blending does simulate the traditional left blend. There is one caveat to keep in mind about joins and blending when considering data aggregation. Joins combine data and aggregate after the fact. Blends aggregate first and then combine the data. In other words, it's all about the order in which you combine the data.

Working with clipboard data

Not all your data may be nice and neatly formatted in a data source such as a relational database, enterprise application, or even an organized file format. You may want to pull in data from an outside source for one-off analysis. Rather than spend hours (or days) trying to craft the perfect data source, and then connecting it to Tableau only to be disappointed, you have a quick solution to test your assumptions on the fly. Tableau allows users to copy and paste a sample dataset directly into a workbook. How, you ask?

In a nutshell, Tableau creates a temporary data source on your behalf so that you can begin analyzing the data. As soon as you paste the data onto the data source page, Tableau creates a new connection to the existing data source. Then, if you paste data on a worksheet, Tableau saves the source to your Tableau Repository. Keep reading for more on how to make all this happen.

TECHNICAL STUFF

Don't get too carried away with what data sources you can copy and paste. You need to stick with your traditional office applications such as Microsoft Word or Microsoft Excel, standard web browser content, or text file-based data. Remember, the data must be translated into comma-separated or tab-delimited values, so formatting is lost upon copying to the clipboard.

To get started with placing a simple dataset directly into a workbook, select a data sample from an Excel File (or a like-kind document), as shown in Figure 4-24, and copy the data from the original source file or website so that it can be saved to your clipboard. As you can see in the figure, the data is structured into columns. For reference purposes, the dataset provides a partial list of the universities that are members of the Washington Research Library Consortium (found at www. wrlc.org).

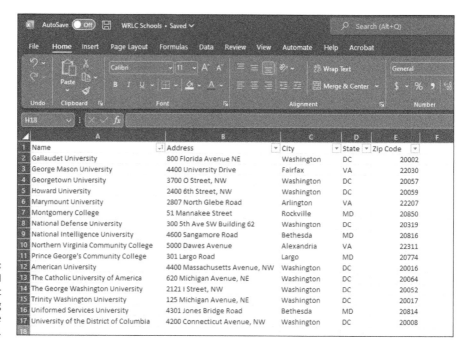

FIGURE 4-24:
An Excel
spreadsheet
with data being
copied to the
clipboard.

Next, follow these steps to copy Excel Data from your clipboard into Tableau
Desktop creating an ad hoc data source:

1. **Open Tableau Desktop and go to the Data Source page.**

2. **Next, go to the Data Menu and either Select Paste Data as Connection or
   Paste Data as Data Source (Figure 4-25).**

   You'll want to select Data as Connection.

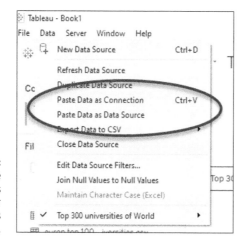

FIGURE 4-25:
Choose
Paste Data as
Connection or
Paste Data as
Data Source.

REMEMBER

A new connection, called Clipboard_221120T195 in this case, is created. A worksheet is also generated consisting of a single table. The worksheet derives field names automatically. In this case, I renamed the field names to more appropriate ones by right-clicking the field name and selecting the Rename option. Note that the field name cannot be the same as the remote field name (the clipboard data field name), as shown in Figure 4-26.

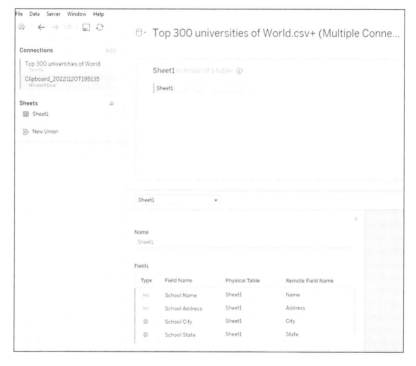

FIGURE 4-26: Changes made to the newly created data connection and workbook.

3. **(Optional) To rename the connection, go to the Data Source pane, locate the newly created Data Source, right-click the connection, and select Rename.**

   In this case, I've renamed the connection as WRLC Schools, as noted in Figure 4-27.

4. **To rename the worksheet, go to the Flow pane and right-click the data source. Select Rename, which allows you to enter a unique name in the Sheet type instead of the generic, Sheet1.**

   I've renamed Sheet 1 to Top 15 WRLC Schools as the logical table name.

After you have saved all your changes, the data source can easily integrate into the existing model, assuming that you've made the necessary relationship tweaks such as streamlining the data in Name, City, State, and Country to be consistent. Figure 4-27 presents the full integration of the Top 15 WRLC Universities into the data model.

FIGURE 4-27: Multiple data connections integrated into a single data model.

Chapter **5**

Ready, Set, Data Prep: Readying Your Data for Prime Time

I f you ask a thousand data analysts what they spend the most time completing, from sourcing data to data visualization and reporting, most folks will say data preparation. Unless you craft the dataset on your own, ensuring that every field maps perfectly to a *T*, you seldom have pure data entry. Tableau recognizes that this issue is one of the complexities in the data life cycle, which is why one of the first products introduced in the solution stack was Tableau Prep Builder. For those needing to twist and bend their data so that it can be shaped and integrated for mass consumption, Tableau Prep Builder is your one-stop shop to handling all these data life cycle activities, from combining, shaping, and cleaning the data before analysis in Tableau Desktop to publishing to Tableau Server or Tableau Cloud.

Tableau Prep Builder is, first and foremost, an Extract, Transport, Load (ETL) tool that connects data from various sources. After connecting to and combining the data sources, users can drag and drop tables into the Flow pane to shape and cleanse the data using a combination of operations such as filtering, pivoting, joining, and unioning data to get it in tip-top shape.

In this chapter, you discover the key capabilities necessary to build flows, from inception to execution, in Tableau Prep Builder.

Dabbling in Data Flows

Flow is the one term I deliberately did not cover in Chapter 1 when discussing Tableau Fundamentals. That's because the concept is too extensive to compartmentalize into a paragraph. Instead, it requires an entire chapter because Tableau Prep Builder is synonymous with the data flow. So what is a data flow, exactly?

You have likely heard a smidge about Extract, Transform, Load (ETL). If so, you understand that moving data through one or more cycles or flows is the basic concept of ETL. The flow in Tableau Prep Builder refers to the movement of data between the source and its destination, whether it's the extracted file or a published server, for end-user consumption.

Over the following several pages, I take you through the step of the flow life cycle, including connecting data in Tableau Prep Builder, configuring the dataset, adding data, building and organizing flows, and maintaining flows.

Connecting the data dots

You recognize that your data needs a little TLC. A few simple data tweaks inside the database or the file won't cut it. In that case, you must first connect your data to Tableau Prep Builder. To do so, you need to make sure your data source can connect to one of several options available:

>> One of the 100+ built-in connectors provided by Tableau

>> Custom connectors built using the SDK, ODBC, or JDBC offering

>> Prebuilt data sources compatible with Tableau

>> Tableau Data Extracts or Catalogs

Assuming that all the datasets pass muster and you've successfully mastered connecting your data (covered in Chapter 4), you're ready to move on to the Tableau Prep Builder panes, and most notably the Flow pane, to create your first flow.

Going down the data flow pathway

After you've connected your data source, the real fun begins. Your first step is to create an input step, and then you can go on your merry way down the Prep Builder pathway of creating flows. The more steps you create, the more actions the data must undergo in the life cycle.

TECHNICAL STUFF

Are you scratching your head yet? I've just mentioned the word *step*, but you didn't start a flow. Thought that may be confusing! As soon as you associate a data source with Tableau Prep Builder, you've created a data ingestion point so that your data can start flowing down its eventual path. Multiple input steps can exist, as can multiple data files. I cover some of these nuances shortly.

ON THE WEB

Throughout this chapter's examples, I utilize a specific dataset on salary predictions, found at `https://www.kaggle.com/datasets/thedevastator/jobs-dataset-from-glassdoor`.

If you've added a single file, Tableau Prep Builder automatically adds the input step into the Flow pane (shown in Figure 5-1). All attributes associated with the file are displayed in the Input pane.

The Flow pane is your main workspace to interact with your data visually and build the flows. The Input pane is where you complete all configurations from the time data is ingested. As noted previously, you can see fields, data types, and data-set examples from the Input pane.

Should you want to add multiple files or sources, each data source becomes a new flow, as shown in the Flow pane in Figure 5-2.

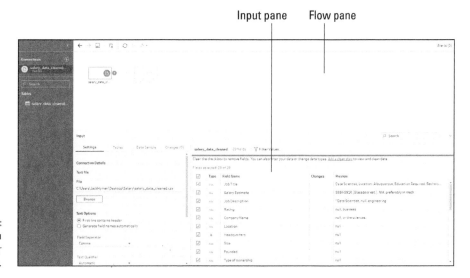

FIGURE 5-1: The Tableau Prep Builder workspace.

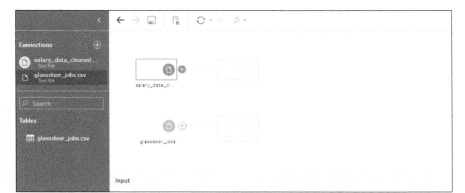

FIGURE 5-2:
Adding more
than one data
source creates
additional
flows within
the Flow pane.

FIGURE 5-3:
Recent flows in
Tableau Prep
Builder.

After you create a data flow, you find that Tableau makes it easy to locate the flow right from the Start page of the Tableau Prep Builder application, where you see all recent flows (Figure 5-3). If you're using Tableau Prep Builder on the web, head over to Explore. From there, you can select all web-based flows recently published or created on the internet.

Configuring the data flow

Configuring the dataset after the data connection has been established is the first step in the preparation process. You might not know at this very moment how much work needs to be done to your flow, but you'll get a sense as you start to configure. As soon as you add the input to the flow, you'll be able to evaluate what data should be included in the final output.

If you are utilizing an Excel or text file, you can make changes directly from the input step. Other data sources, such as those meaty databases and enterprise applications, require some of the changes discussed to be completed in the data source. It varies by platform.

From the input step, what can you do exactly? If you click the specific item in the Flow pane, your options appear in the Input pane. Such options, indicated by their corresponding letters in Figure 5-4, include the following:

>> **Data Source:** Rename the data source, refresh the data source, and describe the data source.

>> **Settings:** Establish data connection-specific configurations.

>> **Tables:** Select one or more tables to include in Input pane.

>> **Data Sample:** Produce data samples based on changes made in Input pane.

>> **Changes:** Review all changes made in the Input pane.

>> **Profile pane:** Remove fields from the dataset or modify fields, including changing data types and field names

>> **Filter Values:** Apply filtering functionality.

>> **Search:** Search for specific fields.

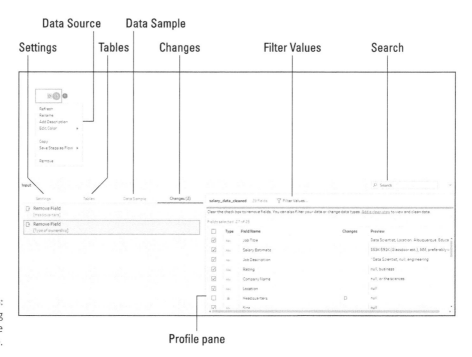

FIGURE 5-4: Configuring data in the Input pane.

Going with the data flow

Connecting the first data source is easy-breezy. Adding data is where things become a bit more challenging. You have several options: Refresh the native data in the input step; edit the connection to re-recognize the data source and its changes; or create a union among files or database tables in the input step. Read on to find out more about each of these options.

Refreshing data in the input step

When your data source is still active, data changes are inevitable. You'll want to refresh the data, whether it's added to an Excel spreadsheet or becomes more entries to another file structure. To refresh the file input steps, you can do one of the following:

>> Go to the Flow pane at the top menu.

>> Click the Refresh button (Figure 5-5, left image) to refresh all input steps.

>> If you want to refresh only a single input step, locate the drop-down arrow near the Refresh button and then select the input step from the list that requires refreshing. You can also select the input step by right-clicking and pressing Refresh (Figure 5-5, right image).

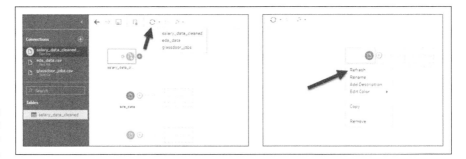

FIGURE 5-5:
Input step
Refresh
options.

Extract input step updates

What I am about to tell you might sound a bit counterintuitive, but it's one of the quirks of Tableau Prep Builder. Suppose you have a Tableau extract or perhaps a database-driven source. In that case, it's best to edit the connection instead of refreshing the data source described in the previous step because data changes can throw off the integrity of the connection if data updates are frequent. You want to be as efficient as possible without having to restart all over again under these conditions.

To ensure the freshest data, follow these steps:

1. **In the Connections pane, right-click your preferred data source.**

2. **In the Flow pane, that appears, select Edit on the step for which you'll be editing the connection source.**

   The menu will allow you to edit the source or add additional sources to an existing flow.

3. **Reconnect to the original data source by signing into the database or selecting the Tableau extract.**

TIP If you believe that your file in the previous step did not refresh properly, reconnect to the data source instead.

What happens when things still don't seem one hundred percent? The folks at Tableau suggest you remove and re-add the step to the flow. Tableau at first indicates that an error exists if you have a complex flow, but this situation is entirely correctable. The steps to ensure that removal and re-addition are successful are as follows:

1. **Go to the Connections pane.**

2. **Right-click the source and select Remove.**

3. **The flow temporarily pauses where the source was formerly.**

4. **Create a connection to the updated file source.**

5. **Drag and then drop the table to the Flow pane to initiate the creation of a flow; then you can add one or more input steps (see Figure 5-6).**

6. **Drag and then drop the new data source onto an Add symbol within a flow to allow it to reconnect with the flow.**

7. **Depending on the source type you've just dropped and added back in to the data flow, you may want to remove the source in the Flow pane, instead of creating a new data source.**

WARNING

FIGURE 5-6:
Removing and adding a new input step.

Creating a union among files or database tables in the input step

Input unions, which are a way to display many tables being queried at a single time, are in their own class because you can create them in Tableau Prep Builder only, unlike the other approaches I've mentioned. Don't worry, however. You can complete some functionality on the web, such as scheduling an input union to run using Tableau Cloud.

A lot of users decide to use Tableau because they want to evaluate many data sources, so they need the ability to cleanse and prep multiple files or database tables. At the same time, with data source complexity comes the desire to search and filter across all the data sources. To create a union with data, if the data sources are files, they must be in the same directory. Before I explain how to create a union, here are some other rules that you must consider:

REMEMBER

>> The ability to union data is not available for Tableau extracts.

>> Files can be added only to the same folder that matches specific filter criteria, or the files added to the same folder won't appear automatically within the union.

>> Files don't automatically appear; you need to save your flows and open them again.

>> Packaged flows aren't automatically added as new files, even if they are in the same folder. Instead, you need to open the flow file in Tableau Prep Builder and select the files. Only then can the files be repackaged.

>> If you want to union a database table, the data sources must be in the same database; the database must also support wildcard searches (not all databases offer these features). Those that do support wildcard searches include Amazon Redshift, Microsoft SQL Server, and Oracle. A limited number of open-source databases offer union options.

>> After creating a union, you can refresh the input step if you decide to add or remove tables or files. Otherwise, you can update your flow with available data.

Although there are a few limitations unioning data, the pros still outweigh the cons. Recognize that you are trying to query multiple tables simultaneously with a union, yet you will visualize the data just one time, which can be complicated to achieve. Why, you ask? Except for .csv and Excel files, Tableau Prep Builder does not establish a data union relationship for all files in the same directory. You'll need to manually handle creating file connections to the data source.

For `.csv` and `.xls` files, Tableau automatically creates the union on your behalf. Suppose you feel that a better union relationship is available, or that not all the files are necessary. In that case, in the Input pane, you can specify additional filters to find the files and sheets that should be included in the union (see Figure 5-7). You can filter the file being unified in various ways, including by filename, file size, date created, and date modified to tailor files based on specific attributes.

FIGURE 5-7:
The Union filter for files in the Input pane.

In Figure 5-8, you'll see that when you add a new step into your flow, all the files are added to the dataset in the file path, which is located in the Profile pane. All fields are added automatically and are visible in both the Profile pane and Data Grid. To add a new step into your flow, follow these steps:

1. **Click the Connect tab on the toolbar.**

   The Connections pane opens so that you can create or access a data connection.

2. **Click the Add Connection button (the plus sign; see Figure 5-8).**

   The Connect pane expands, providing you with various types of connections to create.

3. **In the Connections pane, select the Text File type under To a File; then select your file.**

   You'll find information pertaining to the file within the Input pane (also shown in Figure 5-8).

4. **Click the Tables tab so that you can be assured that both tables connect in the next step.**

5. **Drag the table from the Connections pane and roll it over the existing table.**

6. **Drag the table to the Union (not Join) option below the existing table.**

   The relationship between the original table and the new table, which forms a union, can be seen in the Flow pane, also shown in Figure 5-8. Until the union is created, you cannot see the relationship.

7. **Go back to the Input pane and confirm that the data source and relevant data are available under the Settings tab. If you are not satisfied with the data source, click Browse and find the appropriate file located on your desktop or a shared drive and then double-click the file to open it as part of the existing connection.**

   After you make the modifications, go back to the Tables tab and click Apply. All panes and data source details update immediately. The most notable change is the Field pane, reflecting the updates from the file union.

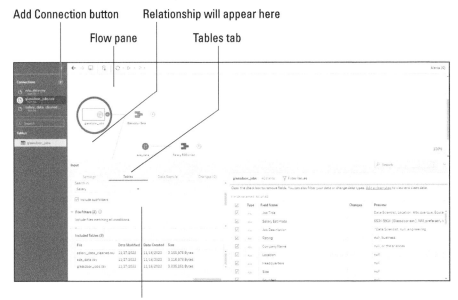

Add Connection button   Relationship will appear here

Flow pane   Tables tab

Find information about the file in the Input pane

FIGURE 5-8: The state of the file after an insert step is created.

TIP

Establishing a union for tables follows the same protocol except that instead of creating a union among files, you are creating a union among multiple tables from one or more data sources. The slight modification occurs in Step 4, whereby the tables aren't files but database tables.

Joining data and input steps

Specific to database-related data, both the desktop version and Tableau Cloud can detect and show users which fields in their tables are unique. Tableau Prep Builder also identifies related fields and shows the names of these fields.

One of three options, as noted in Table 5-1, appears as part of a new column called Linked Keys, which is part of the Input pane.

TABLE 5-1 **Join Relationship Types for Input Step Data Flows**

Relationship Type	Description
Unique identifier	The field is unique for each row in the table. A table can have multiple unique identifiers. Values cannot be blank or null under any circumstance.
Related field	The fields have a relationship to another database table. Multiple related fields in a table can exist.
Both unique identifier and related field	The field is recognized as unique in a table. The field also relates to one or more other tables in a database.

One of the neat things about the linked keys is that you can quickly identify and add related tables to a flow or even create joins as part of the input step. So long as the database connector is supported where tables are defined, linked key relationships are widely available. To successfully leverage linked keys, use the steps that follow. If all you need to do is create a join relationship, click the + (plus sign) icon in the Flow pane and select Add Join; then you can skip most of these steps. However, if you do need to bring multiple data source types together, follow these steps:

1. **Connect to the database that contains the relationships for fields, which may include unique identifiers (primary keys) and related fields (foreign keys).**

2. **Click the field marked as a related field or as a unique identifier and related field in the Input pane.**

   A list of related tables appears in the Profile pane.

3. **Review the tables and hover your cursor over the table you want to add or join to the input step.**

4. **Click the plus sign to add a table to your flow, or if you already have multiple tables available, click the Join button to join two or more tables together.**

Nurturing a flow

To get to the stage of cleansing and preparing your data, you must face a deluge of data, as you now understand if you've read the previous sections. Cleansing requires you to remove all the errors that might be found in your dataset, causing a potential result set to be skewed. The problem could be words that are inappropriately capitalized, items with too few or too many spaces, misspellings, or even extraneous numbers after a decimal. Those are just a few specific reasons you may need to clean your data. When you reach the point of cleansing and preparation, you should be ready to add new steps to the flow, insert new steps, and organize steps. Also, at this point, you can add *context,* meaning a way to individualize items to the flows. Context can be integrated into a flow through the use of the colors, descriptions, and naming conventions needed to support a flow layout. See Figure 5-9. Each of these attributes can be included as part of the specific flow, which incorporates two data sources, a single cleaning step, a pivot step, and a singular output.

Whether you intend to add a step at the beginning or insert a step anywhere throughout a flow, these options are accessible by right-clicking or pressing the + (plus sign) next to a step (highlighted) in the Input pane, as shown in Figure 5-10. Even removing a flow requires only one step of right-clicking the input step and selecting Remove. Here are the available options:

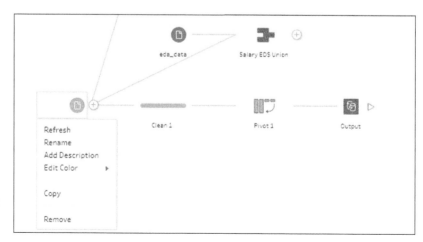

FIGURE 5-9: Formatting a flow step.

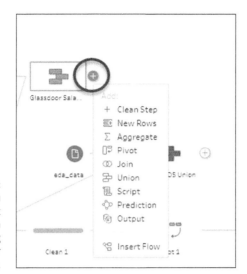

FIGURE 5-10:
The menu options that appear when right-clicking to add or insert a step.

>> **Clean Step:** Allows you to add a step that supports cleaning actions.

>> **New Rows:** Generates new rows to a sequential dataset that fill in dataset gaps.

>> **Aggregate:** Helps to bring steps together between existing fields and change the level of detail provided.

>> **Pivot:** Creates a pivot step between two existing steps to perform actions such as converting column data to rows or rows data to columns. Users can also create wildcard pivots to add additional data to an existing pivot automatically.

>> **Join:** Creates a join step between existing steps. There are two ways to create joins, either manually from the menu or by dragging and dropping steps on top of an existing step to create a join.

>> **Union:** Creates a union between tables. Like a join, there are two ways to create a union step, either by using the Add option or by dragging and dropping to an existing step.

>> **Script:** If you need to utilize a scripting language such as R or Python in a flow, you use this option; however, as of this writing, Tableau Cloud does not support using script steps.

>> **Prediction:** If you have access to the Einstein Discovery–powered models, you can incorporate predictive modeling capabilities into your flows.

>> **Output:** Allows a user to create an output step to save an extract or a .csv file, or to publish output to either Tableau Server or Tableau Cloud.

>> **Insert Flow:** Enables you to add flow steps already created in a previous flow into your current flow. The insertion occurs directly on the Input pane canvas (Figure 5-11) or as part of a step between or at the end of a flow (refer to Figure 5-10).

To remove a flow step, right-click to bring up the option to remove a step (the link) between two inserts (see Figure 5-12).

FIGURE 5-11: Inserting a step into a flow.

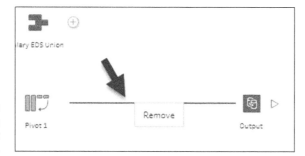

FIGURE 5-12: Removing a step from a flow.

Grouping flows

Suppose you have a set of steps in your flow that are connected and repetitive. The flow might have steps occurring across many lanes, as shown in Figure 5-13. In that case, you can consolidate the connected steps into a single group.

To begin a group, you click the two or more steps in the single flow that you want to group. Then right-click the steps you've selected and select Group from the menu that appears. The result is a folder consolidating all the steps into a nice, neat package, as shown in Figure 5-14. Notice how each group flow is represented with a different color, offering you context indicating that two separate flows are occurring.

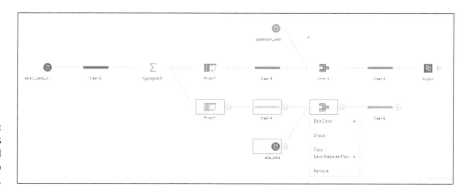

FIGURE 5-13:
Selecting items to be included within a group flow.

A group flow folder

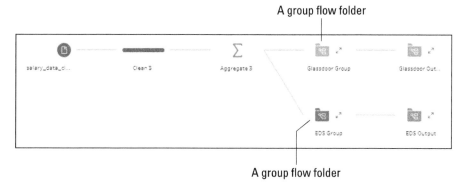

FIGURE 5-14:
Presenting when all steps are compressed into a group flow folder.

A group flow folder

With a group flow, you can

>> Click the double arrows next to the folder, which is the same as a group, to expand or collapse a group.

>> Expand a group anytime and add more steps to the existing group before collapsing the folder, to create a compact group.

>> Expand a group anytime and remove unwanted steps in an existing group before collapsing the folder.

>> To format the group, manage the group settings such as expand or ungroup, copy group steps, or remove a group, right-click the group folder, as shown in Figure 5-15.

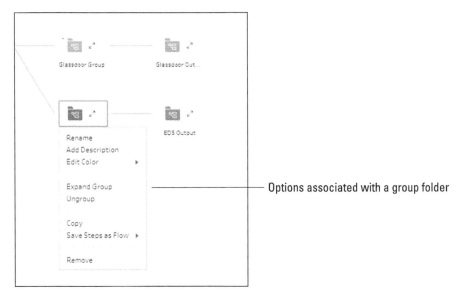

Options associated with a group folder

FIGURE 5-15:
Options available when you right-click a group flow.

Filtering flows

One of the features touted by Tableau is its ability to filter data with a single click. You can hide data using the Keep Only or Exclude options on a specific field in a profile card, Data Grid, or result card. Alternatively, you can select from numerous filtering options at the field level when you require more complex filtering.

Users can filter data at any step within a flow. For example, suppose you want to change a specific value. In that case, you can edit the value within the field or isolate the value with a null by directly clicking the field, assuming that you have a cleaning step available to present the field, as seen in Figure 5-16. You'd use the cleaning step in Tableau when your data requires refinement. Each time a flow cycles, the step will look to complete activities such as filter, rename, split, group, or remove fields.

Many filtering functions are available at the field level. You find these options by clicking the ellipsis, referred to as "More Options" in Tableau Prep Builder. Some of the options you can choose from are shown in Figure 5-17 and include the following:

- ≫ **Rename Field:** Enables a user to rename a specific field.

- ≫ **Duplicate Field:** Enables a user to duplicate a field and all the values within that field.

FIGURE 5-16:
You can edit a field value by directly updating within a cleaning step.

>> **Keep Only Field:** Hides all fields except for the ones selected.

>> **Hide Field:** Temporarily hides the specific field selected from the dataset.

>> **Remove:** Removes the field entirely from the dataset.

FIGURE 5-17:
Filtering options that appear after clicking the ellipsis next to a field.

The menu also offers options to complete more complex filtering, cleaning, grouping, creating calculated fields, and splitting of values. You can also create calculated fields or publish a field as a data role. In the following sections, we will address these items.

Advanced filtering options

There are four filtering categories. The first, Calculated Value, lets you narrow down string data or create calculated values based on numerical fields, depending on the field type. For the example shown in Figure 5-18, I've created a CONTAINS filter, and all jobs must have a Location field containing CA and a Headquarters field containing CA.

After you create a string that contains the calculated values for the filter, click Apply. You can see the changes appear in the dataset after you've created a targeted filter.

FIGURE 5-18:
A calculated value filter.

The Selected Values Filter allows you to search a specific field value and then narrow down the values using the Keep Only or Exclude parameters to tighten the results further. In the example shown in Figure 5-19, the parameter searched on the left is MD (for Maryland). On the right, the Exclude field indicates the removal of all Baltimore, MD instances from the dataset. If you wanted to keep only specific values, you would go to the Keep Only option and select from the remaining cities in the state of MD.

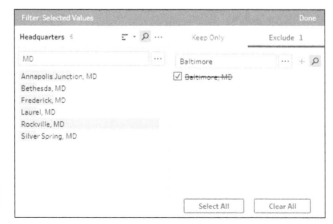

FIGURE 5-19:
Using the Selected Values filter.

Wildcard Search works similarly to Selected Values; however, you could filter on specific values. Then, on the right side, using Boolean parameters, you can further narrow down the options by Contains, Starts With, Ends With, or Exact Match. Again, the parameters can be set for you to Exclude or Keep Only. In the example shown in Figure 5-20, the initial search looks for all Headquarters locations containing the value GA. On the right side, the qualifying parameter is set to keep only those entries that end with the letters GA. As a result, only three locations match these criteria.

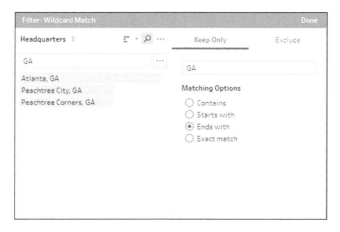

FIGURE 5-20:
The Wildcard
Search filter.

The remaining filter is Null Values. It offers only two options: to narrow the dataset to null and non-null values. You may wonder why someone would heavily restrict values to null values, but it's the quickest way to evaluate what data does not exist in a field because creating restrictions quickly helps reduce anomalies.

Data cleansing options

One of the difficulties when trying to clean a massive dataset is formatting items to a specification. When you have hundreds, thousands, or millions of rows of data for a specific field, cleaning the data in one fell swoop for consistency is ideal. For example, Tableau Prep Builder offers an array of options to clean text formatting, regardless of whether the text contains numbers, letters, or special characters. Examples of what you can do with text-formatting features in Tableau Prep Builder include:

>> Make Uppercase

>> Make Lowercase

>> Remove Letters

- » Remove Numbers
- » Remove Punctuation
- » Trim Spaces
- » Remove Extra Spaces
- » Remove All Spaces

Suppose you had one entry that was Vancouver BC. Another entry was Vancouver, BC. A third was Vancouver Bc. The formatting here presents three different scenarios. To ensure consistency, you'll want to consider streamlining all entries to one format. In this case, the entry should be Vancouver BC. You would follow these steps to make all entries conform to that format:

1. **To thoroughly clean the operations, select Remove Punctuation on the drop-down menu.**

2. **Type** BC **in the search box, which acts as a filter, and make sure the** BC **is all uppercase.**

3. **Select Remove All Extra Spaces.**

   In this case, where the comma is located, you should truncate from two spaces to one.

Using Split Value

Some users find that when they filter, they wind up with too many rows of data in a field. In those cases, you may have a way to classify specific data better. With the Split Value Filter, Tableau Prep Builder can use its recommendation engine to split values based on patterns and known behaviors. Alternatively, you can select which rows should be made into a new column, leading users to go from one column to two or more columns.

An example of using the Split Value Filter for one of the location fields is to split headquarters locations from A–Z to A–L and M–Z.

Calculating values

Users may need to create new data fields from existing data to calculate values. Tableau Prep Builder offers four primary calculation types: Custom Calculation, Fixed Level of Detail (LOD), Rank, and Tile. Table 5-2 explains the value for each calculation type and when it is appropriate to use.

TABLE 5-2
Calculated Field Options

Type	Description
Custom Calculation	Allows a user to use just about any mathematical calculation type and parameterize the data for creating a new field. Example options include POWER, RADIANS, ROUND, and 100+ calculation opportunities.
Fixed Level of Detail	Helps change the granularity of fields in a dataset, especially when looking for multiple levels of data specificity.
Rank	Helps identify the top N or bottom N values for selecting rows with similar data. You can present the data by partition, Order By, Rank Order, and DESC/ASC.
Tile	Helps to identify distribution by field visually and then the number of groups. When applying the tile approach, you can use the Calculation Editor to manipulate syntax or the Visual Calculation editor to select the fields, allowing Tableau Prep Builder to author calculations on your behalf.

ON THE WEB

Given the number of calculation options available in Tableau, you have hundreds of ways to slice data mathematically and create two fields. Rather than review every calculation in detail, go to `https://help.tableau.com/current/prep/en-us/prep_calculations.htm` to quickly reference the formulaic approach that best suits your needs.

Validating Data

Data cleansing isn't a once-and-done operation. You need to find a method to ensure that the data is constantly valid. To help you do so, Tableau Prep Builder introduced data roles, which give you a quick way to spot whether field validity exists. The data role identifies what your data values represent so that Tableau Prep Builder can automatically recognize associated values and validate them. Values that are not valid are then highlighted as being out of scope.

Tableau offers out-of-the-box *data roles*, which identify exactly what your data represents, such as a string, date, or number value; those data roles are often sufficient for most datasets. You can also create custom data roles. The requirements to ensure that roles operate are beyond the scope of this book, but I introduce them here because they are so useful.

To begin to get a sense what data roles do, say you have a variety of fields you need to validate. Tableau Prep Builder compares the expected value against the value defined for the data role in the field, using what it knows from its recommendation engine as well as existing data patterns. All values that do not match are marked with a red exclamation mark as a warning sign.

You can narrow down the field to only valid or invalid values using the filtering tools discussed earlier in the chapter. Narrowing the field using such filtering options allows users to take quick action on updating erroneous data. If you have assigned a data role to one or more fields, you can then apply other filtering options, including Group Values, to the group and match the invalid to the valid fields based on various contexts, such as spelling.

Assigning roles to data

As with data types, you can assign data roles to a given field (Figure 5-21) under the Filtering drop-down menu. Data roles identify what data values represent so that Tableau Prep Builder can ensure that your values are accurate and indicate which ones are erroneous. To assign a data role, go to the Data Type menu found on each field, and then, at the very bottom, select the Standard Data Role.

FIGURE 5-21: Standard data roles.

For the example in Figure 5-22, the goal is to identify data roles that are in error. The geographic context is being evaluated in this case. The example with BC, as we discussed previously, is not a state identified in the U.S. but is a province in Canada (British Columbia), and the scope of the search is U.S.-only states. On the other hand, ARK is not a state abbreviation for Arkansas, nor is it recognized by the recommendation engine. AR would be recognized by the recommendation upon modification of ARK. The exclamation mark indicates erroneous data.

REMEMBER

You may be wondering what the paper clip and exclamation mark next to ARK in Figure 5-22 mean. A paper clip indicates that the value is part of a group of values, whereas the exclamation mark indicates that the value contains a likely error, based on the Tableau recommendation engine.

To dig a bit deeper into why errors might exist, click the ellipsis on the right corner of a field. Select one of the filter types in the drop-down menu except for Null Values to filter all data that is valid, and select Null Values to filter data that is invalid or missing. Then select the appropriate cleansing options, such as Make Uppercase or Make Lowercase, to correct any errors that you might find. In the case of the error shown in Figure 5-22, only one field, ARK, is in error. To fix that error, you would change all entries from ARK to AR by first searching for the value using the Selected Values filter. Then, utilize the cleaning option and apply options such as Make Uppercase and Remove Punctuation, if applicable.

FIGURE 5-22:
Identifying erroneous data using data roles.

TIP

With geographic data, in particular, you may want to group values because of the potential for repetition. For every field that you apply a Standard Data Role to, I suggest also using Group Values to identify patterns and make changes quickly. To accomplish this, click the ellipsis (More Options). And then locate Group Values. You'll select either Spelling or Pronunciation + Spelling to better group values of a valid and invalid nature together.

Publishing output as a data role

Sometimes, you might have a field that contains specific data that you feel should qualify as its own data role. The result is a custom data role. To create a custom data role, you'll need to save it to either Tableau Server or Tableau Cloud.

For example, to classify the employee population based on size, follow these steps (depicted in Figure 5-23):

1. **Select the field that should become a custom data role.**

2. **Click the ellipsis (More Options) and select Publish as Data Role.**

   The proposed list of data options appears, based on the field selected.

3. **Enter your credentials to either Tableau Server or Tableau Cloud.**

   This step allows you to save the data role based on the established flow parameters.

4. **Upon credential validation, click Run Flow to incorporate the custom data role.**

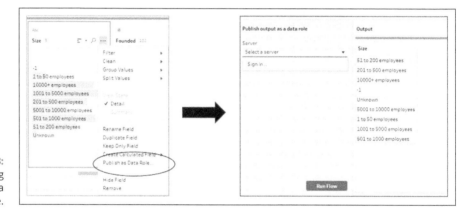

FIGURE 5-23: Publishing output as a data role.

ON THE WEB

Although Tableau has a host of data roles included, many users find creating custom data roles to be an added benefit for highly complex data that doesn't fit the available roles. Publishing output as a data role doesn't fit some of these use cases. To learn about all the requirements to fully manage the custom data role life cycle, go to https://help.tableau.com/current/prep/en-us/prep_validate_data.htm.

Saving Prep Data

Saving your work often is paramount to successfully using any software application and Tableau Prep Builder is no exception. A nice feature with Tableau Prep Builder is the ability to automatically save your data when creating or editing flows on the web. For the desktop, though, you need to save items manually.

A significant consideration that links data freshness and saving items in Tableau Prep Builder is how often a flow is executed. Of course, you can run flows manually and, if you want, save items periodically by utilizing a schedule with Tableau Server or Tableau Cloud. This section presents a variety of approaches to automate saving data across Tableau Prep Builder, but it's important to note that server or cloud-based configuration is often required as part of the scheduling cycle.

Saving flows

The first time you decide to save your flow, you're prompted for a bit more information than at later times. A file is saved in the Tableau Prep follow (`.tfl`) format by default, but you can package the local files such as the Excel, `.csv`, `.txt`, or Tableau Extracts to the flow of your choice and share them with others. The saving process is comparable to packaging a workbook for sharing in Tableau Desktop.

WARNING

You can't mix and match your file types and locations. Only files stored on a desktop can be packaged with a flow. Data from databases or web-based data sources not local to the desktop using a connection are not included in a Tableau package.

To save packaged files, follow these steps:

1. **Select File ⇨ Save As (see Figure 5-24).**

2. **Select the File Type drop-down menu and select either Tableau Flow Files or Packaged Tableau File Flows.**

   Select Packaged Tableau File Flows in this case.

   A pop-up box indicates that all the relevant files using the Salary data have been saved and packaged with the flow you've created. Keep in mind that only the local files are included.

3. **Click OK.**

Your file is now saved to the folder location preferred on your desktop.

TECHNICAL
STUFF

There is no difference between using the Save As option for Export Packaged Tableau File and the File ⇨ Export Packaged Tableau File command.

FIGURE 5-24:
Saving Export Packaged Tableau files.

Automating flows

Changes are automatically saved when you create or edit a flow using Tableau Server or Tableau Cloud. Saved changes include the data source connection as well as inserted, added, and customized steps. So take a deep breath; you won't lose your work. But there are a few catches, of course:

REMEMBER

>> You must log in to the server to which you are saving your flows.

>> You need to head to the Push menu (click File ⇨ Push) to set up the Publishing parameters if you want to publish a flow to a different server's project.

>> Draft flows are visible to only one person: you! You must publish them before they are available to others to collaborate and share. That's only the half of it. You also need to set permissions to access the project; permissions are not configured when you click Publish.

>> Until a flow is published, you see the badge Never Been Published next to a badge showing Draft.

The most important consideration to keep in mind about automated flows is that when a flow is published, and you then decide to edit and republish the draft, each new version of the flow is kept in the Revision History dialog box, accessible on the Explore Page of either Tableau Server or Tableau Cloud from the actions menu.

Viewing outputs on Tableau Desktop

Trial and error is par for the course in cleansing and preparing data. So, it should not be a surprise that users want to take a test drive of their data in Tableau

Desktop. When you open a flow in Tableau Desktop, Tableau Prep Builder creates a .hyper file accompanied by Tableau data source files. All these items are saved in the Tableau repository of your data source file, allowing you to tinker with the data at any time.

Folks assume that all their data is brought over in test mode, but that's the furthest thing from the truth. Users get only a data sampling of the working flow, including all the changes. Recognize, though, that until you save the workbook as a part of a packaged workbook, the dataset remains limited. In other words, the only way to see everything is to add an output step in your flow, saving the output file to a specific location or publishing the flow to a data source.

To view a data sample from Tableau Prep Builder in Tableau Desktop, right-click where you want to view the data in the flow, specifically on a targeted step. Then select Preview in Tableau Desktop, shown in Figure 5-25. The file then compiles by producing an output file. Finally, Tableau Desktop opens on the Sheet tab.

FIGURE 5-25: Accessing Preview in Tableau Desktop.

Crafting published data sources

If you are reading this section, it probably means you are ready to create a published data source. You have reached the last step in the cleansing and preparation cycle (unless you are looking to make some advanced data enhancements described in Chapter 6).

The published data source requires a bit of configuration. Here is how to get there:

1. **Locate the +(plus sign) icon on a step where you want to produce an output.**

2. **Select the Output option (see Figure 5-26).**

   An Output Pane opens, showing you a data snapshot (see Figure 5-27). To the left, you have some options to choose from: Save Output to a File; Published Data Source; or Database.

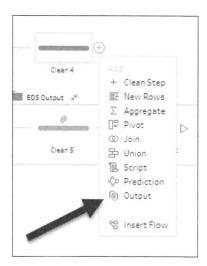

FIGURE 5-26: Selecting the output to run.

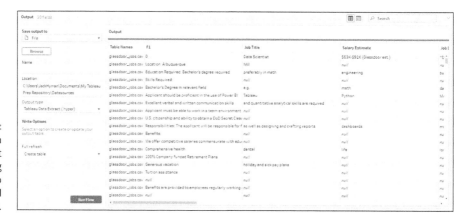

FIGURE 5-27: Snapshot in the Output pane, along with ways to save published data sources.

Depending on the output type, you will be required to configure one or more parameters using one of these approaches:

- If you select File, you're prompted to select the location where the file is saved and the output type. Also, you need to determine the Write type, either Create Table or Append to Table.

- To create a Tableau Extract, set the Save Output to Save As File and the Output Type to Tableau Data Extract (.hyper).

    Selecting Published Data Source requires you to log in to Tableau Server or Tableau Cloud.

If you decide to save the output to a database table, you need to select the connection type, allowing you to utilize 10+ connectors. Alternatively, you can point to a Custom SQL Query.

The most efficient way to save and publish work is to use Tableau Cloud. To publish the data source, follow these steps:

1. **Go to the Save Output drop-down menu and select Published Data Source.**

2. **Pick one option from the drop-down menu, either Select a Server or Sign-In.**

3. **Upon selecting Sign into Tableau Online with your user credentials, you're prompted to log in to Tableau Cloud.**

4. **You can either enter the Tableau Server address or select Tableau Online, but because you want Tableau Cloud in this case, select Tableau Online.**

5. **Click Connecting.**

    A pop-up screen appears asking for your username and password.

6. **Enter your Username and Password to log in. (Figure 5-28.)**

7. **At the prompt, select the project to be loaded and extracted, the project's name, and the project's description.**

8. **Press Run Flow.**

    You now have a published data source, putting you well on your way to using the Published Data Source in Tableau Cloud.

FIGURE 5-28:
Log into Tableau Cloud to configure a published data source.

Chapter **6**

Structuring Data for Liftoff

After you've completed the preparation and cleansing phase covered in both Chapters 4 and 5, your data is on its way to being in tip-top shape, and you're just about ready to make the transition from Tableau Prep Builder back to Tableau Desktop. But first, you need to know about a few remaining items in the bag of magic tricks — fundamental concepts that, whether you are in Tableau Prep Builder or Tableau Desktop, can get you from data glut to harmony.

In this chapter, you take a final quick tour around Tableau Prep Builder to explore features that help streamline your data before heading to Tableau Desktop and Tableau Cloud for the remainder of the book.

Dipping into Data Structure and Results

As Chapters 4 and 5 show you, particular prerequisites must be followed when ensuring that data can be readied for evaluation in Tableau Prep Builder. It doesn't matter if the data is system generated or stored in a never-ending number of formats, from file to the database; not all data formats can be treated equally.

That's because some formats have well-defined data structures, yielding meaningful results sets. Other times, the cleansing process requires you to transform data from disarray to — guess what — structure! You can have one table or many. The point is that you don't need to do this work across the various data systems; you can complete it all within Tableau Prep Builder.

Data preparation and, by default, working with the data structure involve the process of getting data from chaos to order so that it can be analyzed in Tableau. The goal is to create a structure for rows and columns and ensure cleanliness and correctness in data types and values.

Peering into Data Structures

When data is in its raw form, you have control over the data structure because you manipulate and move things all over the place. As soon as you transition to a Tableau product, though, you lose a bit of that control. Tableau assumes that you have access to the raw data as well as sufficient access within the toolset to shape the dataset using Tableau Prep. Some situations won't allow pivoting (explained in more detail in "Pivoting with data: Tall versus wide," later in this chapter), aggregating, or blending data because of how Tableau ingests and presents the data. You can conduct the analysis, but to be successful, you'll need to change how you approach your data, from how you generate calculations to formatting your rows and columns. The following sections address some of these data structure complexities.

Rows and records

It might seem odd to talk about rows and records in this chapter, but I want to cover some points about data structure and placement of data because your goal should be to focus on data granularity.

As you prepare your data, you should adhere to the following best practices concerning rows and records.

>> Each row should contain a unique identifier (UID).

>> Each row should have a unique purpose.

>> Each time you have a value such as ExTableName(Count) as a field, you should know precisely what that value adds to a row.

Your data structure is likely poor if you fail the litmus test for each condition. The top image displayed in Figure 6-1 shows an example of the data structure almost but not quite meeting the litmus test on the left side. To establish a patient's medical conditions, four data requirements are captured in the medical record: weight, height, temperature, and blood pressure, and date is recorded. Although each row of data indicates health care data that is independent and unique, certain fields, such as the Patient ID (PID), must be included to ensure 100 percent uniqueness.

In this case, condition one is not met. Each row may appear unique, but what happens if two patients have the same patient profile, including weight, height, temperature, and blood pressure captured on the same day? In that case, a user would be unable to differentiate the record from one patient to another, so condition two is not met because each row does not have a unique purpose. In the case of condition three regarding calculated fields, the name of a field should be clearly labeled. The example has no calculated fields, so that condition does not apply to this use case. By simply adding the PID row, shown in the bottom image of Figure 6-1, your data structure passes the litmus test because each patient's records can be grouped in conjunction with a unique record ID (not seen).

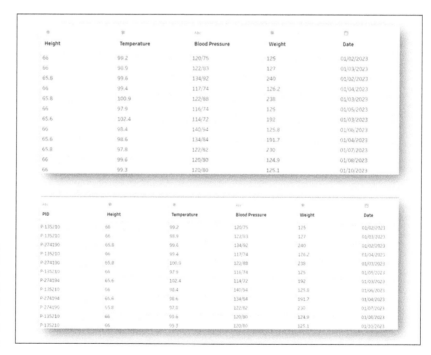

FIGURE 6-1: A rows and records example that doesn't meet all three best practices for data structure.

Columns and fields

In the previous section's example, a column is introduced when you need to make a record set unique to a specific individual or subject such as a product type. In that example, the creation of the PID allowed the patient's records to be aggregated. Hence a unique identity capturing an entire medical history is now available. Combined with a record ID, which is not seen in Tableau Prep Builder, each row is then deemed unique. Fields and columns are considered interchangeable terms, especially in Tableau Desktop. But for Tableau Prep Builder, you should address a data field relative to how data is grouped with data and their relationships. An analyst must articulate the field's association in terms of domain groups. For example, the domain of shoes may have four different groups: men's, children's, women's, and unisex (see Figure 6-2).

On the other hand, the more granular items that fall under each domain, such as sneakers, boots, and slippers, are all item types, not shoe classifications. In other words, the shoe domain is limited to a focused classification, not an expansive list of options. Here's another example: Education, College, and Grades. College is a type of schooling (education). The Grades category is too broad and could fit in various ways, so the concept needs to be narrower.

A column should have broad domain appeal so that the data within the field can be specific yet reliable. Referring back to Figure 6-1, you can see that each column has consistency because Weight, Height, Temperature, Blood Pressure, and Date have the same parameters. Assuming that the data contains a UID (which it does because it is hidden), and combined with a Patient ID (PID) to group like patient data together, the result is on its way to being a solid data structure.

FIGURE 6-2:
Focusing
on targeted
domains in
structuring
column-based
data.

Categorizing fields

Depending on which application within the Tableau platform you use, fields appear differently in the Data pane. In Tableau Desktop, fields are either treated as a dimension or measures, indicated by lines in a table in the Data pane. Furthermore, dimensions or measures are considered discrete or continuous, using a color-coding scheme of blue fields for discrete and green fields for continuous. Blue and green indicators are referred to as pills, as mentioned in Chapter 1.

WARNING

If you have difficulty seeing colors or want an alternative way to discriminate blue from green, you can't. The blue/green pills are a set-in-stone feature within Tableau.

To better understand how to categorize field-level data, take a look at Table 6-1.

TABLE 6-1   **Field Types Categories**

Type	Definition
Dimension	Refers to a qualitative field type, meaning it is described as not measurable. Examples of dimensions include City, State, Hair Color, or Brand. Notice that none of these is a numerical term. Dimensions are associated with being discrete because qualitative data describe items.
Measure	Refers to a quantitative field type, meaning it's described as having data points that can be measured using numbers. Examples of measures include income earned, number of clicks, or quantity. In Tableau Desktop, measures are aggregated by default using SUM. You can change the way data is aggregated. Measures are generally continuous, but not always.
Discrete	When you are looking for distinct values, you are describing discrete data. Restaurants such as McDonald's and Starbucks are two specific (discrete) brands.
Continuous	Continuous data is associated with constant numeric values and order. Examples of numeric order include distance, time, and weight. In Tableau Desktop, continuous values are presented on the axis.

REMEMBER

An axis in Tableau is created when you drag a measure that can be aggregated onto the View. You'll see an axis because there will be a label with a measure's name, and it will include a range of values. Tableau creates an axis to scale based on your dataset.

In Figure 6-3, the Year field is set to continuous, creating a horizontal axis along the bottom. The green pill for both fields shows that both the row and column are representative of continuous fields. The line across the time horizon also indicates a continuous measure.

Figure 6-4 shows that the Year field has been set to Discrete. The field creates a horizontal header of an axis. The blue background (using the blue pill) and horizontal headers illustrate that the data is discrete.

TECHNICAL STUFF

Tableau Prep Builder does not distinguish dimensions and measures because it's a data-cleansing and preparation tool. In cleansing and preparation, you must know (generally speaking) the difference between discrete or continuous values to help shape the data as required.

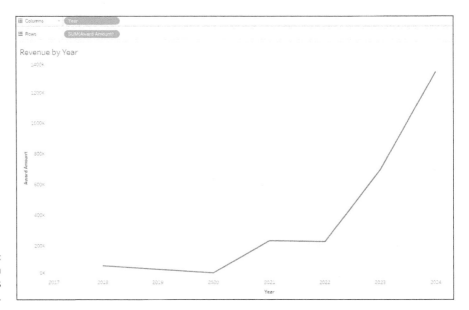

FIGURE 6-3:
Example of a
continuous
measure.

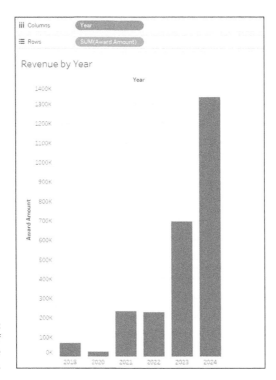

FIGURE 6-4:
Example of
a discrete
measure.

Structuring for Data Visualization

For proper and compelling visualizations, the underlying data must be structured in such a way as to make it logical for both users and Tableau itself. Properly structured data ensures that aggregations and other calculations are computed accurately, which is the foundation for visualizations.

The following sections show you how to group data for optimal readability and data analysis. In the case of binning and histograms, you see how to group data that follows a pattern into bins, or focused groupings using a histogram-based model. Data tends to follow a structured pattern or data distribution for large datasets. When the data falls outside the normal range of values, interpreting the validity of outliers — the odd values in the dataset — is important to improve data visualization quality. The last section covers how you present your data to avoid data redundancy and quality concerns. When creating a wide formatted dataset, data does not repeat in at least one column, usually the first. An example is a unique record ID. If you utilize tall datasets, minimizing the use of columns, you will have data repetition, likely resulting in a need to cleanse your data with a tool such as Tableau Prep Builder.

Binning and histograms

Fixed values are continuous. Your age is an example. It doesn't change for 365 days, so there is a distance between one year and the next. Think about the time. Can you change the fact that there are 60 minutes in an hour, 24 hours in a day, or seven days a week? Not a chance.

When someone asks a 42-year-old person how old they are, do they exclaim from the rooftops, "42 years old, 7 months, 23 days, and 13 hours old?" Okay, that is a bit extreme, but generally people say their age in terms of their latest birthday (or they say 39 going on whatever). A cute little seven-year-old may get into the nitty-gritty of years, months, and days, but they won't when they get older.

Speaking of one's age this way is an example of *binning* — in this case, by using a time-bound reference, age. *Binning* is a way to group related values together rather than have an exorbitant number of distinct, redundant values. When you create a fixed value despite having a more precise answer available, you lump all the facts into a grouping of sorts. How many surveys have you taken in which you were asked to select your age: 18–24, 25–34, 35–44 and so on? That type of grouping is another example of binning.

Tableau Prep Builder uses histograms to visualize the distribution of numerical data using binning. The histogram is similar to the bar chart, but it spans a grouping across a continuous axis, such as the range of ages in a survey or time horizons. The height of the bar, as represented by the bar's rectangle shape, is determined by the frequency of values using the count function.

In the example presented in Figure 6-5, you see two variables, Mobile Devices and Age.

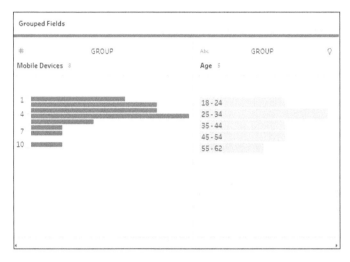

FIGURE 6-5:
An example of
binning and
histogram
structures.

I've binned both variables to show you two perspectives. The summary view illustrates that owners of mobile devices aged 18–62 own anywhere from one to ten devices. Each bar represents the aggregation of values, demonstrating how often a user may have a specific number of devices. Of the range of ten possible answers, there are eight unique binned values that Tableau has determined should be grouped together for the count of mobile devices. Each bar represents the number of people within the sample with a given number of mobile devices. For example, there might be five respondents with four mobile devices, whereas one respondent in this example has ten or more.

For the detailed view of the age of those owning mobile devices, each group was aggregated, illustrating the binning of range-bound data. The detailed view shows in the survey response how many respondents participated in the mobile device survey. For example, 6 of the 30 respondents were aged 25–34, representing the largest bar in the model. The binning was derived by evaluating the ages reported by the participants and then aggregating the results into the appropriate groups.

Distributions and outliers

After your data is consistent enough to be evaluated, having been cleaned in Tableau Prep Builder, you'll want to complete an activity that allows you to understand its range of possible values, known as *distribution*. This is also the time to determine whether you have any one-off data points, known as *outliers.*

Distributions give you an idea of how your data is shaped within the histogram. Depending on the size of the dataset and the range of the bins within the histogram view, ensuring that your data is complete can be tricky. You can be sure that the shape is rock-solid only if you know your data; otherwise, the distribution won't make sense.

Take, for example, the dataset discussed in the previous section, "Binning and histograms." I cover two variables: the number of mobile devices and age. Any number of variables in that dataset would be acceptable, right? Not really. Age is range-bound, as is (presumably) the number of devices a person owns. Is it possible for a person to own 1,000 mobile devices? Yes, it's possible but not likely. If you saw a maximum of 10, and then someone said they owned 1,000 devices, that is most certainly an outlier. For the user with 1,000 devices, that outlier should be discarded because it will throw off the entire visualization, given that it is a single anomaly.

You can gain a perspective on data ambiguity using a data example everyone is all too familiar with. The number of times the search term *COVID-19* appeared on Google starting in January 2020 is one for the record books. Upon the lockdown in China, followed by the United States and numerous other countries, the search term *COVID-19* peaked on March 12, 2020. It was the number one search trend before the news, weather, music, and sports (really) until April 26, 2020. Since then, *COVID-19* has been considered a common search term on Google. So, what do we learn from this trend? There was a date-based trend that had *COVID-19* as the predominant search term, not at a single point in time. In this case, the data should not be discarded because a unique trending distribution over a given period exists.

To zoom in a bit more: March 2, 2020, to April 26, 2020, should for all purposes be considered an outlier because the value is extreme relative to other search values in Google's search engine history. Although some may say that Google exaggerates their numbers from time to time (they don't; robots do the counting), errors within a range are possible. For this example, it's not likely, though, given the nature of the global lockdown. The outliers are correct, given that the outliers were part of a trend over a particular period, not a single blip on the radar, which indicates that natural data anomalies can be introduced into binning and histogram data.

ON THE
WEB

To review the COVID-19 Google Search dataset, go to `https://trends.google.com/trends/story/US_cu_4Rjdh3ABAABMHM_en`.

Pivoting with data: Tall versus wide

Most data analysts are accustomed to exploring wide spreadsheets with many columns of data and few rows. The wide-versus-tall debate often leads folks like you and me to manipulate our data sources because complex data makes us feel unsettled. In a typical business productivity application, pivoting functionality helps you shape your data from tall to wide and vice versa. For those using Tableau's pivot functionality, the word *pivot* suggests going from people-facing (wide) to machine-readable (tall or long) by transforming columns into rows.

ON THE
WEB

Pivoting data is a complex exercise in both Tableau Desktop and Tableau Prep Builder. Depending on the quality of the data source and needed searchability, the requirements vary greatly. To learn more about data pivot-based preparation requirements in Tableau Prep Builder, go to `https://help.tableau.com/current/prep/en-us/prep_pivot.htm`.

Have you ever seen publicly accessible government data before? It's dizzying for any expert analyst to interpret, never mind anyone not in that field. There are numerous top-level agencies in the United States and hundreds, if not thousands, of government departments and branches that roll up under the 15 or so big agencies. So it goes without saying that the interpretation of data would yield a separate column representing each agency's data. Then you'd have a minimum number of rows of data depending on how many years of data is available. Manageable, but quite the eye sore.

The table in Figure 6-6 shows a dataset provided by the White House. I've reformatted the complex dataset to be readable in Tableau using Microsoft Excel. You can access the raw data files at `https://www.whitehouse.gov/omb/budget/historical-tables/`. The dataset contains the Executive Branch Civilian Full-Time Equivalent Employees count as a percentage from 1981–2023. Given there are 11 agencies where data is reported over a 42-year period, the dataset is a good example of a wide dataset because there are 43 columns and just 11 rows of data.

If you read the document as is, you can understand which agencies support the most personnel relative to the U.S. Executive Branch budget. However, to successfully cleanse the data and bring it into either Tableau Desktop or Tableau Prep Builder, you must do the following:

>> Ensure that the dataset has a single field per column.

>> Ensure that each agency has only a single data point per year based on a percentage of total employees.

	DoD	Agriculture	HHS, Education, Social Security Admin.	Homeland Security	Interior	Justice	Transportation	Treasury	Veterans	Other
1981	44.9	5.6	7.3	1.8	3.8	2.3	2.5	4.8	10.2	16.8
1982	47.2	5.4	7.1	1.8	3.5	2.2	2.6	4.6	10.4	15.3
1983	47.4	5.3	7.1	1.9	3.5	2.3	2.7	4.7	10.5	14.7
1984	48.0	5.2	6.8	1.8	3.5	2.4	2.7	4.9	10.5	14.2
1985	48.7	5.0	6.5	1.8	3.4	2.4	2.6	5.0	10.5	13.9
1986	49.3	4.9	6.3	1.8	3.3	2.6	2.6	5.2	10.4	13.6
1987	49.0	4.9	6.0	2.0	3.3	2.6	2.6	5.4	10.5	13.6
1988	47.7	5.1	5.8	2.2	3.3	2.7	2.7	6.0	10.5	13.9
1989	48.0	5.1	5.7	2.2	3.4	3.0	2.7	6.0	10.0	13.8
1990	46.3	5.1	5.6	2.2	3.3	3.0	2.7	6.0	9.8	15.9
1991	45.9	5.2	6.0	2.3	3.4	3.4	2.8	6.3	10.3	14.4
1992	44.9	5.2	6.2	2.5	3.5	3.6	2.9	6.2	10.6	14.6
1993	43.6	5.3	6.4	2.5	3.7	3.8	2.9	6.2	10.9	14.7
1994	42.3	5.4	6.4	2.6	3.7	3.9	2.9	6.3	11.4	15.1
1995	41.7	5.3	6.5	2.7	3.7	4.2	2.9	6.6	11.6	14.8
1996	41.2	5.3	6.7	3.1	3.5	4.4	3.0	6.5	11.7	14.5
1997	40.7	5.4	6.9	3.4	3.6	4.8	3.1	6.4	11.5	14.3
1998	39.5	5.4	7.1	3.7	3.7	5.1	3.2	6.3	11.6	14.5
1999	38.3	5.4	7.1	3.7	3.8	5.3	3.3	6.4	11.6	15.1
2000	36.4	5.2	7.0	3.7	3.7	5.3	3.1	6.3	11.2	18.1
2001	37.4	5.6	7.4	4.0	4.0	5.5	3.3	6.6	11.9	14.3
2002	37.0	5.5	7.2	4.6	4.0	5.5	3.5	6.6	11.9	14.1
2003	35.5	5.6	7.0	7.9	3.9	5.4	3.2	6.3	11.6	13.5

FIGURE 6-6: A wide dataset from white-house.gov.

Although presenting this dataset may look easy in Excel, porting the data into either Tableau Desktop or Tableau Prep Builder complicates the data's appearance because your data is transformed. Each field will be represented in a separate column. In other words, each agency will have a distinct row (single field), and each year will have a distinct column (many fields). The dataset here is wide, as shown in Figure 6-7.

Wide Date Example

Year

	2004	2005	2006	2007	2008	2009	2010	2011	2012	2013	2014	2015	2016	2017	2018	2019
Agriculture	5.50	5.40	5.30	5.20	5.00	4.80	4.50	4.40	4.30	4.20	4.20	4.20	4.20	4.20	4.10	3.90
DoD	35.70	35.70	36.10	36.00	35.80	35.50	34.80	36.70	36.60	35.90	35.60	35.50	35.30	35.20	35.40	35.60
HHS, Educa..	7.00	7.00	6.90	6.80	6.70	6.60	6.50	6.70	6.60	6.60	6.60	6.80	6.80	6.80	6.70	6.60
Homeland S..	7.50	7.80	7.90	8.10	8.40	8.60	8.10	8.50	8.80	8.90	9.00	8.80	8.90	8.80	9.00	9.20
Interior	3.90	3.80	3.70	3.70	3.60	3.50	3.30	3.40	3.30	3.30	3.20	3.10	3.10	3.10	3.10	3.00
Justice	5.60	5.60	5.70	5.70	5.70	5.50	5.30	5.50	5.50	5.60	5.50	5.60	5.60	5.70	5.50	5.40
Other	13.40	13.40	13.40	13.20	12.90	13.40	16.10	12.60	12.50	12.50	12.40	12.30	12.10	11.90	11.70	11.60
Transpor-t..	3.10	3.00	2.90	2.90	2.90	2.90	2.70	2.70	2.70	2.70	2.70	2.70	2.60	2.70	2.60	2.50
Treasury	6.20	6.00	5.90	5.90	5.70	5.50	5.30	5.30	5.10	5.00	4.90	4.70	4.50	4.50	4.30	4.20
Veterans	12.00	12.10	12.10	12.60	13.30	13.80	13.40	14.10	14.40	15.20	15.90	16.40	16.80	17.00	17.60	18.00

FIGURE 6-7: A wide dataset in Tableau Desktop.

If you were to swap rows for columns in the Excel worksheet, you'd then create tall data. Now, technically you could have pivoted this data in Tableau Desktop. However, I want to show you how having a column for each agency and then listing each agency's percentage per year appears. The dataset is a tad overwhelming.

Tableau Desktop consolidates your dataset from the Excel document, which is in the tall format, to a compressed set of five rows of data (years) and four distinct columns representing the sum result of each agency. In Figure 6-8, I don't post all agencies in this dataset, but only a subset.

Compared to the Excel spreadsheet shown on the left in Figure 6-8 containing 20 rows and 3 columns of discrete data, Tableau Desktop has transformed the dataset by listing dates in a single column and having each agency represented as its unique column versus row, as shown in the wide data example in the previous section. Because each row has some form of unique attribution: date, agency, and percentage of the employee population, the dataset is optimized to be readable as a machine-ready format, hence the definition of tall data.

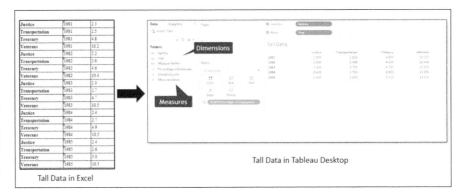

FIGURE 6-8: Tableau transforms an Excel spreadsheet into a Tableau-readable tall dataset.

Normalizing Data

One last topic that might pique your interest before I wrap up the topic of Tableau Prep Builder is a discussion on normalizing data. Generally, you don't think about normalizing data when addressing a single table. Relational databases often contain several tables sharing a common bond. Each table contains one or more unique identifiers, known as primary and secondary keys, on a per-record (row) basis. By joining keys, records become related so that information can be contained in a single table. If you can link the tables to find commonality, you can reduce data duplication.

Think about when you go to a doctor. Every doctor has an electronic health record system containing medical data on you, their patient. Some common data elements include name, date of birth, phone number, and perhaps your unique patient ID. There are two possibilities for how your data can be presented. The first aggregates all data into a single table, as shown in Figure 6-9. Although this approach may be ideal if all clinicians operate in the same medical practice, it is not likely because most patients go to many doctors across many medical practices.

For these reasons, separating the datasets into more discrete blocks that compartmentalize data into groups is more suited to patient-centered data. The primary key (indicated by the arrows in Figure 6-10) synthesizes the record association between two tables. However, you want to look at group-level information for more precision in grouping records for trend analysis. The examples of State in the Demographic Data table and Blood Type and Blind in the Medical Data table are distinct groups that offer individual-level information with grouping opportunities.

When you break down tables into more discrete datasets, there is often the possibility of common fields within one or more columns. This process is called *normalization*. When you normalize data, you are helping to reduce redundant data found in the database.

FIGURE 6-9: A single table before normalization.

PID	Patient Last Name	Patient First Name	Patient Phone	Age	Blind	Blood Donor	City	State	Zip Code
1Z4Q4J	Smith	James	617-555-1234	32	No	Yes	Phoenix	AZ	72901
2Z4Q4J	Jones	Barbara	617-555-1412	49	No	Yes	Scotsdale	AZ	72922
3Z4Q4J	Brown	Randall	202-555-1922	52	No	No	Washington	DC	20005
4Z4Q4J	Irving	Rebecca	202-555-9151	19	Yes	No	Bethesda	MD	20814
5Z4Q4J	Washington	Simon	757-555-2412	48	No	Yes	Virginia Beach	VA	23455
6Z4Q4J	Clayton	Maura	703-555-3933	22	Yes	No	Arlington	VA	22201
7Z4Q4J	Gibson	Brooklyn	404-555-0667	17	No	Yes	Atlanta	GA	30318

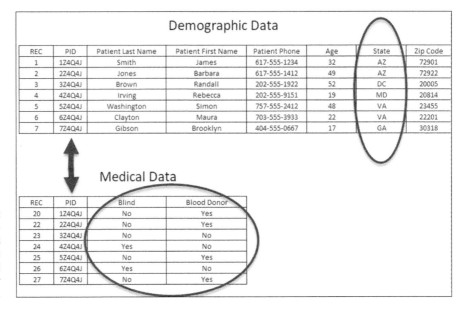

FIGURE 6-10: Tables are broken to address the group and individual-level information for normalization.

Demographic Data

REC	PID	Patient Last Name	Patient First Name	Patient Phone	Age	State	Zip Code
1	1Z4Q4J	Smith	James	617-555-1234	32	AZ	72901
2	2Z4Q4J	Jones	Barbara	617-555-1412	49	AZ	72922
3	3Z4Q4J	Brown	Randall	202-555-1922	52	DC	20005
4	4Z4Q4J	Irving	Rebecca	202-555-9151	19	MD	20814
5	5Z4Q4J	Washington	Simon	757-555-2412	48	VA	23455
6	6Z4Q4J	Clayton	Maura	703-555-3933	22	VA	22201
7	7Z4Q4J	Gibson	Brooklyn	404-555-0667	17	GA	30318

Medical Data

REC	PID	Blind	Blood Donor
20	1Z4Q4J	No	Yes
22	2Z4Q4J	No	Yes
23	3Z4Q4J	No	No
24	4Z4Q4J	Yes	No
25	5Z4Q4J	No	Yes
26	6Z4Q4J	Yes	No
27	7Z4Q4J	No	Yes

Normalization requires that each table maintain a minimum of one shared unique field that can be combined to bring the data back together.

When the two tables are separated, as seen in Figure 6-10, the Patient ID (PID) is the common field that joins the tables. However, the tables have redundant data fields containing YES/NO (Blood Donor, Blind) or States that can undoubtedly be consolidated. If you have duplicated data among the records but no PID, the record set will most certainly shrink. But combining the patient data tables using the PID as the unique identifier, the PID creates a dataset that is normalized because all patient records among two or more tables are grouped together using the unique value. If you have duplicate PIDs, consolidation of the record set is inevitable.

In summary, as you are prepping and packaging your data for liftoff, remember that with normalized data, each row has a unique identifier. Also, each table must have a minimum of one column that can be used to connect tables to create key-based relationships.

3
Telling the Data Story in Tableau

Familiarize yourself with the key Tableau Desktop features and functionality, including menus, toolbars, and cards.

Develop compelling visualizations for reporting, dashboarding, and storytelling using Tableau Desktop.

Extend the power of the visualization by adding analytics functionality and mathematical capabilities using Tableau Desktop.

See how to make Tableau Section 508/WCAG compliant.

Present data using dashboards and stories within Tableau Desktop.

Chapter **7**

Touring Tableau Desktop

O f all the applications in the Tableau product suite, Tableau Desktop is by far the one you'll use most as a data analyst. Tableau Desktop was the first application developed back when its founding company started in the late 1990s. It remained the industry leader because of its rich feature set. To create reports, dashboards, KPIs, and stories, you must use Tableau Desktop.

In this chapter, I walk you through the key features of Tableau Desktop so that you can transform data into visualization masterpieces, allowing you to tell a story with your data.

Getting Hands-On in the Tableau Desktop Workspace

Tableau Desktop touts itself as an all-inclusive data analytics and business intelligence solution. *All-inclusive* is the key phrase, because all activity is completed in the Tableau workspace, which consists of menus, toolbars, data panes, cards, shelves, and sheets. A *sheet* can represent one or more worksheets, dashboards, and stories.

In Figure 7-1, notice the conglomeration of capabilities built into the Tableau Desktop, including

- **Workbook name:** The name of your workbook, which may consist of worksheets, dashboards, and stories. The workbook name in Figure 7-1 is PSC Code for Tableau.

- **Cards and shelves:** A drag-and-drop interface in the workspace used to add data among one or more views. In the figure, the card Product Or Service Codes has been dragged from the Rows shelf to the Filters shelf. Doing so allows a user to create a filter for Product Or Service Codes.

- **Views:** The primary canvas where visualizations (referred to as a *vizzes*) are created. The figure shows a listing of Federal Agencies that purchased products or services under PSC Code 7030 or DA10. Each bar represents the SUM dollar amount obligated for the specific agency.

- **Toolbar:** The central location of commands and navigation aids to complete your analysis.

- **Start:** Your ability to connect to new data sources begins with the Start icon.

- **Side Bar:** Provides direct access to the Data and Analytics panes.

- **Data Source tab:** This tab serves as the central location to access the Data Source pages so that you can view your data.

- **Sheet tab:** Tabs in Tableau Desktop provide access to various workbook pages, whether a worksheet, dashboard, or story.

- **Show Me:** Enables you to select the appropriate viz, based on the number of dimensions and measures included on the cards and shelves. Assuming that a viz is active, you'd click once, and the viz updates in the View area.

I reference these specific areas of the Tableau Desktop throughout this chapter. These are the critical launch points to managing data, creating visualizations, and conducting analysis.

Making use of the Tableau Desktop menus

Menus in Tableau are one way to access all the features available to your workspace. Whereas the toolbar visualizes vital features, the menu categorizes each feature based on business functionality. For example, all worksheet, dashboard, and story capabilities fall under their respective menus. In contrast, you can access a complete set of analysis capabilities on the Analysis menu. The following sections dig a bit deeper into each of the menus and the critical capabilities within Tableau Desktop.

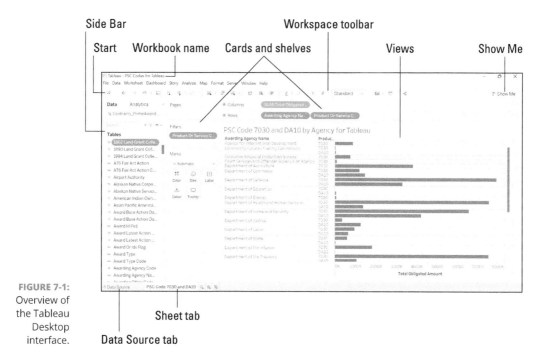

FIGURE 7-1:
Overview of
the Tableau
Desktop
interface.

File menu

The File menu (Figure 7-2) is the central point where you save Tableau Desktop products and export Desktop files to alternative file formats. You can also import data into Tableau, set your data locale, and configure outputs to be print-ready. If you want to start a new workspace (choose New), open an existing workspace (choose Open), or close the current workspace (choose Close), you can complete each of these essential functions directly from this menu.

Data menu

Data is at the heart of Tableau Desktop. The features that are available as part of the workspace vary somewhat from those you can access on the Data Source page. When you want to fully exploit all the features within a data source that's already connected to Tableau Desktop, you go to the worksheet and click the Data menu. Most features are greyed out unless you are copying and pasting across multiple data sources. You can connect to a new data source from the Data menu, as you can by clicking the Tableau icon.

FIGURE 7-2:
The File menu.

Most configurable features on the Data menu can be accessed under the active Data Source page. Active options include adding, removing, or extracting data from the data source. In addition, you can publish a data source and append existing data sources. You also find functionality such as configuring data source names and ensuring that referential integrity exists on the Data menu within a workspace, as shown in Figure 7-3. After you create a new data source for the Tableau workspace, you see a Data menu that varies slightly (see Figure 7-4). Each option in this menu allows you to complete a more detailed data-related task that you can see within one click.

Worksheet menu

The Worksheet menu combines all the features needed to create, format, and build interactive experiences for a given worksheet. The Worksheet menu breaks out into subsections (see Figure 7-5), which include these capabilities:

>> **Creating a new worksheet:** Allows a user to create a new worksheet.

>> **Managing the worksheet:** The menu items Copy, Export, and Clear enable you to copy (images, data, and crosstabs), export (images, data, and crosstabs), and clear datasets of various formatting, sorting, and filtering anomalies.

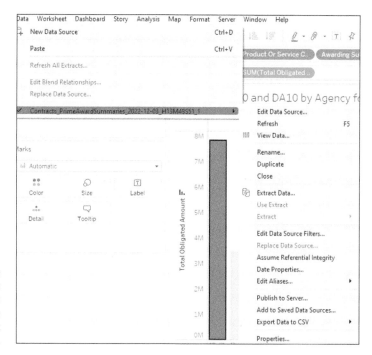

FIGURE 7-3:
The Data Source menu under the Worksheet menu.

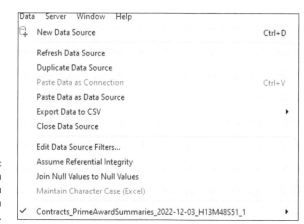

FIGURE 7-4:
The Data Source menu on the Data Source page.

» **Applying interactive elements:** You use the Actions menu to create interactive relationships among data elements, dashboard objects, and other worksheets within Tableau Desktop or on the web. The *tooltips* (a way to include text-based data in a pop-up format) are also part of this section of the Worksheet menu and are worksheet specific. Tooltips are briefly discussed in terms of integration in both Chapters 10 and 11.

» **Formatting a worksheet:** Here you find the following submenus related to labeling and marking a worksheet:

- **Show Title:** Allows you to present the title on a view.

- **Show Caption:** Allows you to better understand the visualization through a textual description authored entirely by Tableau.

- **Show Summary:** A type of card that helps you understand the breadth of the Tableau dataset included within a view.

- **Show Cards:** Enables you to select which areas of the interface should be visible (or not). For example, a Filters card can be shown or hidden.

- **Show View Toolbar:** To maximize the screen real estate, you may want to hide the toolbars on the top. In this case, you can show or hide the toolbars.

- **Show Sort Controls:** Data can be presented as either ascending or descending. To ensure that the sort order is present, you want to make sure that the Show Sort Controls is enabled.

» **Adding metadata to the worksheet:** If you need to add context or duplicate the crosstabs, this menu segment includes all the firepower under two options:

- **Describe Sheet:** Allows you to see details about elements used in a visualization.

- **Duplicate as Crosstab:** Allows you to insert one or more worksheets into a workbook, and then populate the sheet with a cross-tab view of the data from the original worksheet.

» **Enabling updates:** There are two options to choose from: Auto Updates and Run Update. You can have the system auto update the data source in real time, or you can select Run Update to update when you prefer.

TIP

Many of the features listed also have like-kind buttons on the toolbar. With the menu, you get all the features. On the toolbar, you're limited to the critical capabilities for a worksheet.

Dashboard menu

Similarly to the Worksheet menu, the Dashboard menu is divided into sections, using a horizontal line to break up features. Given that a dashboard's purpose combines worksheets, you don't see many formatting-related options on the Dashboard menu. Instead, the Dashboard menu focuses on how to present the data on various devices such as desktops or tablets. Because dashboards also present a variety of datasets, Tableau Desktop allows you to add grids to each worksheet so that you can complete a more detailed analysis. The Dashboard menu (Figure 7-6) is broken out into key sections, as follows:

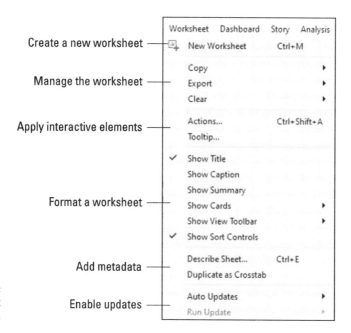

Create a new worksheet —— New Worksheet   Ctrl+M

Manage the worksheet ——⎧ Copy ▶
                        ⎨ Export ▶
                        ⎩ Clear ▶

Apply interactive elements ——⎧ Actions...   Ctrl+Shift+A
                             ⎩ Tooltip...

Format a worksheet ——⎧ ✓ Show Title
                     ⎪ Show Caption
                     ⎪ Show Summary
                     ⎨ Show Cards ▶
                     ⎪ Show View Toolbar ▶
                     ⎩ ✓ Show Sort Controls

Add metadata ——⎧ Describe Sheet...   Ctrl+E
               ⎩ Duplicate as Crosstab

Enable updates ——⎧ Auto Updates ▶
                 ⎩ Run Update ▶

Worksheet   Dashboard   Story   Analysis

FIGURE 7-5:
The Worksheet menu.

- >> **New Dashboard:** Allows you to create a new dashboard.

- >> **Device Layouts:** Allows you to choose desktop, phone, or tablet.

- >> **Grids:** Provides a matrix design to organize and present specific visual elements on a canvas, enabling you to understand how they relate to one another.

- >> **Formatting and Images:** Allows you to format the dashboard with text-based elements or to add external images.

- >> **Titles and Actions:** Allows you to add a meaningful title or *actions,* a means of adding context or interactivity to a dashboard.

- >> **Updates:** Allows a user to configure Auto Updates or run a manual update on a dashboard dataset.

- >> **Current Layout:** Presents the current layouts available.

To save and export a dashboard as a graphic, which is a static picture showing data, you can either copy a worksheet as a viz or export a worksheet to create a single snapshot of the data in the form of a .png graphic file.

TIP

Sometimes users hide the dashboard title because data may not be entirely related to all the visualizations. Select the Show Title option if you want to show the dashboard title.

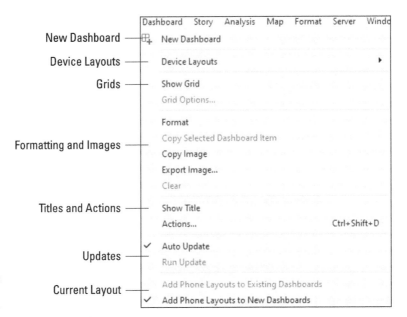

New Dashboard

Device Layouts

Grids

Formatting and Images

Titles and Actions

Updates

FIGURE 7-6:
The Dashboard
menu.

Current Layout

Story menu

The Story menu, shown in Figure 7-7, appears to have few options. You can format, copy images, export images, clear the story, and enable or disable the title and backward and forward buttons, and that's seemingly all you can do — unless you look at the expandable cards. In contrast to some other features with full menus, the story features take advantage of cards instead. For example, when you select Format, a card appears on the left side of the Tableau Desktop interface. That card enables you to format the story experience using options such as the following:

>> **New Story:** Allows you to create a new story

>> **Format:** Offers various formatting options including background enhancements, navigation enhancements, and font/image options

>> **Title and Navigator:** Allows you to add a title and create the story's navigation using story points

>> **Updates:** Allows you to refresh the data

WARNING

You find out more about creating a story later in the chapter, in the section "Differentiating between a Dashboard and a Story," as well as at length in Chapter 10. Be warned though that standard design terminology in everyday analytics platforms does not apply to a story, as I just described. The story is one of the areas in Tableau that require you to learn a bit more lingo.

New Story

Format

Title and Navigator

FIGURE 7-7:
The Story
menu.

Updates

Analysis menu

The Analysis menu is full of bells and whistles. As with other menus, it has distinct sections, as shown in Figure 7-8. You can explore the analysis features more fully in Chapters 8 and 9, which go deeper into data visualization, but here's an overview of the Analysis menu sections:

» **Labels/Measures/Marks/Data:** This menu section enables you to label, view, and explain your data by applying different approaches. You can either aggregate measures or keep them distinct.

» **Percentage Of:** Depending on the measurement type selected, each measure on a worksheet is expressed as a percentage of a given measure within one or more panes in a view.

» **Summarization, Trending, Values, and Layouts:** This segment offers a real hodge-podge of analysis options, enabling you to establish grand totals, look at trend-line analysis, show/hide particular values created, and show/hide empty values if applicable in a dataset.

» **Legends, Highlighters, Filters, Parameters:** This is another section with a boatload of tools that enable data filters, support data parameterization using calculations, and offer more aesthetic approaches to your presentation by highlighting data or adding legends for data awareness.

» **Calculated Fields:** If the data doesn't exist, you can create targeted fields to enhance the dataset with calculated fields. This section is also where you go to create a calculated field (or edit the field if one has already been created).

» **Cycle Fields/and Swap Rows and Columns:** These two options are grouped but have polar-opposite impacts on the data. Whereas you use Cycle Fields to flip-flop the order of the rows and columns in the dataset, often changing the accuracy of data, you use Swap Rows and Columns to change the visualization from left/right to top/bottom. The data is merely presented from a different visual perspective.

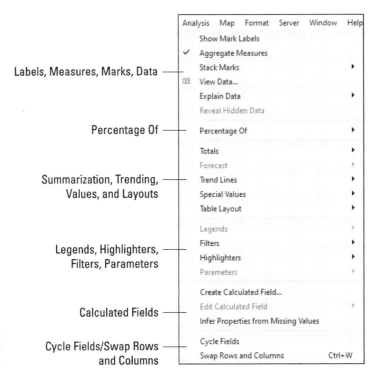

Labels, Measures, Marks, Data

Percentage Of

Summarization, Trending,
Values, and Layouts

Legends, Highlighters,
Filters, Parameters

Calculated Fields

Cycle Fields/Swap Rows
and Columns

FIGURE 7-8:
The Analysis
menu.

Map menu

Unless you are using one of the map-based visualizations, the Map menu is of little value to you. Likewise, if your dataset has no map data such as city, state, or county, you can skip this menu. But if you do have some demographic-oriented data, you'll find that Tableau's mapping functionality is second to none. You have various ways to display your map output, whether in light, dark, or normal mode, using the following options shown in Figure 7-9:

>> **Background Maps:** Offers map-rendering types such as street, outdoor, satellite, light, dark, offline.

>> **Background Images:** Allows you to add a custom background to your map. For example, you can add a state seal if you're creating a map for a specific state in the United States.

>> **Geocoding:** Lets you integrate geocoding targets into a Tableau map visualization.

>> **Edit Locations:** Enables you to edit the map targets to be more specific, based on a geographic region such as a state or country, depending on geographic parameters in the map type.

>> **Map Legend:** Lets you add color variations to a map.

>> **Background Layers:** Allows you to add textures to your map such as land cover, terrain, coastlines, or streets or highways based on map granularity.

>> **Map Options:** Lets you select which controls should be enabled or disabled in the Tableau Map Viewer, such as search, layer control, pan and zoom, scale, and units of measure.

TIP

When you need to look for more granular details, you can get down to street level, outdoor, or satellite views so that your data appears in 2-D or 3-D. If you prefer to add third-party mapping data sources, you find such options within the Background Maps menu (WMS/Mapbox Options).

You can also add multiple layers to your maps, depending on how many datasets are integrated into a single workspace. Suppose, for example, you have three worksheets. Each worksheet can be a layer of a map brought together as a single visualization.

FIGURE 7-9:
The Map
menu.

Format menu

You can format any object from this single menu in Tableau. No questions asked.

The single menu is your single source to locate formatting options, which is helpful if you don't know which card controls which formatting function. Most features in Tableau use the point-and-click method, so you can simply highlight an item in a specific card, go to the Format menu, select the formatting feature you want, and then follow the prompt. Options such as Font, Alignment, Shading, Borders, and Lines align to the more traditional formatting activity on a document. Visualization-rich formatting options also appear on this menu, including these:

>> **Panes:** Enables the Worksheet, Dashboard, or Story Format panes.

>> **Format:** Enables the specific panes for fonts, alignment, shading, borders, and lines.

>> **Animation:** Enables the Animation pane for you to integrate interactivity into your Tableau workspace.

>> **Lines, labels, and captions:** Allows you to enhance your visualization using reference lines, drop lines, annotations, titles, captions, or field labels. Each menu option enables a new pane.

>> **Visualization enhancements:** You can enhance visualizations with the use of legends, filters, highlighters, or parameters.

>> **Themes:** Enables you to create a targeted look and feel to workbooks and cells.

>> **Copy/Paste Formatting:** Lets you capture formatting once and reuse it.

>> **Clear:** You can clear the formatting of the worksheet, dashboard, or story.

Figure 7-10 shows the Format menu.

WARNING

You may notice some repetition of option names on certain menus. For example, the Format menu contains many Analysis options such as Highlight, Filter, Legends, and Parameters because they are also deemed to be formatting options. Although they appear to replicate options of the same name elsewhere, they actually vary in feature functionality. On the Format menu, options are specific to data formatting, whereas on the Analysis menu, they relate to creating or evolving the data elements.

Server menu

You can think of the Server menu, shown in Figure 7-11, as your candy store for all things relating to public and server data. This menu enables you to access the most popular Tableau Public datasets, publish your own datasets for the world to explore via Tableau Public, or take the traditional approach by using Tableau Server (or Cloud) for publishing workbooks, data sources, and filters. The menu specifically points out what features are unique to Tableau Public versus Tableau Server and Tableau Cloud.

You also can access the free Tableau Bridge Client from this menu so long as you have a Creator license.

TIP

Sign in before you do anything to save time if you intend to use Tableau Server, Tableau Public, and even Tableau Cloud. Simply click the first option, Sign-In. If you haven't signed in to one of these applications, you'll be prompted every time you try to publish your data.

REMEMBER

The Tableau Online Link is embedded on each Tableau Server connection page so that you can create a connection to Tableau Cloud.

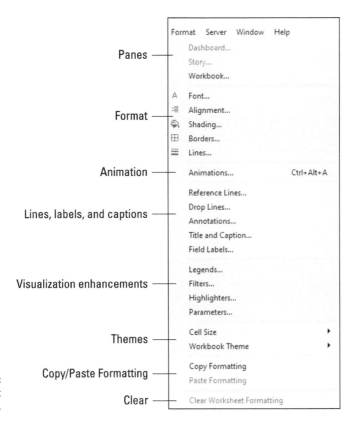

Panes

Format

Animation

Lines, labels, and captions

Visualization enhancements

Themes

Copy/Paste Formatting

Clear

FIGURE 7-10:
The Format
menu.

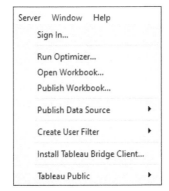

FIGURE 7-11:
The Server
menu.

Window menu

You can use the Window menu (Figure 7-12) as your cheat sheet for accessing all your worksheets, dashboards, and story tabs. Instead of going to the bottom of the screen to find all your worksheets, dashboards or stories, click the Window tab to the Window menu on the Tableau toolbar to see how many items you've generated. If you want to focus on a specific item, select that item with a single click.

The other feature offered by the Window menu is the capability to show and hide standard features, such as toolbars, status bars, and sidebars. Again, it takes only a single click on the menu option to make one of these bars appear or disappear — nothing less, nothing more.

FIGURE 7-12:
The Window
menu.

Help menu

Chapter 14 goes into more detail about many of the Help menu items shown in Figure 7-13, so I don't belabor them here other than to say that they are free self-help training and education resources. Tableau heavily emphasizes using self-help resources. As you can see in the figure, the menu offers Open Help (Forums), Get Support (Ask the Community or Pay for Support), Watch Training Videos, and Check for Product Updates.

REMEMBER

You find a few features in Help that most users would expect to find on a different menu, such as File, which is typically where application preferences and licensing details are located. Not with Tableau. You modify all your application-wide settings, preferences, licenses, and language selection choices using the Help menu.

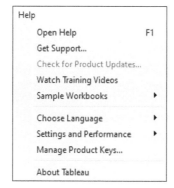

FIGURE 7-13:
The Help
menu.

Tooling around in the toolbar

The toolbar appears across the top of Tableau Desktop (see Figure 7-14). Although it's not as robust as the menus, the toolbar clusters key features that are necessary to manipulate and analyze data and fully exploit the visualization options available. As you work through the toolbar, you notice that it is divided into sections. The first section is specific to creating data sources and handling standard application functions such as undoing and redoing previous actions. The following list describes the tools found on this first section of the toolbar, also shown in Figure 7-15:

FIGURE 7-14:
The full Tableau Desktop toolbar.

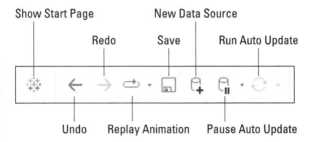

FIGURE 7-15:
Tools on the first section of the Tableau Desktop toolbar.

>> **Show Start Page:** Enables a user to go back to the Start page.

>> **Undo:** Reverses the most recent actions in a workbook. A user can reverse an unlimited number of times, back to when Tableau was most recently opened.

>> **Redo:** Repeats the last actions reversed, assuming that you've selected the Undo button at least one or more times.

>> **Replay Animation:** When you have one or more states within a visualization, you can see the various states by pressing this quasi-Play button. Various speeds are available with the Replay Animation button.

>> **Save:** Saves changes made in a workbook.

>> **New Data Source:** Opens the Connect pane to create a new connection or to enable a user to access an existing saved connection.

>> **Pause Auto Update:** Allows you to control where Tableau updates the view when you make changes.

>> **Run Auto Update:** If running a query, you can manually update your data to make changes, assuming that Auto Update is turned off.

The next section of the toolbar functionality, shown in Figure 7-16, centers around creation and filtering tasks. You must put your magnifying glasses on to see the itsy-bitsy menus. Each toolbar option has a drop-down menu with sub-functions. For example, the first button allows you to create a new worksheet. When you click the button, options appear for creating a new dashboard or new story. Depending on what feature you're using (worksheet, dashboard, or story), the other two toolbar buttons vary in drop-down capability. The second button always creates a duplicate feature, and the third is intended for clearing a sheet, residual formatting, and filters.

Duplicate

FIGURE 7-16:
Core work-
sheet,
dashboard,
and story
functionality.

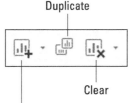

Clear

Drop down to create new worksheet, dashboard, or story

The next segment of buttons, shown in Figure 7-17, is nifty because these buttons enable you to manipulate visualizations and data sort order. The Swap button allows you to swap rows and columns order visually without touching a single data cell. The Ascend and Descend buttons enable visualization sort order differentiation; one is for data to ascend, and the other is to descend. Depending on the visualization type you're applying in the canvas, the data presentation may be entirely text based or a mix of visual and text, with the items displayed as descending or ascending.

Swap Rows and Columns

Sort Descending

FIGURE 7-17:
The swap and
sort order
functionality
on the Tab-
leau Desktop
toolbar.

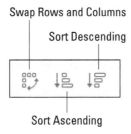

Sort Ascending

After you've nailed down the visualization (viz) type you prefer, formatting to perfection is an essential ingredient for the data analyst. You use the next series of buttons (see Figure 7-18) to format your visualizations. These buttons, which are loaded with various options, appear from left to right in the figure:

- **Highlight:** Enables you to highlight selected sheet features. You can define how values appear in a menu.

- **Group Members:** Allows for creating groups of selected values by combining selected values. When you select multiple dimensions, you can choose whether to apply them to one grouping or all groupings.

- **Show/Hide Mark Labels:** Click to show or hide all markings on a current worksheet. An example of a marking is to provide a text-label equivalent on a viz.

- **Fix Axes:** You can lock the axis or show specific ranges. You can also establish a dynamic axis that can adjust based on a minimum and maximum value established within a view.

- **Fit:** Select from the drop-down menu how the view is sized within a window. Several options include Standard, Fit Width, Fit Height, or Entire View.

WARNING

I can't stress enough that Tableau has many hidden menus. Within the visualization formatting toolbar options, you have three complete sets of options — one for worksheets, one for dashboards, and one for stories. Although the icons are virtually the same, the capabilities are vastly different.

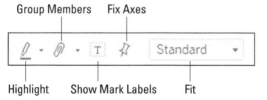

FIGURE 7-18: Visualization formatting buttons.

The rightmost section of the toolbar, shown in Figure 7-19, consists of a series of shortcuts for users to execute presentation and publishing actions quickly. The first button, Show/Hide Cards, offers a menu of every available card that can be shown or hidden. When you click the down-pointing arrow to make the drop-down menu appear, you can single-click each card and rapidly enable or disable an option.

You use the next button, Presentation Mode, to put your worksheet, dashboard, or story into presentation mode. Think of this button as creating the ultimate executive presentation view with one click.

The final button on the Tableau Desktop toolbar is Share Workbook with Others. Ring a bell? This is a code phrase for publishing to one of several Tableau server-based platforms such as Tableau Public, Tableau Server, or Tableau Cloud. After clicking the button, you need to enter the Tableau Server URL or select the Tableau Online link. You are then on your way to publishing your workbook, dashboard, or story to the masses.

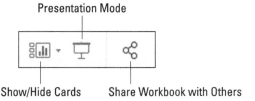

FIGURE 7-19: The rightmost section of the Tableau Desktop toolbar.

Understanding sheets versus workbooks

Much like other business productivity suites, Tableau uses the same naming nomenclature and file structure of the workbook and sheet file structure. A workbook (package) can contain many sheets. A sheet can be in the form of a worksheet, dashboard, or story:

>> **A worksheet** contains a single view of data along with shelves, cards, legends, data, and analytics panes along the Side Bar.

>> **A dashboard** is a compilation of views across many worksheets. The Dashboard and Layout panes are available on the Side Bar.

>> **A story page** takes a sequence of worksheets or dashboards and integrates navigations to piece together a cohesive message that cannot be told on a single screen or page. The Story and Layout panes are also available on the Side Bar.

You have several ways to create new sheets in a workbook, but the easiest one is to head straight to the tabs at the bottom of the Tableau Desktop interface. To create a worksheet, dashboard, or story, go to the bottom of a given workbook, near the status bar. You'll see three different icons with + (plus signs): one to create a new worksheet, one to create a new dashboard, and one to create a new story (see Figure 7-20).

FIGURE 7-20:
Click a + (plus sign) button to create a worksheet, dashboard, or story.

Create a new story

Create a new worksheet

Renaming sheets

To rename a worksheet, dashboard, or story within a workbook, you double-click the tab at the bottom of the workbook and then type in the alternative title in the highlighted space. If you're renaming a sheet, you type the new name in when the tab turns to a different color. When you're done entering the new name, press the Enter key to commit the change.

Deleting sheets

Just because you may *want* to delete a sheet doesn't mean you'll be able to. A few conditions must be met before you can remove a worksheet from a workbook:

» At least one worksheet must exist within a workbook.

» If you've used a worksheet as part of a dashboard or a story, you've committed the data to the workbook until you remove the dashboard or story. Your only option is to hide rather than delete the worksheet.

» If you have used a worksheet as a viz within a tooltip, you can hide it or delete it, but any associated data with a viz is lost upon deleting the worksheet.

If you consider all these conditions and are still okay with proceeding, select the active sheet that you want to delete from a workbook. Right-click the active sheet, select the Delete option, and click OK when prompted. If worksheets are dependent on what you are attempting to delete, you'll be notified to hide or unhide, delete, or cancel the worksheet.

Integrating Filters and Actions

You may have realized by now that you can do a bit of data massaging after seeing the big picture of a visualization. If you want to direct your users to specific functionality or enhance a visualization by enabling them to slice and dice their data a bit more, you can add filters and actions to a worksheet, dashboard, or story.

The following section tackles filtering and action integration.

Filtering for the needle in the haystack

Say you have 1 million records in your Tableau dataset, but you're trying to find those ten records that contain a specific string in a particular column. Filtering in Tableau can help you target those very specific data points when your dataset is robust. For example, in Figure 7-21, I've opened the Filter menu by right-clicking the Product Or Service Code dimension.

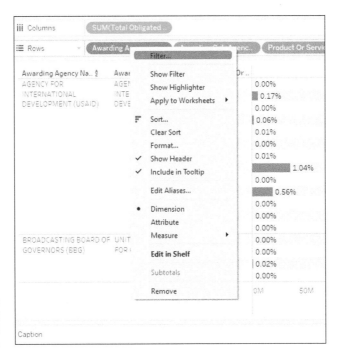

FIGURE 7-21:
Establishing
a filtering
parameter.

Upon going to the Product Or Service Code dimension, I clicked the Wildcard tab and decided to create a Contains filter. I typed **D** as the Starts With parameter so that any instance where the letter *D* appears at the beginning of the Product Or Service Code will be deemed a viable part of the result set. If the *D* happens to be the second character or even last character in the string, Tableau will not include the Product Or Service Code as part of the output.

To create a filter, follow these steps:

1. **Right-click a dimension or measure and select Filter.**

2. **Go to the Wildcard tab.**

   A screen appears, allowing you to create a filter.

3. **Select the Starts With parameter.**

4. **Enter the match value in the field.**

In this case, I entered the letter *D*.

5. **Click OK.**

In my example, only the values that start with *D* as the first letter appear in the list.

You can repeat this exercise as often as you want to get to a very tightly bound range of data.

In the example shown in Figure 7-22, I added a parameter by searching for only those transactions awarded to companies where the letter *A* is also part of the state name for Tableau as well as where the Product Or Service (PSC) Code contained the letter *D*. This is noted in the Filters card section.

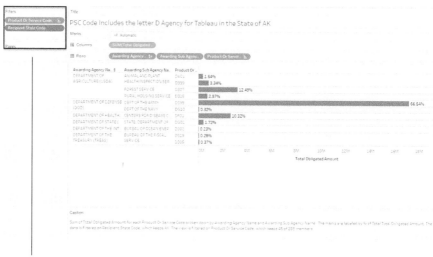

FIGURE 7-22:
An example of a highly filtered result set along with high-lighted Filters cards.

Filters card

REMEMBER

When the Filters screen appears, you have a wide range of filtering options, including the following:

>> **General filtering:** Targets all data in the specific dataset as all or nothing.

>> **Wildcard filtering:** Allows you to search based on parameters such as Contains, Starts With, Ends With, and Exactly Matches.

>> **Condition Filtering:** Targets data based on formulas as numerical values.

>> **Top Filtering** helps you identify fields relative to a value measure, such as the top 10 percent.

As you can see, the possibility of filtering is quite robust.

Activating your viz with actions

Another kind of filtering activity, called an *action,* isn't data related, but you may be interested in applying it to your viz to provide context and interactivity. An action enables you to interact with your visualization through a mechanism such as interacting with a targeted *marking* (placing individualized data points on a visualization), hovering over an item such as a graphic, or clicking through a menu. The navigation changes across one or more views based on how you set up the activity and its response.

Here's an example of using an action. Say that you have created a dashboard that provides employees in an organization with a revenue forecast for each office in the organization. You can add an action to display relevant artifacts that may attribute demographic data to the specific geographic target on the map. Another option may be to allow a user to click the map in order to drill down into a more detailed view of organizational data, such as who is in the territory and how much each territory member has produced to achieve the territory revenue target. When you create a filter for each worksheet, a separate filter allows the user to gain a better sense of the finite details for a single visualization. However, if you're looking to see the impact of filtering across many visualizations, the use of actions can be helpful, especially if you want to evaluate trends among your data.

Within the dataset, the user can use a traditional filtering approach to understand the data at a finite level better. The reason is simple: You can zoom in or out at any time to see the macro or micro view of the organization's financial picture.

To create an action, select Worksheet (above the Tableau Desktop toolbar) to open the Worksheet menu, and then select the Actions submenu. Then you need to figure out whether to apply the action to the entire workbook or one specific worksheet.

As noted in Figure 7-23, you can execute a variety of actions, including these:

>> **Filter:** Allows you to create a drill-down approach to filtering across one or more visualizations.

>> **Highlight:** Allows you to select and value its position in one or more visualizations.

>> **Go to URL:** Allows you to go from a visualization to an external source such as a website or application.

- **Go to Sheet:** Allows you to go from the current sheet to another sheet within a workbook.

- **Change Parameter:** Allows you to change a parameter value through direct interaction with a viz, such as by selecting a mark or clicking an item. Parameters can be applied to items such as reference lines, calculations, and filters.

- **Change Set Values:** Allows you to set a multistep condition (think if-else or do-while, if you're a programmer) in order to trigger an action.

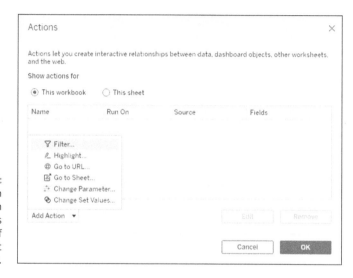

FIGURE 7-23: Choose an action from the Actions submenu of the Worksheet menu.

ON THE WEB

To understand how to complete the detailed configuration for each action type listed, you need to go to the Tableau documentation at https://help.tableau.com/current/pro/desktop/en-us/actions.htm. Actions options are constantly updated with each iteration of Tableau Desktop, so check back often to learn about the new opportunities available.

Getting Guidance from Tableau for Your Visualization and Analysis

Have you ever thought about what is really behind a dataset? Sure, you'll look at a dashboard, report, or even a Tableau story and pick at a point here and there, but your typical data analyst doesn't truly take advantage of all the analysis points (really). When you use Tableau Desktop, and for that matter, Tableau Cloud, your analysis guides the author and reviewer in discovering relevant data, from apparent trends and patterns to the missing data points that may seem ambiguous. (See Chapter 3 for more on the author role in data preparation.) The user experience provides a conglomeration of tools from the Show Me pane across various queries and data lenses to help better explore your data. At the end of the day, your goal should be simple: Craft a shared narrative that helps tell a relatable story across views, dashboards, stories, and reports for the decision-maker.

When you make a data point available as a column or row in Tableau Desktop, the application determines which visualization technique best suits your dataset without writing any custom code. You can find the best-fit visualizations in the Show Me pane, seen in Figure 7-24, which suggests the required dimensions or measures in each row or column to create a recommended visualization type. Tableau Desktop offers 24 out-of-the-box visualization types, which Chapter 8 covers. Examples include pie charts, scatter plots, tree maps, area charts, and line charts.

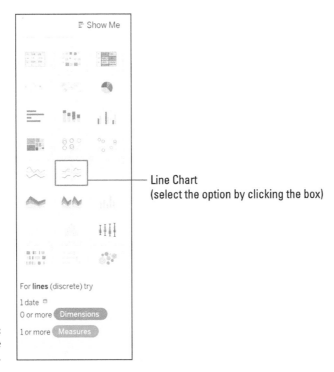

Line Chart
(select the option by clicking the box)

Differentiating between a Dashboard and a Story

Chapter 10 is dedicated to helping you create dashboards and stories, so this brief section's purpose here is to clarify the difference between a worksheet and a dashboard or story.

The dashboard

The workbook and its worksheets are obviously important, but there is only so much a worksheet can accomplish. You may, for example, need to compare a variety of data views simultaneously, such as the revenue produced by various departments of an entire company in one view. Or perhaps you want to break out a geographic region using a map view in a second view. In a third view, you may even want to pinpoint the product or service accelerating revenue growth in a specific region. Instead of having separate worksheets present the data, you can create a single view of the data. That single view is your *dashboard.*

You create dashboards similarly to how you create a worksheet, using the tabs at the bottom of the workbook. Data in sheets and dashboards are connected at the hip. If you modify a sheet, your dashboard reflects the change and vice versa.

In Figure 7-25, I've combined several of the previous worksheets presented in this chapter into a single dashboard and added a filter.

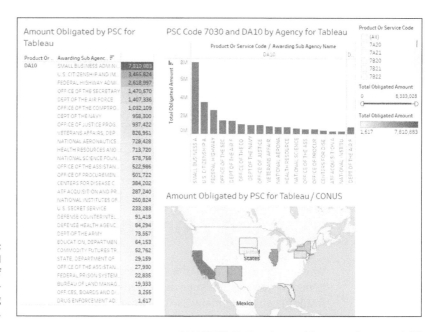

FIGURE 7-25: A dashboard made up of three worksheets along with a filter.

The story

A story is a sequence of visualizations; it could be a worksheet or dashboard coming together to convey information. The story is intended to tell a narrative, provide context, and demonstrate how outcomes are derived. You can also use a story to present a streaming use case, from the conception of data to the conclusion.

Like the worksheet and dashboard, a story is nothing more than a sheet in Tableau. Therefore, the mechanics used to create, name, and manage the story don't deviate from the worksheet or dashboard. The big difference is in the sequencing of the worksheets. You'll need to correctly name and label every worksheet because each one becomes a story point — a navigation point in the story sequence.

Figure 7-26 shows which of the continental 48 United States had recognized federal sales of Tableau between 2018 and 2022. The second story point (not shown) shows a breakdown in how much was spent by each federal agency.

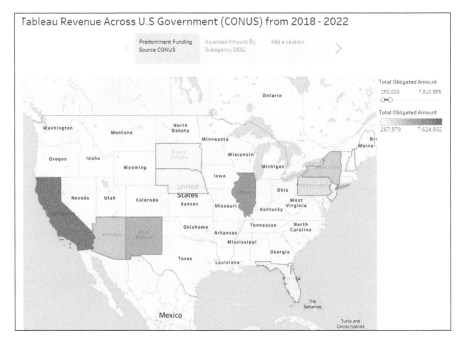

FIGURE 7-26: An example of a story consisting of multiple worksheets.

Customizing the Workspace

Worksheets are a compilation of cards, shelves, legends, and vizzes, to name a few items. As you explore your data, you'll need to create several worksheets, which result in collecting many cards, utilizing many shelves, and opening many panes in Tableau Desktop. Unless you are showing your worksheet, dashboard, or story in Presentation Mode, the various parts in Tableau Desktop may cause chaos and confusion. The old saying "less is more" applies here. Hiding (or at least reducing the footprint) to a bare minimum via customization is a lesson you'll want to learn from the get-go.

Rearranging workspace cards

Worksheets contain many cards. Each card can contain shelves, legends, and one or more object controls. With Tableau, you can rearrange and even hide these cards to create a custom workspace and keep it looking orderly. To move a card, follow these steps:

1. **Point your cursor at the title area of a card you intend to move.**

2. **As the cursor changes to the move symbol (a four-directional arrow), click and drag the card to its new position.**

   As the card is being dragged across the canvas, you'll notice that on the worksheet, the card's position is highlighted with a blackened frame.

Figure 7-27 shows an example of rearranging a workspace. In the top image, the Rows and Columns shelves are above the visualization. However, in the bottom image, the Rows and Columns shelves have been moved to the left column, which shifts the placement of the Filters shelf and Marks card.

Putting your data in motion using Presentation Mode

Imagine you've completed a data analysis but don't want to put the results in a static document such as a PowerPoint, Word, or PDF file. The reasons not to put them in such a document are many, but often it's because of the level of granularity a report or dashboard may offer a user if they drill down into their Tableau Desktop dashboards, stories, and reports.

You can put your data in motion using the Presentation Mode features in Tableau Desktop. Instead of seeing the various cards, toolbars, menus, and analysts' capabilities, Presentation Mode allows you to hide everything on a sheet except for the View area and its legend, filter cards, worksheet tabs, and parameter controls.

Columns shelf moved   Columns and Rows shelf

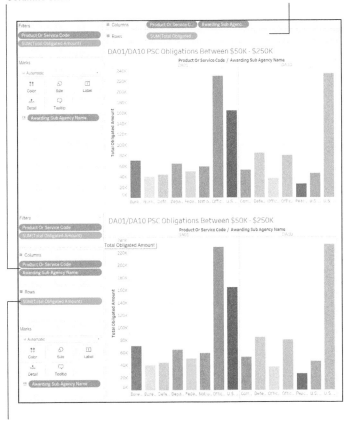

FIGURE 7-27:
Rearranging
shelves and
cards in a
workspace.

Rows shelf moved

You can switch in and out of Presentation Mode by clicking the Presentation Mode button in the toolbar. Alternatively, you can access Presentation Mode on the Window menu with a single click. Presentation Mode offers a variety of control buttons found on the bottom right side of the interface, as shown in Figure 7-28 and described here:

>> **Show Filmstrip:** Each sheet is represented as a thumbnail at the bottom of the workspace.

>> **Show Tabs:** Shows each sheet tab in sequential order at the bottom of the workspace.

>> **Previous/Next Sheet:** Allows you to move forward and backward across the sheets in a workbook.

>> **Enter/Exit Full Screen:** Enables you to expand or minimize the workbook from the entire screen to just part of the screen.

>> **Exit Presentation Mode:** Allows you to return to the workbook to continue making edits to one or more worksheets using the menus and toolbars available. You can see the Data pane while in Presentation Mode.

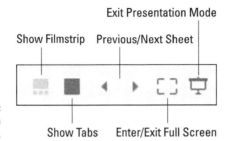

FIGURE 7-28:
Presentation
Mode controls.

Showing and hiding workspace features

Fortunately for you, you can turn almost every feature in Tableau Desktop on or off with a single click, as easily as flipping a light switch. You may want to suppress features because the workspace can become cluttered with extraneous cards, shelves, and filters.

TECHNICAL
STUFF

There are three main levers you can turn on and off in the workspace:

>> **Showing or hiding toolbars and status bars:** Select Window to open the Window menu from the toolbar, and then select or deselect the toolbar or status bar you want to enable or disable from showing in a workspace. (See Figure 7-29.)

>> **Showing or hiding windows and panes:** The left side of the workspace allows you to view the Data pane for worksheets, the Dashboard pane for dashboards, or the Dashboards and Sheets pane for stories. To show or hide these features, click the Minimize button, which is the up or down arrow in the right corner of each pane. The pane is minimized until you re-click the up or down arrow to maximize the interface size. An example of how to show or hide a pane using the shelves and cards is shown in Figure 7-30.

>> **Showing or hiding cards:** The Tableau Desktop interface contains many cards by default. As you add new features from the moment you create the data connection, the cards keep stacking up in the workspace. To hide (or show) cards, go to the toolbar and click the Show/Hide Cards button (refer to Figure 7-19, earlier in the chapter). You can select (or deselect) each card you want in the interface. To reset the workspace to its default card settings, click the Show/Hide Cards button on the toolbar, as shown in Figure 7-31, and then click the Reset Cards option.

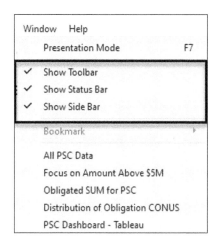

FIGURE 7-29:
Show or hide
toolbars and
status bars
through the
Window menu.

FIGURE 7-30:
Use the
Minimize
button to
show or hide
windows and
panes.

Show/Hide Cards

FIGURE 7-31:
Reset to the
default work-
space through
the Show/Hide
Cards menu.

Chapter **8**

Visualization Foundations in Tableau

Ta-da! It's the moment you've probably been waiting for and what most people often want to jump to straight away: creating the visualization (viz) in Tableau. Tableau makes it easy to figure out whether a visualization requires a measure or dimension, and whether the data should use discrete or continuous behavior using the Show Me recommendations, which include more than 20 choices. But one of the challenges people often face is having skipped the data cleansing or realizing that "whoops," our data has some flubs. That realization is perfectly okay, however, because Tableau allows you to filter and hide data anomalies. Before you take a deep dive into the visualization realm, I want you to consider that your dataset size and quality drive the visualization. At the same time, Tableau is fantastic at interpreting the data; only *you* know whether the visualization and explanations are on the money.

This chapter covers selecting and parsing a large dataset in Tableau Desktop. After you understand the principles involved, you can move on to creating each visualization type in the Show Me pane, with the focus on the importance of data types using measures and dimensions. To show you some ways to spruce up the visualization, I explore some of the customizations provided in Tableau. And finally, you find out how to publish your visualization to Tableau Online.

Finding the Ideal Dataset

Data comes in all shapes and sizes. You'll need to be flexible and work with your dataset, so be open-minded! You'll also want to be sure of a few things when utilizing a tool such as Tableau.

WARNING

A single clean dataset may not be your answer, either. You'll likely need to introduce a few sets if you're trying to solve a complex problem, and you may need to play cleanup between Desktop and Prep Builder. If you are an enterprise user, having a data dictionary to accompany the dataset is quite helpful. As you discover in Chapter 9, calculations are often required to expand upon specific points.

An effective dataset should

>> **Contain the elements you need:** The dataset has many variables to compare data.

>> **Contain disaggregated Data:** Data should not be just one type. You want numerical and non-numerical data collected from multiple sources, measures, and variables.

>> **Contain numerous dimensions and measures that can be leveraged as discrete or continuous:** Data can't be just qualitative or quantitative based.

>> **Have a data dictionary or metadata:** Headers and footers for a dataset are a starting point. Does the dataset explain what the values of each column mean?

>> **Be usable for a business intelligence tool (hopefully):** Data can't be too cumbersome or messy because if it is, you'll have problems creating a viz.

Connecting to the Data Source in Desktop

For the remainder of the book, I use a dataset from usaspending.gov, the definitive source for U.S. government spending, for examples of using Tableau features. The dataset follows the rules of an ideal dataset (for the most part) specified in the previous section; it contains more than 270 fields to choose from. So yes, it's an extensive dataset. The use cases for the examples vary, but they all focus on one topic: Tableau sales within the federal government taking place from 2007–2022.

TECHNICAL STUFF

The dataset contains about 1,800 records. Over the next several chapters, the examples use more than 40 fields from this dataset. To get access to the dataset, go to `https://files.usaspending.gov/generated_downloads/Prime AwardSummariesAndSubawards_2023-03-30_H02M04S45012058.zip`.

To connect to the usaspending.gov data, you'll need to unpack the data from the Zip file. The dataset you want to use is the Prime Awards Extract. After you've extracted the Prime Awards `.csv` file to your Desktop, follow these steps to expedite the loading of data into Tableau Desktop.

1. **Click the Tableau icon or choose File ⇨ New Menu.**

    The Connect page appears.

2. **Select Text File.**

3. **Locate the file** `Contracts_PrimeAwardsSummaries_<Date>.csv` **and double click the file.**

    Your data source is now loaded into Tableau Desktop, as you'll see because Sheet1 is added as a data source on the Data Source tab.

TIP

The Connection screen appears, allowing you to change your data using the Prep editor. Don't worry about this now; you'll make modifications along the way using filtering and calculation techniques instead of removing data right now.

4. **Create your first worksheet by heading to the Worksheet tab at the bottom of the page.**

Introducing the Visualizations

A visualization, referred to as a *viz* for short in Tableau, is the graphical representation of data in tables, pivots, charts, graphs, plots, or maps. Tableau provides a wide range of visualization types and customization options, allowing users to choose the best way to display their data and convey their message. Often, Tableau provides best-fit recommendations based on your data when you drag and drop fields from a data source onto the source. Based on the fields dragged and dropped onto the canvas (the visualization-specific workspace area) from the highlighted area in Figure 8-1, a desired visualization type can form in the Show Me pane, shown in Figure 8-2.

The appearance and formatting of the visualization can be customized using the options in the Marks card and the Formatting pane.

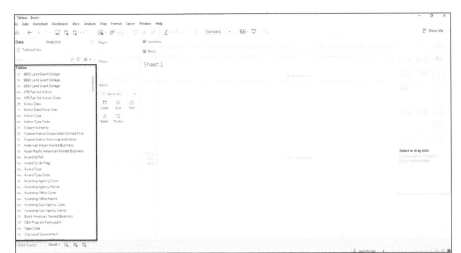

FIGURE 8-1:
The Tableau Desktop canvas, including data fields on the left.

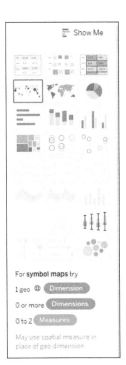

FIGURE 8-2:
The Show Me pane's best-fit examples.

The text table

The text table places one dimension on a Rows shelf and another on a Columns shelf. You then complete the view creation by adding more measures to the text as you see fit. A text table leverages the *text mark type*, which is a way to display numerical data in a text-based manner when dimensional data exists. Tableau uses the *mark type,* which is a way to add color, size, shape, and typeface, assuming that the view is constructed using dimensions exclusively (remember that it's automatic).

Two dimensions in the dataset are Awarding Agency Name and Recipient State Code. To create a text table visualization, drag both dimensions to the Rows shelf, and drag one dimension into the area of the mark, which is Total Obligation. The result is a visualization, as shown in Figure 8-3.

TECHNICAL STUFF

You may be wondering why you move items into the marks area versus to a Rows or Columns shelf. If you add fields on shelves, you are creating visualization structure. To increase the level of detail and control the number of marks in the view, which may include increasing or decreasing data granularity, you'll want to add data to the Marks cards. By adding specific fields to Marks cards, you are encoding the visualization with context using color, size, text, or numerical translation.

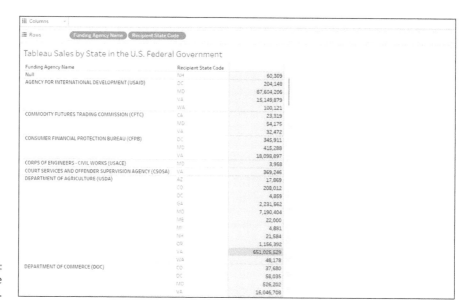

FIGURE 8-3:
A text table visualization.

The heat map and highlight table

A heat map in Tableau is a visualization that uses color to encode values in a table or matrix. This type of map helps to compare the relative values of data points within a dataset and identify patterns and trends. The highlight table in Tableau is a visualization type that displays the values of a single measure or a series of measures, in a table format, with the ability to highlight the highest or lowest values.

Creating a heat map

To create a heat map in Tableau, you need one or more dimensions and measures. The example in Figure 8-4 uses one measure and two dimensions. To create the heat map in this example, follow these steps:

1. **Drag one dimension to the Columns shelf (Recipient State Code), and drag the other dimension to the Rows shelf (Funding Agency Name).**

The measure is to the left of the chart, as shown in Figure 8-4 under Marks: SUM(Total Obligations Amount).

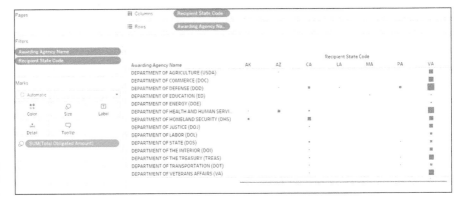

FIGURE 8-4:
A heat map
visualization.

2. **Right-click each of the dimensions and select Filter; next, select the desired parameters; and finally, click OK.**

Two filters for this visualization now appear under the Filters card:

- One wildcard on Awarding Agency Name, where anything containing the word *Department* should appear

- A filter on the Recipient State Code

In this example, any state containing the letter *A* appears. As you can see, the viz is significantly filtered. The marks that are proportionally larger than others indicate greater spending.

Using a heat map to assist in understanding who is getting more money may be helpful for a scientific presentation or to wow someone. However, with business reports, it's all about the data. That's why you'll want to use a highlight table instead.

Creating a highlight table

You can have the values in the table sorted in ascending or descending order. You can format the table to display the values differently, using colors, font sizes, or symbols to highlight specific values. A highlight table can quickly identify trends or patterns in the data and compare values across different categories or dimensions. It's a valuable tool for presenting data clearly and concisely and can be easily included in dashboards or reports. Figure 8-5 presents the same dataset created in the heat map in the highlight table. You can see many of the most significant awards in the State of Virginia. Volume-wise, large orders were also placed in California and Washington State (headquarters to Salesforce and Tableau, respectively).

To create a highlight table, follow these steps:

1. **Drag the Recipient State Code Field to the Columns shelf and the Awarding Agency Name to Rows shelf.**

   Both fields are dimensions.

2. **Drag the Total Obligated Amount to the Marks cards twice.**

   The field automatically becomes SUM(Total Obligated Amount). Both of these items are measures.

3. **Enhance the measures whereby one of the fields reflects the text marking and another reflects the color marking.**

4. **Right-click both dimensions and create a filter for each:**

   a. **For the Recipient State Code, go to the wildcard and pick only states where the letter *A* is in the State Code name.**

   b. **For the awarding agency name, select only those where the word *Department* exists in the name.**

   The dataset dramatically shrinks and the result is a highlight table, as shown in Figure 8-5, with the State of Virginia seeming to have the most dollars obligated across key departments in the U.S. federal government.

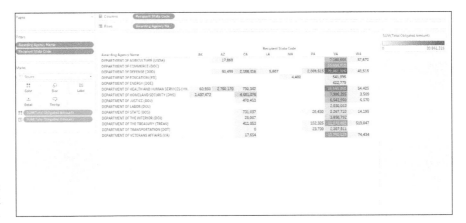

FIGURE 8-5:
A highlight
table.

Maps with and without symbols

There are two map types in Tableau, a map without symbols and one with symbols. The only differences between them are the formatting options and sophistication of the data in terms of the colors, styles, and symbols. On a normal map, the symbol used is almost always a circle, but the symbols used with a symbol map can vary.

Regardless of what type of map you use, a map in Tableau is a visualization that displays quantitative values on a geographical map using symbols (again, often these are circles). Maps often contain symbols whose size, shape, and color can vary to represent different values in the dataset. A legend is often used to help interpret the map. It's important to use symbols appropriately; using too many or mixing different sizes, shapes, and colors can make the map hard to understand.

TIP

Proportional symbol maps, which use symbols scaled in size according to the data values, can help compare limited datasets across a geographical area. However, you should take care to ensure that the symbols are distinct from the actual size of the location. It's also essential to ensure that the variables on the map are related.

Figure 8-6 shows a symbol map. To create a symbol map that shows the depth of symbols, colors, size, and size based on the data points or map, like the one in Figure 8-7, as well as illustrates more traditional map details such as terrain and streets if you zoom in close enough, follow these steps:

1. **From the dataset on the left pane, drag Recipient State Code and Recipient City Name to the Rows shelf.**

2. **Drag Total Current Value of Award to the Rows shelf.**

The difference between Step 2 and Step 1 is a measure versus a row. The measure automatically SUMs the Total Obligation per City and State Symbol.

3. **Right-click the measure and select Edit Filter.**

4. **Enter a range of values from 50,000 to 1,000,000.**

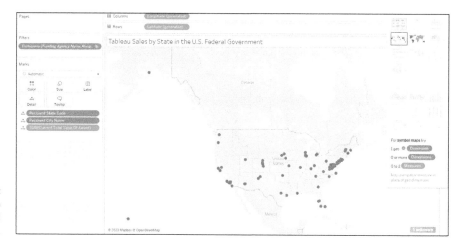

FIGURE 8-6: A symbol map with limited detail.

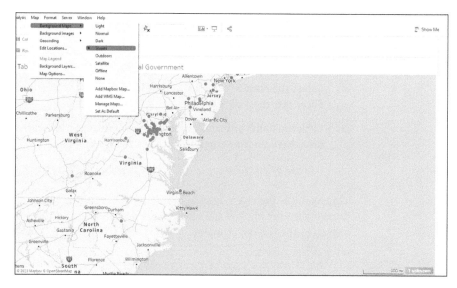

FIGURE 8-7: A symbol map with more details, including street view.

If you select the symbol map from Show Me, you can see very distinct circle sizes depending on dollar amounts. Selecting Maps initially differentiates the map by shades, which is normal behavior. As you can see in Figure 8-7, though, by going to the Maps menu, you can change and adjust the background, in effect also removing the color scheme. You then see more density relative to the area. For the example in Figure 8-7, bigger circles appear for the activity occurring in the Washington, D.C., metro area, where more significant procurements occurred.

The pie chart

A *pie chart* in Tableau is a visualization that displays data as a circle divided into wedges, with each wedge representing a proportion of the total. The pie chart helps show the breakdown of a measure or dimension into its parts. It compares the relative sizes of different categories. Pie charts require one or more dimensions and one or two measures.

To create a pie chart with the usaspending.gov dataset, follow these steps.

1. Select the NAICS Code field from the Data pane and place it in the Columns shelf.

2. Drag the Total Obligations from the Data pane to the Rows shelf.

3. Go to the NAICS Code and right-click Filter.

   A Filter window appears, allowing a user to create a General, Wildcard, Condition, or Top filter.

4. Select the NAICS Codes 541511, 541512, 541513, 541519 under the General Filter tab; then click OK.

5. Click the Label button under Marks and select Show Mark Labels. Click anywhere on the screen to hide the Show Mark Labels screen.

   A pie chart is created.

This example pie chart, shown in Figure 8-8, enables you to understand the proportionality for all Tableau sales under NAICS Codes 541511, 541512, 541513, and 541519 in the U.S government.

WARNING

Pie charts are not among the friendliest graphics in Tableau. You need to use tooltips to interpret data where you have several measures and dimensions. You can have only one label, which is numerical and therefore a measure. Figure 8-9 shows an example of including a tooltip.

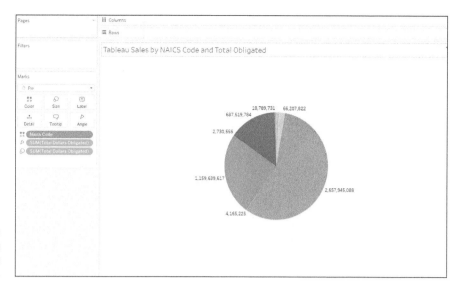

FIGURE 8-8:
A pie chart
with filters
applied.

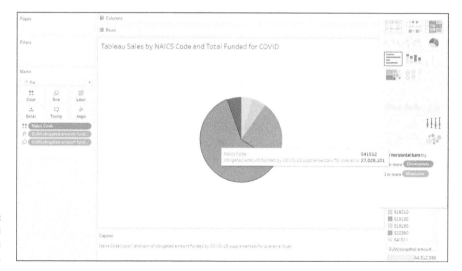

FIGURE 8-9:
Including a
tooltip in a
pie chart.

The bar chart

Tableau offers three types of bar charts in Tableau: horizontal (which is standard), stacked, and side by side. Here are some differences among the three:

» **Standard, horizontal bar charts** display the values of a single measure for different categories or groups. They help to compare the values of the measure across the categories. Horizontal bars require a single dimension.

>> **Stacked bar charts** display the values of multiple measures for different categories or groups, representing each measure differently. They help to show the contribution of each measure to the total value for each category. A stacked bar chart requires one or more measures and at least one dimension.

>> **Side-by-side bar charts** display the values of multiple measures for different categories or groups, with each measure displayed in a separate bar next to the other. This type of chart helps to compare the values of multiple measures for each category. It would be best if you had one or more dimensions and measures for a side-by-side bar chart.

To create both the standard and stacked bar charts (using the same usaspending. gov dataset used throughout the book), follow these steps:

1. Select the NAICS Code field and place it within the Marks card.

2. Drag the Total Obligated Amount field to the Rows shelf.

3. Click the Wildcard tab and select the Contains option in the menu that opens.

4. Enter 541 in the Match Value textbox.

    This step filters the NAICS Code field for all values containing 541 as part of the NAICS Code.

5. Click Apply.

6. Click the Show Me button on the top-right side to open the Show Me pane and select either Horizontal (Standard) Bars or Stacked Bars to see examples like those in Figures 8-10 and 8-11.

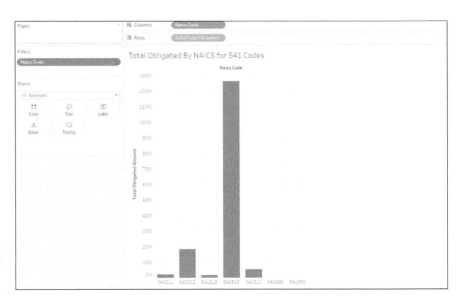

FIGURE 8-10: A horizontal (standard) bar chart.

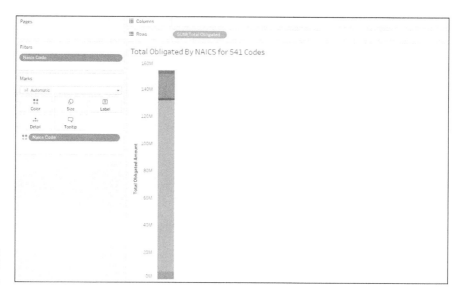

FIGURE 8-11:
A stacked
bar chart.

The only option for those looking to compare several data points using a bar chart is the side-by-side bar chart. Figure 8-12 shows an example of what you see when a second measure, called Total Potential Value of Award, is dragged to the Rows shelf. Tableau automatically SUMs the value. Although the field is dragged to the Rows shelf, it's ultimately transformed into measure values relative to measure names. Notice in the figure that two columns are being evaluated, which results in the automatic generation of a legend, also shown in Figure 8-12.

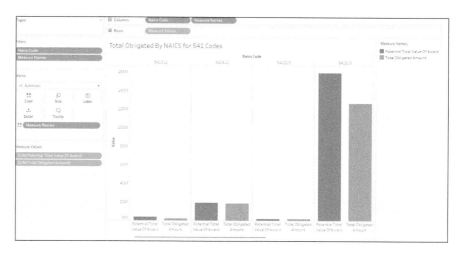

FIGURE 8-12:
A side-by-side
bar chart.

The treemap

A treemap offers you a way to visualize and display hierarchical data using nested rectangles. The area of each rectangle is proportional to the quantity it represents. The rectangles are arranged in a way that avoids overlap, so it's easy to see the structure of the data. Treemaps can help to compare proportions within a hierarchy and to identify data patterns. People often use them to display data about categories, such as sales by product, geographical regions, or customer segments.

In Tableau, a treemap may also include colors that indicate proportionality and importance relative to the dataset.

Using the same dataset (usaspending.gov), follow these steps to create a treemap:

1. **Select the Recipient State Code, Recipient City Name, and Total Obligated Amount fields.**

2. **Place all the fields in either the Rows or Columns shelf.**

3. **Select the Recipient State Code, right-click, and click Edit Filter.**

4. **On the drop-down list that appears, clear all options except for V.**

   The result is a treemap that shows the volume of sales among cities in the State of VA between 2007–2022 (see Figure 8-13). The city of Reston had the most significant sales volume, with more than $50M in sales. On the other hand, Gainesville, which is not visible or labeled in the corner, has the slightest impact. Notice that the gradient legend in treemap's right corner helps to show the value scale.

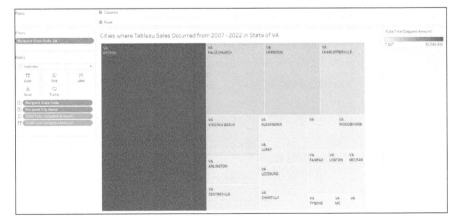

FIGURE 8-13:
A treemap.

Circles and bubbles

People often confuse circles with bubbles in Tableau, but they shouldn't. Also, the names of these diagrams are a bit misleading because the Circle view visualization in Tableau is a traditional scatter plot. The scatter plot displays data points as circles (or other shapes) on a two-dimensional grid. A single circle represents each data point, and the circle's position on the grid represents the values of the data point along the x and y axes. You often use scatter plots to visualize the relationships between different datasets or to identify patterns and trends in the data. For example, you may want to use a scatter plot to visualize the relationship between a company's revenue and its profits, or to identify stock market trends. Scatter plots are a valuable tool for exploring and understanding data. You can customize them in various ways to highlight different aspects of the data.

A second type of circle visualization is the side-by-side Circle view. This type of visualization displays two datasets as circles. One set of circles is positioned next to another to compare the values of two datasets or to show how two datasets are related. You often use side-by-side Circle views to compare data about categories, such as sales by product, geographical regions, or customer segments. You can also use them to compare data about individual observations, such as the size of a company and its revenue or profit.

The last of the circle-type charts is a bubble, even though bubbles and circles are the same. The bubble chart in Tableau is a visualization that displays data as circles shown on a two-dimensional chart. Each bubble represents a single data point, with its position on the chart determined by its values on two numeric axes. You can also use the bubble size to encode additional data, such as the volume of a particular product sold or the population of a particular city. People often use bubble charts to compare multiple datasets, identify trends and patterns, and find outliers in the data. Bubble charts can help to visualize data with three or more dimensions, such as data that includes a third numeric or categorical variable.

Using the usaspending.gov dataset, the following steps show you how to create each circle chart using the same variables in each: Recipient State Code, Current Total Value of Award, and Total Obligated Amount.

1. For the Circle view, place the two measures on the Rows shelf and the dimension on the Columns shelf.

2. On the bottom of the page, you see that nulls exist. Click the nulls link to indicate that you want to filter all values (see Figure 8-14).

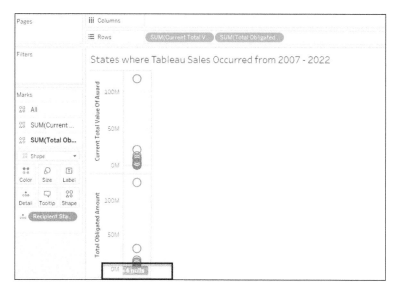

A pop-up menu appears, asking you to filter or show data at the default position.

3. **Click Filter Data (see Figure 8-15).**

The resulting chart shows that one state has a disproportionate amount of sales relative to the rest. The next step creates a filter to give you a better sense of reality.

4. **Go to the Filters card and select SUM(Current Total Obligations).**

5. **Right-click SUM(Current Total Obligations) and select Edit Filters.**

6. **Enter the range of values $50,000 – $2,500,000 in the textbox (see Figure 8-16) and then click OK.**

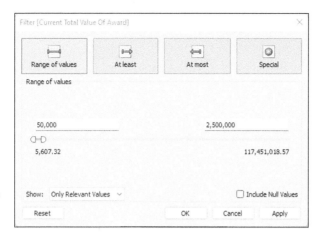

FIGURE 8-16:
Set a range of values in the filter.

After you follow the preceding steps, you can click the Circle views, Side-By-Side Circle views, or Bubble Chart views visualization in the Show Me pane to see different interpretations of the data using the same dimensions and measures utilized. Regardless of the view, you'll see three consistent circle and bubble charts appear, presenting the same message in terms of sales value by state, given the range $50,000–$2,500,000 NET from 2007–2022 using the Circle view, Side-by-Side Circle view, and a bubble chart, as shown in Figures 8-17 through 8-19.

FIGURE 8-17:
A Circle views visualization.

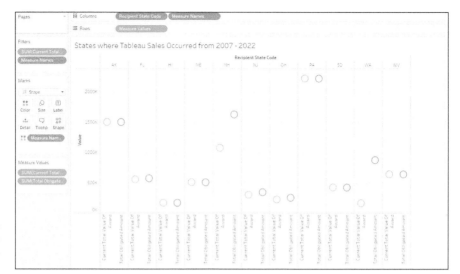

FIGURE 8-18:
A Side-By-Side
Circle views
visualization.

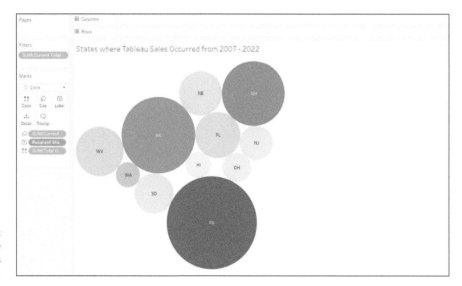

FIGURE 8-19:
A Bubble
Chart views
visualization.

The line chart

In the Show Me pane, Tableau offers three types of line charts: discrete, continuous, and dual line. Here's how these three types differ:

>> **Continuous line chart:** With this type of chart, the x-axis is a continuous numeric field or date field. When the x-axis is a continuous field, Tableau automatically creates a continuous axis and plots data using a line.

» **Discrete line chart:** With this type of chart, the x-axis is a discrete field containing a finite number of distinct values. Tableau creates a discrete axis and plots data using discrete data points rather than a continuous line.

» **Dual-line chart:** Also referred to as a dual axis, this type of chart displays two measures on a y-axis. Using this chart type is proper when comparing two measures that have different scales. You may have one measure with a range of 0–100 and another measure that ranges from 200–500. If you try to measure these on the same axis, it would not be easy to see the difference between them. Using dual-scale axes allows you to compare the two values more effectively than using a single-line discrete or continuous-line evaluation.

To create a continuous line chart from the sample dataset (usaspending.gov), follow these steps:

1. **Locate these two data fields: Current Period of Performance and Total Obligated Amount.**

2. **Drag the Current Period of Performance field to the Columns shelf.**

3. **Drag the Total Obligated Amount field to the Rows shelf.**

    A continuous line chart like the one shown in Figure 8-20 appears.

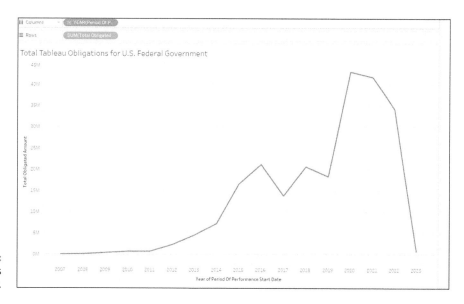

FIGURE 8-20:
A continuous line chart.

Each time you add another field to the Rows shelf — for example, the Potential Value of Award — another line will be added to the visualization. If you want to create a discrete line chart instead, you'll need to apply the changes to the y-axis (Columns shelf), as shown in Figure 8-21.

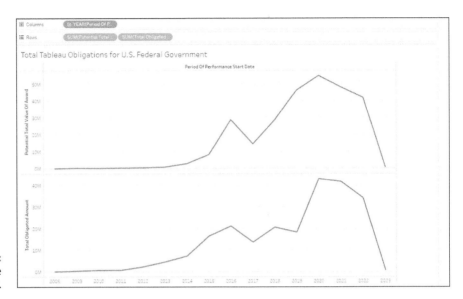

FIGURE 8-21:
A discrete line chart.

You can make use of the dual-line option on the Show Me pane without adding more data points. The notable difference between Obligated versus Potential emerges clearly with this type of chart, shown in Figure 8-22, especially with the different colors for each line.

The area chart

As with the line chart, the area chart offers a continuous and discrete view.

The area chart displays data as a series of points connected by lines, except that between the lines and the x-axis, the space is filled with color or a gradient. You use area charts to demonstrate trends over time or to compare several measures. If you used the data points from the previous section's example, you would see little differentiation between discrete and continuous lines versus area charts except for the areas being filled. Figure 8-23 uses the data points Year of the Period of Performance Start Date and the sum of the Potential Value of the Total Award to show a like-kind line in the area chart.

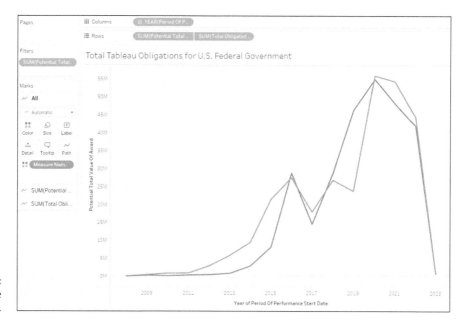

FIGURE 8-22:
A dual-line
chart.

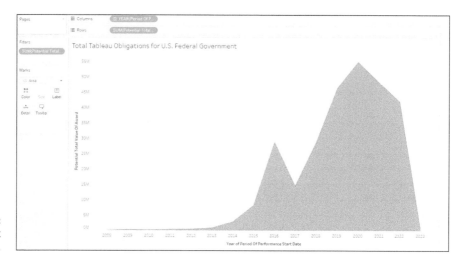

FIGURE 8-23:
An area chart
(continuous).

What happens, though, if you add an extra layer? You may want to understand who is spending the money. You can add an extra layer and create a stacked area chart, which is not an option available on the Show Me pane.

To create a stacked area chart:

1. **From the usaspending.gov dataset, drag the Awarding Agency field to the Marks card.**

   You see many lines instead of a single line.

2. **Click the icon next to the Awarding Agency Name label to differentiate the colors.**

3. **Select the Color option.**

   The result is a stacked area chart like that shown in Figure 8-24. Notice that it's the same shape as the original chart, except there is differentiation because now if you scroll over the chart, you can see which agencies have spent what during a given year. The legend on the right helps you decipher the color coding.

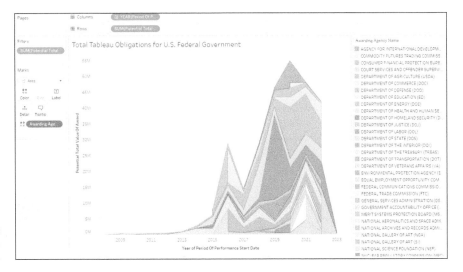

FIGURE 8-24:
A stacked area chart.

TIP

A legend can be challenging to read for a sighted user, never mind a person with color challenges. Tableau does offer an accessible, compliant palette for those needing to meet Section 508 and WCAG standards. Also, the usaspending.gov dataset has many data points. Filtering should help reduce the number of tones and shades for better readability in a stacked area chart.

The dual combination chart

In Tableau, a dual combination is a visualization that combines two separate views of the same data onto a single sheet. Dual combinations help to compare two targeted values given a specific period or value in the exact visualization, or the same measure or dimension across different periods.

To create a dual combination chart in Tableau, you need two measures and one date. Dimensions are optional. To create a dual combination chart using the usaspending.gov dataset as an example, follow these steps:

1. **Drag the Period of Performance Start Date data field to the Columns shelf.**

2. **Drag the Potential Total Value of Award and Total Obligated Amount data fields to the Rows shelf.**

   The initial result is shown in Figure 8-25. Notice the bars and line.

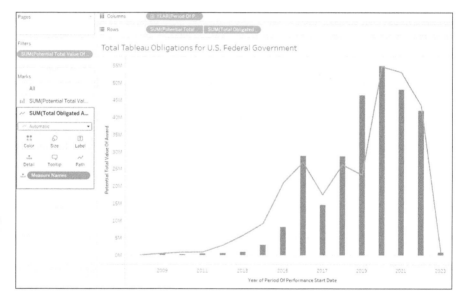

FIGURE 8-25:
A dual combination chart with bars and a single line.

3. **(Optional) You can swap the line for an alternative combination, such as areas, circles, and symbols (Figure 8-26). To accomplish this, go to each value under the Marks card and select one of the following from the drop-down list (by default, the list is set to automatic):**

   - Area Chart for Total Obligations

   - Line Chart for the Potential Total Value of the Award

   In Figure 8-27, you can see the changes made when both fields were changed from a line or bar given the options found under the drop-down menu.

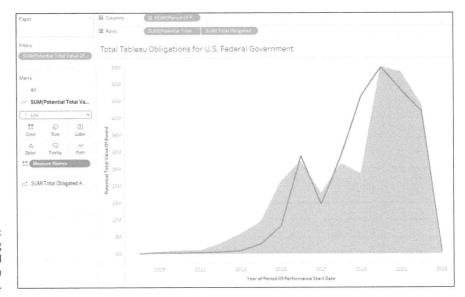

The scatter plot

The scatter plot is appropriate when you want to visualize numerical variables. You can create a simple scatter plot by placing one measure in the Columns shelf and one in the Rows shelf, or create a matrix-based scatter plot by adding a dimension to the Rows and Columns shelves for categorization purposes.

If you take a matrix-based approach, Tableau places the measure as the inner-most field, meaning that the field is to the right of any dimension on a shelf.

REMEMBER

In the following example using the usaspending.gov dataset, you follow these steps to evaluate the number of awards per the NAICS Code and Product and Service Code (which are both dimensions), by including the Current Total Value of Awards and Number of Offers Received fields:

1. **Drag the Current Total Value of Awards field to the Rows shelf.**

2. **Drag the Number of Offers Received field to the Columns shelf.**

3. **Drag the NAICS Code and Product and Service Code fields to the Marks card.**

WARNING

At this point, you see a scatter plot with a highly dense region in the lower-left corner (see Figure 8-28). However, to better understand data, I strongly encourage you to apply filters on the dimensions and measures. Creating a specific filter for each measure and dimension helps you to view all scenarios and achieve greater clarity.

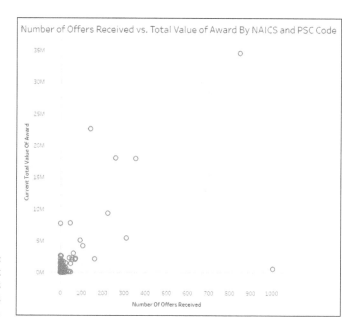

FIGURE 8-28:
A scatter plot with no filters on dimensions or measures.

4. **To apply filters, right-click each of the dimensions or measures and select Show Filter.**

Each filter appears on the right side of the screen.

5. **Adjust the filters as follows:**

   ● **For Product and Service Code: Enter** D.

   ● **For SUM(Numbers of Offers Received): Set the range to 0–100.**

- **For SUM(Current Total Values of Award): Set the range to 250,000–1,000,000.**

- **Keep the NAICS Codes as they are.**

The new scatter plot shows the finite number of Tableau-related acquisitions where the SUM was between $250,000 and $1,000,000 for specific NAICS and PSCs combined. An example is shown in Figure 8-29.

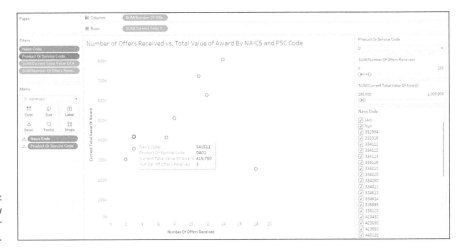

The histogram

Histograms help users understand data distributions. Using a bar chart to group values for data comparison, you can better understand data based on grouped values of continuous measures or bins. In other words, you may have many small transactions. Still, the transactions are lumped together under a single umbrella and classified using a range. For example, all store transactions with a value of less than $99.99 would fall into one range, and transactions above that threshold would comprise a second range.

That's the case in Figure 8-30, where *bins,* a grouping of like-kind values, are grouped for the Current Total Value of the Award, which is the only data field you need to drag to the Rows and Columns shelves. Each of the smaller transactions matched to like-kind properties are paired in bins and then classified, which is the same in the sampling you've just created in the previous section, "The scatter plot."

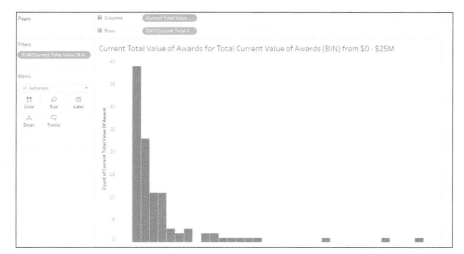

WARNING

You have little control over histogram bins; therefore, you should filter the dataset to target a realistic view of a histogram. Such filtering has been applied to the histogram in Figure 8-30 to keep the range of values from exceeding 25,000,000. All anomalous data ranges have been removed.

The box and whisker plot

The *box and whisker plot,* also called a *box plot,* is a chart type that allows users to display minimum values, 25 percent quartile, median, 75 percent quartile, and maximum range values. Values that exceed the thresholds are called *outliers.* Using a box and whisker plot helps you understand the distribution and spread of your dataset.

To create a box and whisker plot, you need two dimensions on the Columns shelf and one measure on the Rows shelf. Ensure that the Marks card is set to a circle and the reference line is set to a box plot.

After you place your data fields on the shelves, the resulting chart (using the usaspending.gov dataset) looks like the one in Figure 8-31, which illustrates the total value of awards based on a given contract type. As you can tell from the figure, the Firm Fixed Fee and Labor Hours had the bulk of federal dollars allocated during the award period.

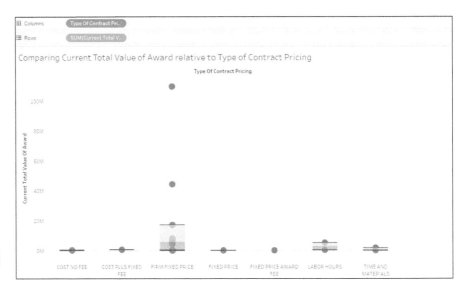

FIGURE 8-31:
A box and
whisker plot.

The Gantt chart

You use a Gantt chart to illustrate the duration of a data point. A Gantt chart requires one date measure in the Columns shelf and one dimension in the Rows shelf. The Tableau Gantt chart is different from the traditional project management tool such as Microsoft Project because you can't create a discrete line item and assign a start date and end date to a specific item. Quite the opposite, in fact. With Tableau, you're looking at the date at a given moment in time. For example, say that a transaction occurred in January 2023. On a Gantt chart, a tick mark would appear, representing the period of January 2023. Depending on the granularity, it could be one mark representing the month (January 2023) or a series of marks representing part of a quarter (Q1 2023). The marks are not spelled out for the duration of the contract; they just show a moment in time. That's the case with the Gantt chart you see in Figure 8-32, with each mark representing a unit of one month.

To create a Gantt chart using the usaspending.gov dataset as an example, follow these steps:

1. **Drag the Month of Period of Performance Current End Date field to the Columns shelf.**

2. **Drag the Type of Set Aside field to the Rows shelf.**

3. **Right-click the Period of Performance Current End Date field, and change the time frame from Years to Months (it's the second option, which includes the month and year notation).**

   Your Gantt chart ticks are now a bit more granular.

4. **Click Gantt Chart on the Show Me pane.**

   A Gantt chart like the one in Figure 8-32 appears.

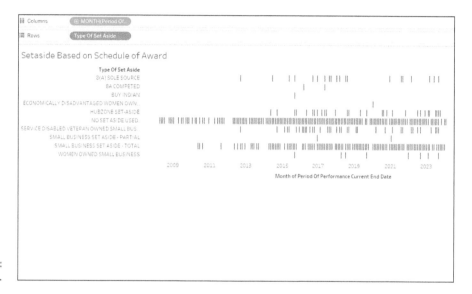

FIGURE 8-32:
A Gantt chart.

TECHNICAL STUFF

Out of the box, Tableau defaults to the Year setting for every tick mark on the Gantt Chart. To change this setting, right-click the date-based measure and then click an alternative parameter such as Year, Quarter, Month, or Day to modify the bounds. The example in Figure 8-33 shows Month as the setting.

The bullet chart

The *bullet chart* displays data in much the same way as a horizontal bar chart, except that it's condensed, given that it contains two data points. A bullet chart compares a single measure to a targeted value. This type of chart is ideal when you're trying to gauge performance over time. The bar represents the tracked measure, and the horizontal line indicates the target value. Knowing the bar's position relative to the line helps you quickly ascertain whether you're on target to meet the measured objective. A bullet chart does allow for the comparison of multiple measures in the same target value.

FIGURE 8-33:
Setting date-based measures for a Gantt chart.

To create an example bullet chart using the usaspending.gov dataset, follow these steps:

1. **Drag the Award Type data field to the Rows shelf.**

2. **Drag the Total Potential Value of Award and Total Obligated Amount data fields to the Columns shelf.**

3. **Select the Bullet Chart option on the Show Me pane.**

   The bullet chart shown in Figure 8-34 appears.

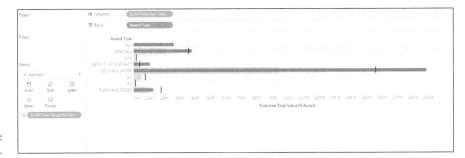

FIGURE 8-34:
A bullet chart.

Converting a Visualization to a Crosstab

I'll bet you didn't know that you can take any visualization in Tableau and convert it to a cross tabulation table, or crosstab, did you? A *crosstab* converts a visualization into a text-based table, showing the data in a textual form. Like the text table discussed in the section "The text table," earlier in the chapter, the crosstab table comprises one or more dimensions and measures. A crosstab can also integrate various calculations for the measure fields, including running totals and percentage totals. To convert a visualization to a crosstab using the usaspending.gov dataset, follow these steps:

1. **Drag the Period of Performance Start Date field to the Columns shelf.**

2. **Drag the Funding Agency Name and Awarding Office Name fields to the Rows shelf.**

3. **Drag the measure Total Obligated Amount to the Labels shelf under the Marks card.**

   A simple crosstab is created (see Figure 8-35).

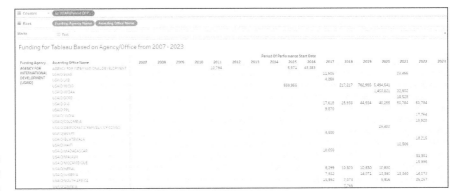

FIGURE 8-35: A simple crosstab table.

To differentiate the significance of values within a dataset, you can color-code your dataset. Color-coding requires you to add the Total Obligation field one more time to the Labels shelf within the Marks card. Then, right-click and select Color.

In the example shown in Figure 8-36, the dataset has been filtered to only one federal agency. Still, the color scheme and range in values and colors are apparent.

TIP

If your range of values is quite broad — say, 0 to a billion — I strongly encourage you to pick a gradient range that's easy to differentiate. Having too many similar shades can confuse people and defeat the purpose of using color.

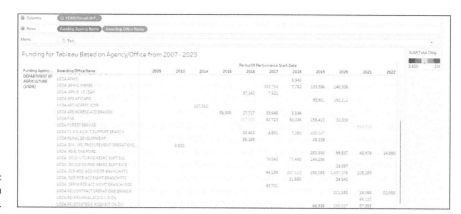

FIGURE 8-36:
A crosstab with
colors.

Finally, you may want to review data using a standard calculation. Out of the box,
Tableau incorporates various calculations that can be autogenerated in a crosstab
table. The options, which appear in Figure 8-37, are frequently updated.

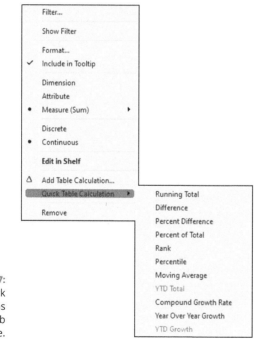

FIGURE 8-37:
Adding quick
calculations
to a crosstab
table.

To add a calculation to the chart to use instead of the dollar values, follow these steps (still making use of the usaspending.gov dataset for this example):

1. **Right-click the SUM(Total Obligated Amount) indicated by the text symbol in the Measure Values card.**

   A list of options appears, including Add Table Calculation, which you'll be selecting.

2. **Select the Add Table Calculations option.**

   A pop-up window appears, enabling you to create a Table Calculation (see Figure 8-38).

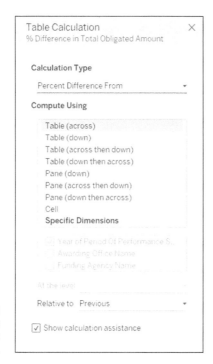

FIGURE 8-38: Table calculation types.

3. **On the first drop-down menu, select Table Calculation Type: Percent Difference From.**

4. **On the second drop-down menu, select Compute Using Table (across).**

   When you close the window, the crosstab immediately changes to show yearly percentages (see Figure 8-39.) The percentages indicate the increase and decrease in total obligated spending relative to the previous year for a given agency and its corresponding office.

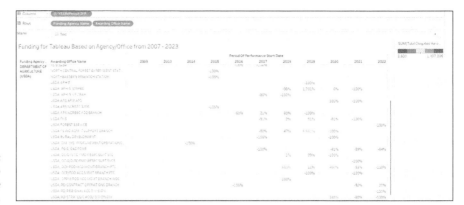

FIGURE 8-39:
A crosstab
using table
calculations.

Publishing Visualizations

Tableau Desktop has several paths for users to take to get their work product from Tableau Desktop to Tableau Server or Cloud. You can complete and publish a worksheet containing your visualization by doing one of the following:

>> On the Server menu, select Publish Workbook.

>> On the toolbar, click the last button, Share Workbook with Others.

>> On the File menu, choose Export your Visualization as a Package.

>> Create a PDF, PowerPoint, or alternative file format for mass use.

If your goal is to share and collaborate with other users in the organization who have Creator, Explorer, or Viewer licenses, publishing the workbook to a Tableau project is your optimal choice. If a system administrator has configured a project on your behalf, follow these steps to save your worksheet using either the Server or toolbar approach; the prompts are the same.

1. **Click the Share Workbook with Others button on the toolbar.**

   A pop-up menu appears (see Figure 8-40).

2. **Select the project.**

3. **Under Name, enter a worksheet name.**

4. **Under Description, provide a document description.**

FIGURE 8-40:
A common
publishing
dialog box for
Tableau Cloud
and Server.

5. **Under Tags, click Add to add tags.**

6. **Under Permissions, click Edit to list who may or may not have access to the file in the future.**

7. **Under Data Sources, click Edit to validate the data source parameters using the Workbook Optimizer.**

   By default, it is usually embedded.

8. **If you are satisfied with what Workbook Optimizer indicates, you can execute publishing directly, or close the window and click the Back button to return to the previous window and then click Publish.**

WARNING

At this point, the file should be ready for publishing. One last step could be to optimize the file. In this case, the dataset used so far contains more than 280 fields, but only a handful have been used for the exercises. That's okay, because you'll use some other fields in subsequent chapters. However, if you want to optimize the dataset, follow the guidance provided using Workbook Optimizer (shown in Figure 8-41), which offers you a way to ensure that the dataset you're publishing is healthy.

FIGURE 8-41:
Workbook
Optimizer.

IN THIS CHAPTER

» Defining the three basic
calculation types

» Applying the principles and
components for creating
calculated fields

» Enhancing visualizations to
identify patterns, trends, and
behaviors in data

Chapter **9**

Analytic Practices in Action

When data is ingested into Tableau, you may, as many users do, find it to represent just the tip of the iceberg. That's because calculations allow you to transform a simplistic data point into a complex equation. You can potentially combine multiple fields while also leveraging functions and formulaic expressions available in Tableau. To create calculations, you need to understand the principles of creating calculated fields in Tableau. In this chapter, you find out how to create complex calculated fields as well as see how to identify patterns, trends, and behaviors using Tableau's built-in Analytics feature.

Understanding Calculations

On the surface, Tableau has three main calculation types: basic expressions, level of detail (LOD) expressions, and table expressions. Each type has variants. Table 9-1 summarizes the difference between the three types.

TABLE 9-1   Calculation Types

Type of Expression	What It Does
Basic	Allows for the transformation of values at the data source level of detail. It can be a row-level calculation or, at the visualization level of the detail, it can represent an aggregate calculation.
Level of detail (LOD)	Allows you to compute values at the data source level and the visualization level; however, you have more granularity in how to manipulate the data using conditions such as INCLUDE (more), EXCLUDE (less), or FIXED (independent).
Table	Allows you to exclusively transform values at the level of detail at the visualization.

To create a row-level calculation that applies a specific condition, use the following formula:

```
SPLIT([Funding Agency Name], '', 2 )
```

If you want to create a column that displays a count or the aggregate of how many agencies procured Tableau, you could use the following aggregate calculation:

```
COUNT([NAICS Codes])
```

You'd place the calculation in the Marks cards while you drag the NAICS Code to the Rows shelf. The result appears in Figure 9-1.

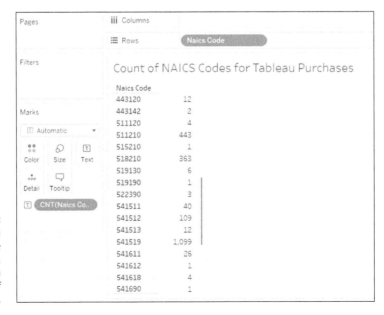

FIGURE 9-1: Using an aggregate calculation, which is a basic type of expression.

A *level of details (LOD)* expression is more concerned with finding targeted details, hence the name "level of details." Your goal in establishing the calculation is to select the appropriate parameter for a given calculation. Say you want to identify the year or month an organization received an award. Here's the formula you could use:

```
{ FIXED [NAICS Code]:(MIN([Period Of Performance Start Date]))}
```

The output you get in Tableau appears in Figure 9-2.

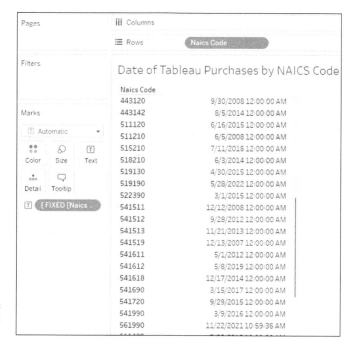

FIGURE 9-2:
A level of detail
calculation.

To visualize data at the level of detail, you need to apply conditions to the equation. Using the same award scenario, say you want to know just one part of the performance period, not the entire period. Perhaps you also want a consolidated view of your data. You can use a function to support such visualization.

For the example in the following equation and shown Figure 9-3, each NAICS code indicates when at least one award occurred during a fiscal year.

```
Year (Period of Performance Start Date)
```

Period of Performance Starts by NAICS Code	
Naics Code	
511120	2015 2018
511210	2008 2009 2010 2011 2012 2013 2014 2015 2016 2017 2018 2019 2020 2021 2022
515210	2018
518210	2014 2015 2016 2017 2018 2019 2020 2021 2022
519130	2015 2019 2020
519190	2022
522390	2015 2019
541511	2008 2015 2016 2017 2018 2019 2020 2021 2022
541512	2012 2013 2014 2015 2016 2017 2018 2019 2020 2021 2022
541513	2013 2016 2017 2019
541519	2007 2008 2009 2010 2011 2012 2013 2014 2015 2016 2017 2018 2019 2020 2021 2022 2023
541611	2012 2016 2017 2018 2019 2020 2021 2022
541612	2019

FIGURE 9-3:
A table
calculation.

Crafting Calculated Fields

Sometimes you may have lots of excellent data. Still, you may not have all the correct calculations to complete a worksheet so that your dashboard or story makes sense despite a data deluge. In these circumstances, you'll want to introduce calculated fields. A *calculated field* allows you to create new fields from data that already exists in your data source. What you are essentially creating is a new field, or column, within your data source that consists of values or members from which calculations are derived.

An example of a good use of a calculated field is when you want your audience to know the percentage of something by comparing two data points. Another example is when you're trying to understand the financial impact of a specific action, requiring several data points. The calculation may combine measures and dimensions to produce a final result.

Tableau allows users to create custom, calculated fields that can become new measures or dimensions. You can take the data from one or more existing data sources and define a calculation, which can be as simple as adding two fields. A more complex calculation can incorporate multiple fields and include functions. Read on for more details of using calculated fields.

Starting with a simple calculated field

Getting your feet wet by playing with known data points and expected behaviors is a significant first step in creating a calculated field. For an example, follow these steps to see how to capture the percentage of the obligation spent to date between two fields: Current Total Value Of Award and Potential Total Value Of Award:

1. **Go to a worksheet in Tableau.**

2. **Choose Analysis ➪ Create Calculated Field.**

   The Calculation Editor opens (see Figure 9-4).

3. **Name the field in the textbox (for example, "Percent Total Award"); then click OK.**

4. **Type the following into the Formula Editor, as shown in Figure 9-4:**

   ```
   SUM([Current Total Value Of Award])/SUM([Potential Total
       Value Of Award])
   ```

   If you've entered the formula correctly, the message The calculation is valid appears.

5. **Click OK when finished.**

   The field is added to the existing list of fields found in the Data pane.

Calculation Field Name textbox

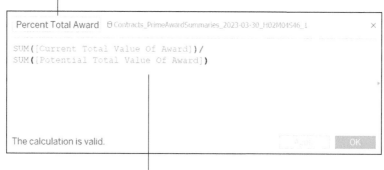

FIGURE 9-4:
Use the
Analysis menu
to open the
Calculation
Field Editor
and enter a
formula.

Calculation Field Formula Editor

TECHNICAL STUFF

Formulas are a combination of functions, fields, and operators. Head to Chapter 13 to reference the essential functions that are useful in Tableau so that you can create optimal formulas.

The new calculated field should now appear in the Data pane. Assuming that the goal was quantitative, the field becomes a measure. If the field yields a qualitative output, the result is a dimension.

To visualize the Percent Total Spent to Date against Agency and Fiscal Year, follow these steps:

1. **Place the calculated field you just created in the preceding steps in the Marks card. Click the field and select Text.**

2. **Drag the Period of Performance Start Date field to the Columns shelf and the Funding Agency Name to the Rows shelf.**

3. **Create a filter with a range of dates set from 1/1/2017 – 12/31/2022.**

   Figure 9-5 presents the result, which includes integrating your newly created calculated field using a Text Table visualization.

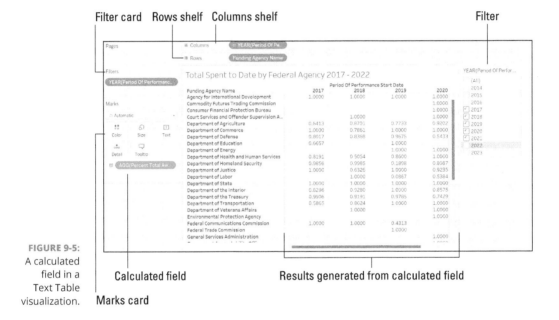

FIGURE 9-5:
A calculated field in a Text Table visualization.

Formatting your calculations

Unlike what you do with visualizations, this section is not about how to color-code your numbers. Instead, you find out how to work with the essential components of a calculation. Each calculation must adhere to a proper syntax to operate as a data field. Table 9-2 describes the attributes of a successful calculation.

TABLE 9-2 The Essential Components of a Calculation

Component	Concept
Function	A statement that converts the value of a data field based on defined conditions
Field	Dimensions or measures available from your data sources
Operators	Symbols that explain an operation
Literal expressions	Known or constant values

Applying these four fundamental concepts, take a look at this complex formula:

```
IF SUM([Total Dollars Obligated]) > SUM([Current Total Value Of
        Award]) THEN "Overspend"
ELSEIF SUM([Total Dollars Obligated]) < SUM([Current Total Value
        Of Award]) THEN "Available"
ELSE "None"
            End
```

The formula says that if the total dollars obligated is greater than the current spend, the word Overspend should appear in a table. If the total dollars obligated is less than the current spend, the word Available should appear in the table. Otherwise, the condition means that funding is exhausted; hence, no more funding is available (None).

Digging deeper into the formula, here are the components that the calculation incorporates:

» **Functions:** IF, ELSE, ELSEIF, END, and SUM

» **Fields:** Total Dollars Obligated and Current Total Value Of Award

» **Operators:** > and <

» **Literal expressions:** Only string literals are used in this formula. They include "Overspend", "Available", and "None".

Figure 9-6 yields the results of the complex calculation created using the equation in this section. If there is a blank for a specific year, no funding is obligated or spent in that fiscal year.

REMEMBER

You are probably wondering why I haven't discussed parameters yet. That's because parameters are nothing more than placeholder variables that you can add to a calculation in place of a constant value.

FIGURE 9-6:
Applying a
calculated
field to a table
using complex
formatting.

Getting the syntax of a calculation right

Calculations are a combination of functions, operators, and fields. The syntax, more affectionately understood as the placement order, requires Tableau to create a proper calculation.

Follow these steps to create a calculation with the elements placed in the proper order:

1. **Start with the name of the calculation.**

   It should be easy to understand. Make sure it is alphanumeric and to the point. The name cannot contain any spaces.

2. **Use an equal sign (=) to start the calculation.**

3. **Create a calculation consisting of functions, operators, and fields that define the targeted calculation.**

4. **End the calculation with a closing parenthesis.**

Here's a simplistic example of a syntax-appropriate calculation:

```
Budget = SUM(Total Dollars Obligated)
```

Table 9-3 provides a more detailed explanation of working with syntax in your calculations.

TABLE 9-3   **Calculation Syntax Considerations**

Component	Syntax
Functions	Varies depending on the type of function. See Chapter 13 for examples.
Fields	Brackets ([and]) surround the calculation.
Operators	**Arithmetic:** These are typical mathematical operators including +, -, *, and /.
	Comparison: Used to compare values as equal, greater than, less than, or combinations of equal/not equal. Operators include >, <, ==, <=, >=, and !=.
	Logical: These are either/or state condition operators. Operators include True and False, AND, OR, or NOT.
	String: Bring two strings together using a + sign. An example is `stringa + stringb`.
	Conditional: Based on conditions in the equation. Typical operators include `IF THEN`, `ELSE`, `ELSEIF`, and `CASE`.
	Aggregate: Special functions like `SUM()`, `AVG()`, `MIN()`, and `MAX()`, when applied to a set of rows or columns, give you an aggregate value.
Literal expressions	**Numeric literals:** Specific numeric values that are written out, such as `1.2345`.
	String literals: Expressions using quotation marks, such as `"None"`.
	Date literals: Specific dates, with a hashtag (#) at the front, such as `#2/3/23`.
	Boolean literals: Either True or False with a hashtag (#) in front, such as `#True` or `#False`.
	Null literals: Presented as `null`.
Parameters	Already defined calculations that are surrounded by brackets, such as `[Completed Calculation]`.

Evaluating Your Data Using the Explain Data Feature

Suppose you intend to take your data to Tableau Cloud or put it on Tableau Server. In that case, a feature called Explain Data extends analysis capabilities. Ironically, you need to configure Explain Data settings in Tableau Desktop, but analysis can be completed only by using a server-based infrastructure.

Explain Data takes the sheets, dashboards, and stories you create and helps you evaluate the dataset for trends, patterns, outliers, and correlations in the underlying dataset. Explain Data builds various statistical models and offers a variety of explanations to users in a visualization.

REMEMBER

You might see the word *viz* appear in Tableau documentation. *Viz* is short for *visualization*. Absolutely nothing changes whatsoever.

Configuring the Explain Data feature involves selecting the datasets and fields that you deem to be in and out of scope before you publish a workbook. After you've uploaded that data to Tableau Cloud, the data is used to run the Explain Data analysis.

After you open your uploaded sheet in Tableau Cloud, select a data point and then head to the Analysis menu. On that menu, choose Explain Data ⇨ Run Now. Alternatively, right-click a numeric value (in this example, it's the numeric value for Department of Education under the year 2019) and select Explain Data, as shown in Figure 9-7.

FIGURE 9-7:
Accessing the Explain Data feature in Tableau Cloud by right-clicking a numeric value.

A data guide appears on the rightmost column of the Tableau Cloud interface, detailing the specific data point, as shown in Figure 9-8. To better understand the full scope of the explanation, you can drill down into each section by clicking each bold header.

You can also evaluate other data fields that may be interesting to know more about. If, for example, you select the section What is Unique About Department Of Education (Ed), 2019 (see the final item in Figure 9-8), Explain Data gives you significant details about the data fields that relate to your data point. For the example in Figure 9-9, those significant details relate to the award or awards given for that fiscal year.

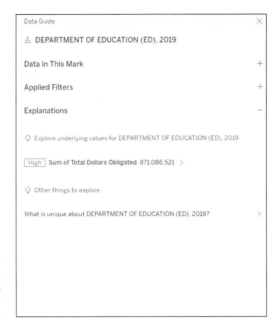

FIGURE 9-8:
The data guide provides details about a data point.

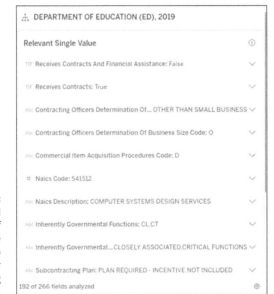

FIGURE 9-9:
A detailed view of alternative fields to consider while using Explain Data.

Spotting Patterns in the Data through the Analytics Tools

The goal of analytics is generally to identify trends and spot patterns in your dataset. It can also forecast opportunities based on the available data. With Tableau, you can conduct a variety of analytics activities, from measuring trends to pinpointing anomalous behaviors. The Analytics pane in Tableau is home to 14 modeling options to help you analyze data through summary, trending, forecasting, clustering, and banding behaviors.

In addition, the Analytics pane provides a second level of analysis to enhance an existing visualization with further insights. Figure 9-10 shows the modeling capabilities available to you on the Analytics pane, and Table 9-4 describes each option in detail.

To apply a modeling option in the Analytics pane, you drag the option over the existing visualization. For any of these analytic options to work, a visualization with data already in place must exist.

TABLE 9-4   **Analytics Pane Modeling Options**

Modeling Capability	Description
Constant line	A line that is associated with a specific measure or value. If a range is from –100 to 100, you can set a constant line with markers at –50, 0, and 50, for example.
Average line	Averages the values across the data and places a line in that location. For example, if the data range is from 0–100, but the average is 32, the line appears at 32, not 50 (the middle).
Median with quartiles	Adds at least one set of median lines and distribution bands in a view. The median appears with two bands representing the distribution, and the quartiles are shaded in gray.
Box plot	As with the box plot chart, you can overlay a box plot on another chart type. Here, each box plot is a bit more discrete in that the user scrolls over the plot to gain insights into the statistical data from the whiskers, means, and quartiles.
Totals	Adds a Total value to a view. Options offered include Subtotals, Column Grand Totals, and Row Grand Totals.
Average with 95% CI	Adds at least one set of average lines with a series of distribution bands. The distribution bands are configured at the 95 percent confidence level.
Median with 95% CI	Adds at least one set of median lines with a series of distribution bands. The distribution bands are configured at the 95 percent confidence level.
Trend line	Adds a minimum of one trend line to a view. Several trend types are available for evaluation, including Linear, Logarithmic, Exponential, and Polynomial. Trend analysis type varies depending on the visualization type.
Forecast	Tableau provides a forecast using measure-based data exclusively, hence numerical values only. Multidimensional data sources are not supported in forecasting.
Clusters	Groups data points together that are similar, which helps identify patterns and trends that may not be apparent if you look at each data point alone. Unsurprisingly, you need several values associated with the same measures to attain a cluster value.
Custom reference line	You add one or more of these lines to enhance the visualization for analytics reference. The reference line can be for one or all measures.
Custom reference bands	You add one or more of these bands to enhance the visualization for analytics reference. The reference band can be for one or all measures.
Custom distribution band	You add one or more of these reference distributions to enhance the visualization for analytics reference. The reference distributions can be for one or all measures.

TIP

In some cases, several selections are available, as shown in Figure 9-11, whereas in other cases, you have a single choice. An additional screen appears for custom parameters, asking you to configure the reference parameters before the analytic reference is placed on the visualization.

A complete visualization containing both the selected trend line and an average line (representing average obligation) appears in Figure 9-12.

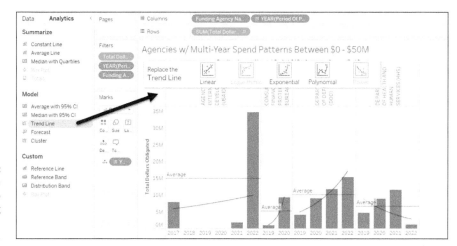

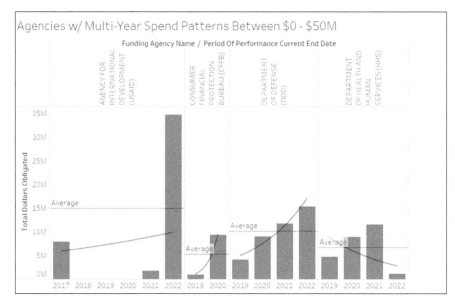

THE EINSTEIN DISCOVERY ANALYTICS TOOL

Powered by Salesforce and incorporated as an add-on to Tableau, Einstein Discovery, now known as CRM Analytics, is an analytics tool that leverages artificial intelligence and machine learning to enhance data analysis through comprehensive statistical analysis and predictive models. It takes your analysis further by efficiently processing millions of rows of data to identify significant correlations and forecasting outcomes. Instead of looking for the needle in the haystack, Einstein Discovery works on your behalf by providing recommendations for improving those forecasts. To access such a feature requires an administrator to purchase the add-on and then activate the feature from the system administrator console in Tableau Cloud or Tableau Server.

WARNING

Patterns, trends, and cluster analysis are relatively easy to implement using Tableau Desktop or Tableau Cloud; the functionality requires little work beyond dragging and dropping. Tableau also offers predictive modeling functionality, but this requires you to know enough about scripting and advanced data modeling. Head to `https://help.tableau.com/current/pro/desktop/en-us/predictions.htm` if you want to find out how to incorporate predictive analytics.

Chapter **10**

Showcasing Data with Dashboards and Stories

ableau is an excellent tool for analyzing data and crafting visualizations, even utilizing a single worksheet and data source. But the real power of Tableau reveals itself when you're looking to share and collaborate on data with others, which provides multidimensional perspectives. Dashboards enable you to bring together several perspectives so that the audience can interact with the data holistically.

In this chapter, you find out how to engage in two forms of data collaboration beyond a worksheet: the dashboard and the story. To ensure that all users can work with the data, you also discover how to make your data accessible by following Section 508 of the U.S. government's Rehabilitation Act as well as the Web Content Accessibility Guidelines (WCAG) compliance standards.

Dashboards in Tableau

Tableau takes the worksheet's static nature and makes it come to life through interactive data visualization. Users can quickly and easily analyze, interpret, and communicate data on a single interface, assuming that they have an appropriate number of visualizations and filters for a single screen. Otherwise, you can create several dashboards and craft a story, which I cover later in the chapter. The dashboard consolidates and displays a large amount of data in a single, organized view, making it easy to identify trends, patterns, and relationships within the data.

You can create dashboards in Tableau by using various visualization types, including charts, graphs, maps, and tables. You can also customize dashboards with filters, parameters, and other interactive elements, such as buttons, which allow users to drill down into the data and explore it in more detail.

Over the following several pages, you find out how to configure, customize, and enhance the dashboard experience using Tableau Desktop and Tableau Cloud.

Configuring the dashboard

Consistency is critical with Tableau. You have several ways to create a dashboard. One is to click Dashboard on the top of the page to open the Dashboard menu and choose the New Dashboard option (see Figure 10-1). Or you can click the New Workbook icon in the toolbar to open the drop-down list and then click the Dashboard button on the Tableau toolbar (see Figure 10-2). The third way to create a dashboard is to head to the bottom of the workspace near the status bar and select the New Dashboard icon, shown in Figure 10-3.

FIGURE 10-1: Creating a new dashboard using the menu.

FIGURE 10-2:
Creating a new
dashboard by
clicking the
button on the
toolbar.

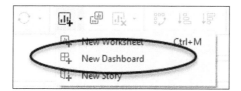

FIGURE 10-3:
Creating a new
dashboard
by clicking
the New
Dashboard
icon on the
bottom of the
workspace.

Whichever way you create a new dashboard, the outcome is always the same: You've added a new dashboard workspace. The interface for your new dashboard workspace (shown in Figure 10-4) consists of many features that enable you to create a multifaceted visualization, including the Dashboard pane and Layout pane.

Interface card (size and type)   Dashboard workspace

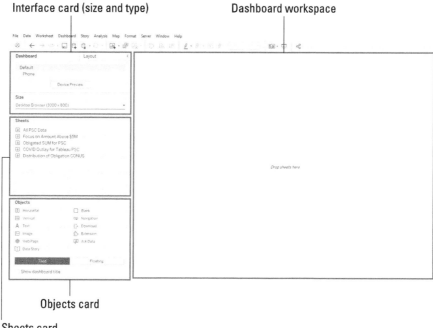

FIGURE 10-4:
A blank
dashboard
workspace.

Objects card

Sheets card

The Dashboard pane contains a few dashboard-specific functions, including

>> **The interface type and its size:** You can choose whether the dashboard is meant for the Desktop or a mobile device based on how many views you expect to integrate into a single dashboard.

>> **Sheets:** A compilation of all worksheets that you can include as part of a single dashboard.

>> **Objects:** Items you can add to enhance a dashboard, including shapes to highlight data points and textboxes for headers and footers.

>> **The dashboard workspace:** The location where you can aggregate various worksheet views on a single page to create a single dashboard.

To create a dashboard, drag one or more sheets from the Sheets card on the Dashboard pane to the Dashboard's workspace (as shown in Figure 10-5). In the Dashboard pane, select the appropriate size for presenting the visualization, rendered for either a desktop or mobile device. A grey workspace indicates that a new object is being added. You repeat this activity numerous times, adding all the sheets from the Sheets card and Objects card that you want until you feel that your dashboard is complete.

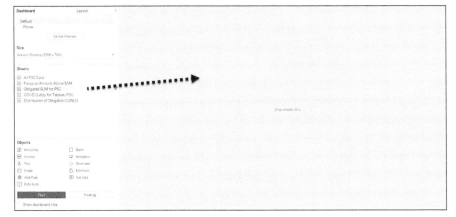

FIGURE 10-5:
Dragging sheets and sizing the visualization in the dashboard workspace.

Customizing the dashboard

To create the ultimate dashboard, you may also want to utilize layout objects, found on the Objects section of the Dashboard pane (under Sheets). For example, you may want to include the horizontal and vertical layout so that when you drag a sheet to the workspace, the page is more aesthetically pleasing and balanced.

To use a layout object, drag one or more objects to the dashboard workspace. Then place one or more sheets from the Sheets card on the workspace to create the desired dashboard result. Figure 10-6 shows an example of a layout using the Horizontal object (Figure 10-6), and Figure 10-7 shows the layout using the Vertical object (Figure 10-7).

FIGURE 10-6: A horizontal layout of sheets for a dashboard.

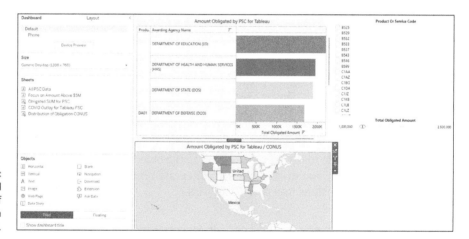

FIGURE 10-7: A vertical layout of sheets for a dashboard.

The Blank object, shown in Figure 10-8, is a glorified spacer that helps to separate the sheets and keep them from being on top of one another. You use the Blank object for other reasons as well. First, it helps you focus on individual visualizations when you're including multiple sheets in your dashboard. More important, though, is that the spacer can also be used for nonlayout-specific objects, discussed in depth in the next section.

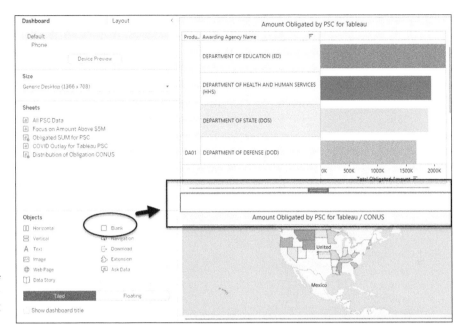

FIGURE 10-8:
The Blank
object serves
as a type of
spacer for
enhancing
layouts.

Adding Objects to Dashboards

In contrast to a worksheet and a story, you can add objects to enhance your dashboard. Because the dashboard represents a collection of various visualizations, you may need to incorporate logos, images, shapes, or even embedded content, such as a web page. The icons in Figure 10-9 represent the various object types that you can incorporate into a dashboard, including text, images, and embedded web pages.

Figure 10-10 shows how to drag the object to the workspace. In the following sections, you discover how to integrate text, images, web pages, button types, and extensions into your dashboard.

Tackling text, fonts, and color

The Text object has many of the same features as your run-of-the-mill text editor, such as selecting fonts, changing font size, and applying bold, underline, italics, and positioning options. The Text object, however, lets you add an object to the dashboard to augment a caption or data story with self-written text. You are not married to sticking with a specific font or size or making the text black; in fact, you can craft a textbox with various font faces, sizes, and shapes if you want, as exemplified by Figure 10-11. As soon as you drag the Text object to the dashboard, a pop-up window asks you to type freely. To format the text, highlight it and then click the button for the formatting feature you need.

Tableau also enables a user to insert prebuilt text, as indicated by the drop-down menu under Insert, which is part of the text editor.

FIGURE 10-9: Choose an option for the dashboard.

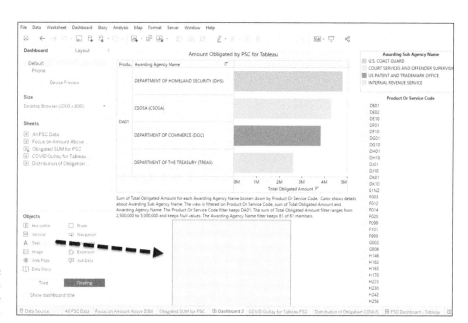

FIGURE 10-10: Drag an object to the workspace.

FIGURE 10-11:
Example
text-box with
formatting
features.

Integrating images and logos

You may want to make the dashboard experience personal to your brand or per-haps add an image that can add value to your dataset that is not self-explanatory using core Tableau features. One idea may be to extract an image from a report and then compare it to your data. You can pull the image directly from a website, or you can upload and insert it into the dashboard. To add an image, which can also act as a logo in a targeted location of a dashboard, follow these steps:

1. **Drag the Image object from the Dashboard pane to the workspace (as indicated by the dotted arrows in Figure 10-12).**

2. **Select one of the corners and drag to expand or contract the image to the appropriate dimension.**

3. **Double-click the image box to open the Edit Image screen.**

4. **Upload the image to the workspace, or point to the URL by selecting Link to Image; then enter the URL.**

   The image uploads from the internet to the dashboard.

5. **At the bottom of the Edit Image Object screen, add appropriate alt text for usability purposes.**

   Alt text helps a user with visual challenges to better understand what an image object describes. Additionally, if you're looking to position an image within the given space provided, you can select the boxes under the options to center or fit the image (or both).

6. **When you're finished adding your image, click OK.**

7. **Drag the completed image to its destination.**

The ideal logo placement is on the left side of the title of your dashboard.

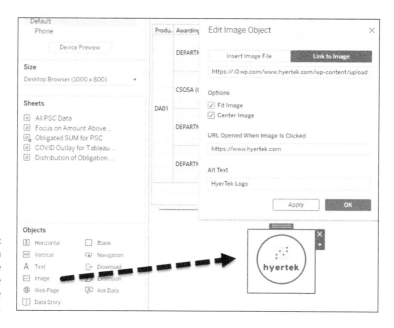

FIGURE 10-12:
Placing a
corporate
logo on the
bottom of the
dashboard.

Weaving in web pages

Including a web page within a dashboard may sound unusual, but it can be useful when you're pulling data from a targeted source or want to provide additional insights into a data point. In that case, you can create a Web Page card on the dashboard. By including procurement data on the dashboard from another source and then allowing a user to compare the Tableau-generated visualizations, you can map the source to aggregate data in a single view. The single view incorporates the various sheets from one or more workbooks and the data source itself (which is usaspending.gov in the example in Figure 10-13).

To add a web page object to your dashboard, follow these steps:

1. **Drag the Web Page object to the dashboard workspace.**

2. **In the pop-up box that appears, shown in Figure 10-13, enter the website parameters (the URL).**

3. **When you're finished, click OK.**

   The Website Object loads the targeted URL into the layout container, which you can modify to fit onto the dashboard comfortably. The *layout container* allows you to group related dashboard items together so that they can be positioned to meet your specific needs quickly.

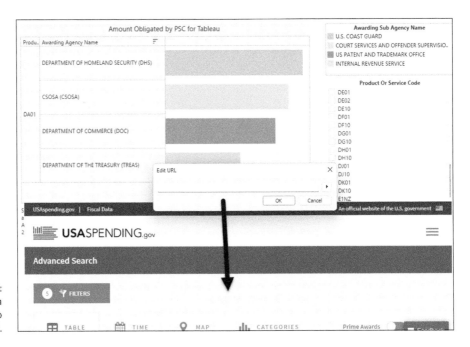

FIGURE 10-13:
Embedding a web page into a dashboard.

Buttoning up the dashboard

Buttons can enhance the interactivity of Tableau dashboard by enabling users to trigger specific actions or events. The two main types of buttons are the Navigation and Download buttons. Navigation buttons enable users to navigate between worksheets, dashboards, and stories within Tableau. Download buttons let users download items from a specified URL by clicking the button. These buttons can add an extra dimension to dashboards by allowing users to interact with the data and navigate through the content in a more targeted and customized way.

You can see both button types near the bottom of Figure 10-14. To configure these buttons, you must fill in all fields on the Edit Button page. Key items to configure include navigation location, button style, and tooltips to describe the button's purpose. The figure also shows an example interface for configuring the Navigation buttons.

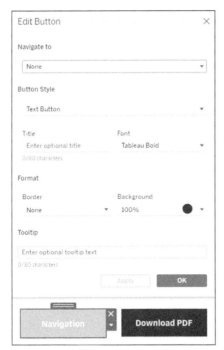

FIGURE 10-14:
Configuring
Navigation
and Download
buttons to
place on the
dashboard
workspace.

Extending the dashboard

Tableau extensions are add-ons that allow you to extend the functionality of Tableau dashboards and worksheets. Extensions can be created by folks like you and me or by other enterprise software organizations to enhance Tableau dashboards or worksheets.

Many extensions are available, including ones that allow you to integrate with external applications, add custom visualizations, or add new features to your dashboards. To use an extension, you need to install it in Tableau and then add it to your dashboard layout just as you do any other dashboard object.

In Figure 10-15, you'll find an example of what the Extensions interface looks like after you drag and drop the Extension object onto the workspace.

**TECHNICAL
STUFF**

Each extension has its own configuration requirements, but the process to select, drag, and drop is the same for all. Follow the developer's instructions to incorporate an extension into your dashboard.

FIGURE 10-15:
Adding an
extension to
the dashboard
using third-
party sources.

Adhering to best practices for dashboard design

When creating a dashboard, it's essential to keep in mind the guidelines for making an effective dashboard. You can't just consider the data, although that is important. You should also strive to balance aesthetic clarity, conciseness, and appropriateness. Also, it would be best to remember that users often face unique circumstances when reviewing visualizations, especially ones full of color that may be complex to understand. Follow these principles, at a minimum, for design best practices. A bit later in the chapter, I talk about applying accessible features to Tableau.

>> **Keep it simple:** A dashboard should include only the most crucial information and be clear of unnecessary details.

>> **Use clear and concise labels:** Use clear and concise labels to help users understand the purpose and context of each view or visualization.

>> **Use appropriate visualizations:** Choose the correct type of visualization to convey the information effectively. For example, use a bar chart to show quantitative comparisons and a pie chart to show proportions. (Chapter 8 covers working with these and many other types of charts.)

>> **Use color effectively**: Color should be used only to highlight important information and create a visual hierarchy; also, using too many colors can be overwhelming.

>> **Test and refine:** Test your dashboard with users to gather feedback and refine it based on their needs and insights.

Following these guidelines, you can create a compelling and informative dashboard in Tableau that helps users quickly understand and analyze data.

Acing Accessibility with Tableau

To ensure that your data views are accessible to a wide range of users, including those who rely on assistive technologies such as screen readers or Braille keyboards, you can use Tableau to build views that adhere to the Web Content Accessibility Guidelines (WCAG 2.0 AA). This is particularly important if you want to make your views as accessible as possible or work in a setting subject to U.S. Section 508 requirements or other accessibility regulations. By following these guidelines, you can make your views easy to use and navigate for all users, regardless of their abilities or the technology they use to access your content.

After you have created your view, you can publish it and embed it into a web page that also adheres to these guidelines.

It would be best if you did the heavy lifting in Tableau Desktop because there are limitations to creating accessible-ready solutions in Tableau Cloud.

For an example of an accessible data view, consider a stacked bar chart that incorporates numerous color schemes. Such a chart needs to include various elements that help make the view accessibility friendly. These elements could be text-based image descriptions known as alt text. Other items to consider including are clear and descriptive headings, and proper formatting and organization of content. Figure 10-16 illustrates all the ways you can support accessibility, from color palettes to captions for people with sight limitations. Figure 10-17 demonstrates that a textual counterpart is available for every graphical representation using the View Data window. Here are some specific suggestions:

>> **Include descriptive tabs.** Each worksheet is a separate object that ultimately gets added to a dashboard or story. Start by making the tabs descriptive because they impact your workbook, dashboard, and story titles.

>> **Use clear titles.** Does Dashboard1 or Story1 have any meaning to you? Not at all. Instead, be explicit about what the visualizations offer the data observer.

>> **Provide captions.** Suppose you don't see certain colors or have no sight. How can you interpret graphics and colors that explain a dataset? The most appropriate way is to incorporate Tableau's automated captions as a supplemental approach to describe the visualization. For users without sight, captions can be read by accessibility readers such as JAWS.

>> **Incorporate filters.** Having a graphic is one thing, but if there is a way to interpret the data, you need to include it. Filters allow for pinpointing of data and better analysis.

>> **Insert categorical legends.** Whether the goal is to interpret the colors or describe a single color with qualitative explanations, a legend guides the reader, especially those who are visually challenged to interpret the content.

>> **Deliver text details with a data story.** The Data Story object, found under Objects in the left pane of the dashboard workspace, gives you a text analysis of your dataset without conducting an ounce of analysis. For those who can't visualize, the data story can cut to the chase rapidly. See "Adding Objects to Dashboards," earlier in this chapter, for details on adding objects like the Data Story.

>> **Use the right color palette.** If you want to be sure that the color palette complies with WCAG-approved colors, head over to the color legend, where you'll modify the color scheme to be compliant (Figure 10-18) by right-clicking and then selecting Edit Color. Select the Color Blind palette to ensure Section 508 and WCAG AA compliance.

WARNING

Tableau can integrate accessibility in many ways, but some require a bit of configuration. Tableau features that may enhance the experience for those with accessibility requirements include:

>> Targeted keyboard navigation

>> The ability to program for specific assistive devices

>> Adding alt text to describe charts and visualizations

>> Considering the needs stated in Section 508 compliance guidelines, which include color contrast requirements.

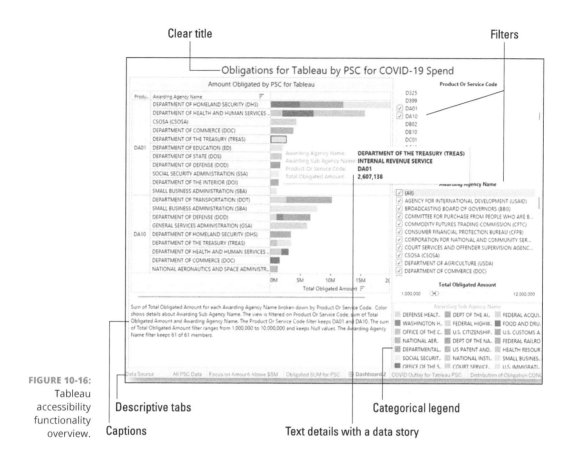

FIGURE 10-16:
Tableau
accessibility
functionality
overview.

Clear title

Filters

Descriptive tabs

Categorical legend

Captions

Text details with a data story

FIGURE 10-17:
The View Data
window shows
the textual
counterparts of
graphic
data
representations.

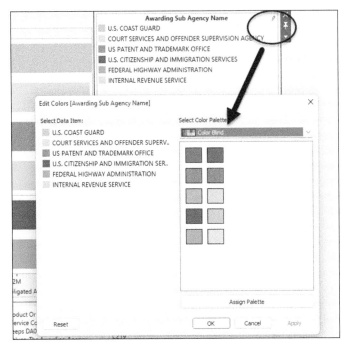

FIGURE 10-18:
The Color
palette set to
Color Blind
mode.

Synthesizing Data through a Tableau Story

The Tableau *story* is a powerful tool for creating an interactive data visualization based on a sequence of information. The story feature lets you easily connect to various data sources, not just one, to build dashboards and charts. You can also share your insights with others by aggregating visualizations using workbook sheets.

REMEMBER

The story is a sheet, not a workbook. The method you use to create, name, and manage the worksheets and dashboards should be consistent with a story. There is a catch, however: A story is a collection of sheets, so you'll need to figure out the sequence of those sheets and create story points. A *story point* is a single sheet representing a single concept throughout the story.

Formatting updates may include the appearance of your charts and dashboards. You can also add interactive elements to the charts and dashboards for each story point, including filters, parameters, and actions.

After you've assembled your story, the final step is to share it with others by publishing it to Tableau Cloud. You can also embed a story on a website or blog.

Planning your story to perfection

Have you ever experienced a dataset as a hodge-podge because no theme connects the data and facts to the scenario? It's happened to me, and I'm sure it has happened to all of us at some point.

Before creating your story, it's essential to consider its purpose and the experience you want your viewers to have. Are you trying to persuade them to take action, or do you just want to offer a straightforward narrative or present an extended use case? Different purposes require different strategies to achieve your goal:

>> **Spurring your audience to action:** The most powerful stories in this category get to the punchline immediately by showing the outcome. A story can present a doom-and-gloom scenario, the ah-ha revelatory moment, or the visionary goal. In each of these cases, you want to start with the result, followed by walking the user through how you got there. Ultimately, you want to remind the user why taking action is essential. Using analytics to give a sales pitch is an example of how to take action.

>> **Offering a narrative:** The good ol' line about a picture saying a thousand words applies here. Simple, straightforward graphics are best for a straightforward narrative, with less interaction and more interpretation. A good narrative focuses on showing the impact before, during, or after a targeted event.

>> **Presenting a use case:** For this type of story, you need to consider whether you want to present data points that build toward a conclusion, or that start with a conclusion and then show the supporting data points. The latter approach can be practical for engaged audiences. Health care use cases are ripe for storytelling using the use case method.

TIP

This tip may sound like it defeats the purpose of Tableau, but I find it helpful to sketch out your story on paper or a whiteboard before building it in Tableau. You are laying out the targeted data points to help identify any potential issues with the sequence and ensure that your story flows smoothly. Another reason an advance sketch is helpful is that it helps you focus on delivery speed and ensure that the dataset fits in the worksheet comfortably, which leads to better readability.

ON THE WEB

Tableau explores numerous ways to tell a compelling story based on the business need. When deciding whether you want to take action, create a narrative, or author the use case, the various approaches can help you laser-focus even more. To discover more about how to craft each story type, start at https://help.tableau.com/current/pro/desktop/en-us/story_best_practices.htm.

Surveying the story workspace

As mentioned in Chapter 7, the story workspace is pretty simplistic. It has only six major areas to be aware of, as shown in Figure 10-19:

>> **Buttons for adding story points:** Click the Blank button in the Story pane to add a story point. Alternatively, if you want to duplicate the behaviors of a worksheet, click the Duplicate button to use a current story point as your starting point.

>> **Story pane:** From here is where you drag relevant dashboards, sheets, and text descriptions within your workbook to the story sheet. You can set the size of your story and its display by going to the Size drop-down menu on the bottom of the Story pane (which is also where you can hide the title, if you want). To hide a feature, just deselect the check box next to its name.

>> **Layout pane:** In this pane, which is next to the Story pane, you can select the navigator style and hide the forward and back arrows.

>> **Story menu:** When trying to format, copy, or export content, including images for a story, you use the Story menu, which you access via the toolbar. Clearing a story in this menu may include hiding the navigator and story title.

>> **Story toolbar:** Mousing over the navigator (described in the next bullet) enables the Story toolbar. You can reverse changes or handle story point updates using the Story toolbar.

>> **Navigator:** Right above the Story view is the navigator, a central hub for editing and organizing the story points. You'll come to the navigator when you want to show your audience how to step through a story. The navigator has a variety of styles, which you can change in the Layout pane.

Crafting the story

Crafting a story in Tableau is a similar process to creating worksheets and dashboards. The difference is that all activities start with the Story tab or menu, as shown in Figure 10-20.

REMEMBER

When you click the Story tab, Tableau opens a screen for a new story (see Figure 10-21). Remember, though, that each worksheet and dashboard previously created are listed in the Story pane. These assets are required first if you haven't created other worksheets or dashboards.

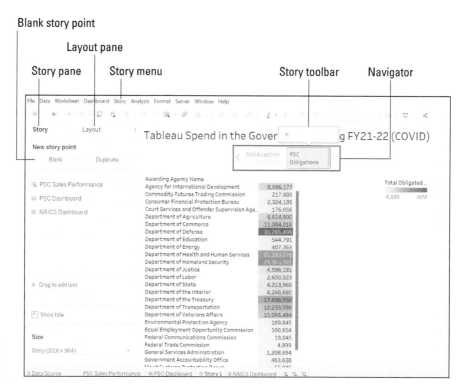

Blank story point

Layout pane

Story pane   Story menu   Story toolbar   Navigator

FIGURE 10-19:
The story
workspace.

Tableau Spend in the Gover [×]   g FY21-22 (COVID)

FIGURE 10-20:
The Story tab.

When you have your assets ready in the Story pane, your next step is to set the story size (Figure 10-22) and apply story points. You can incorporate one story point, or a hundred; each point presents a targeted message.

In the lower-left corner of the screen, select the size interface based on pixels, as seen in Figure 10-22.

> **TIP**
>
> Your story's title is based on the original worksheet name. Titles can be modified by renaming your worksheet.

After setting up the basic story configuration, it's time to start building the story. Double-click a worksheet from the Story pane to add it as a story point. You can also drag and drop the worksheet into the workspace. As shown in Figure 10-23, there is one blank space, indicated by Add a Caption. You can double-click a worksheet or drag it to the circled location. The other two story points integrate existing worksheets. Either you can modify the title of the story (Figure 10-24) or save changes by clicking Update, as shown in Figure 10-25.

FIGURE 10-21:
A blank story
workspace.

FIGURE 10-22:
Select the story
interface size.

Size
Story (1016 × 964) ▼

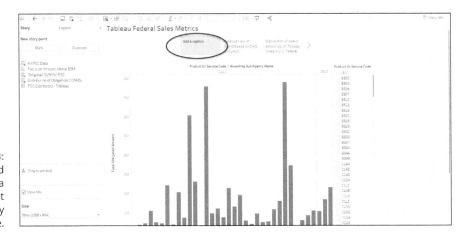

FIGURE 10-23:
Dragging and
dropping a
worksheet
from the Story
pane.

WARNING

Each sheet you add to a story becomes a story point. The story point is directly tied to the worksheet. If you remove the worksheet, your story immediately changes.

After you've landed the story point where you want it, it's time to add captions to the story for descriptive purposes (shown in Figure 10-24). To modify functionality such as filters and story-point order, make changes using the features in the areas outlined in Figure 10-25. The impact of any changes you make is immediate. In this case, the name of the caption was changed, as were the filters in the filters pane.

FIGURE 10-24:
Modifying the
title of a story
point.

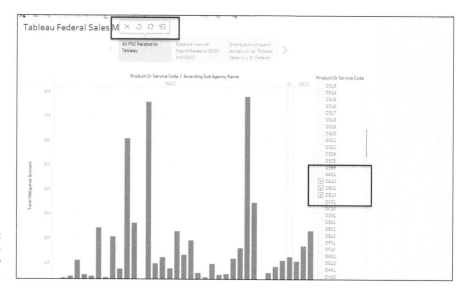

FIGURE 10-25:
Updating the
story with new
filters.

After creating your first story point, drag one of your sheets next to the recently created caption, as indicated by the arrow in Figure 10-26. This adds a new story point to the workspace. The only significant activity you need to complete is modifying the caption to reflect the sheet moving forward. Repeat this action as many times as needed to provide more descriptive explanations of each story point.

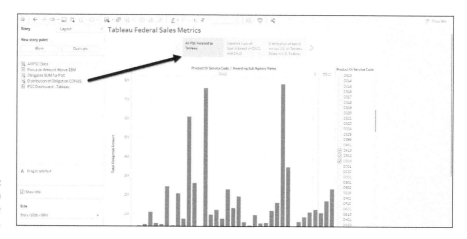

FIGURE 10-26:
Dragging a
sheet to create
a story point.

Formatting the story

Formatting is the most prevalent feature within the story user experience. The changes you make for formatting are more like nuanced modifications to a worksheet and the aesthetics of a story point. Changes you make across the Story and Layout panes are more global to the story. Here are some key formatting concepts to consider:

>> **Navigator options:** Modifying the navigator style can be completed in the Layout pane.

>> **Resizing captions:** Expand and contract the size of your caption from the left and right corners, as you would a typical image. Resizing can only be done in Tableau Desktop.

>> **Sizing dashboards within a story:** It's one thing to size a worksheet, but sizing a dashboard means retrofitting numerous visualizations to a screen. Tableau can do that for you automatically under the Size section of the Layout pane.

>> **Format the story:** The look and feel created in a worksheet may not be desired. Instead, highlight a specific item and choose Format ⇨ Story to open the Formatting pane to modify the format (see Figure 10-27).

>> **Deleting a story.** Select the caption and then click the X. You'll be able to delete the story point quickly. Don't worry, however. Your data won't go missing.

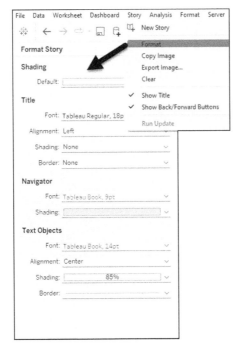

FIGURE 10-27:
Formatting a story using the Format menu.

Enhancing Visualizations with Actions

An *action* is a helpful feature that allows you to add interactivity to your dashboards. Adding logic to your dashboard components allows you to create actions on other dashboard sheets when users interact with the source sheet. Follow these steps to create an action:

1. **Click the Actions submenu under the Dashboard menu and select Actions.**

   The Actions interface opens, allowing you to create targeted actions for a workbook or a dashboard.

2. **Click the Add Action button in the bottom-left corner to choose one of the dashboard action options, as shown in Figure 10-28.**

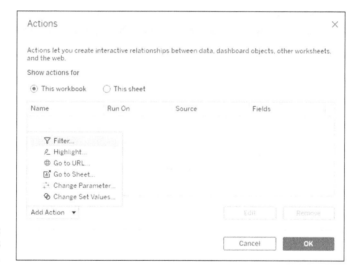

FIGURE 10-28:
The Actions menu.

3. **Select the type of action you want to add.**

   A new screen appears, where you can set up the logic for the action. You can choose the source and target sheets for the action and specify the interaction that triggers the action, such as Hover, Select, or Menu, as shown in Figure 10-29.

4. **Click OK (see Figure 10-30).**

   In the example shown in the figure, a Hover action for a dashboard is being created. In this case, you are setting up an automatic referral to one or more sheets upon hovering over specific views within the dashboard.

As a result, when users hover over any item in the dashboard, they are redirected to a specific worksheet.

Actions give you a convenient way to add interactivity and logic to your data, allowing you to create dynamic and engaging visualizations for your users.

FIGURE 10-29:
Configuring an action.

FIGURE 10-30:
Saving an action.

4
Showcasing Your Data in the Tableau Cloud

Discover the personal features such as Personal Space, Favorites, Recents in Tableau Cloud.

Tackle when it's best to use Shared with Me, Collections, Explore, or Recommendations, all collaborative features in Tableau Cloud.

Configure users and groups as a System Administrator.

Explore key administrative features and capabilities available as a Tableau Cloud System Administrator.

Chapter **11**

Collaboration and Publishing with Tableau Cloud

L ike other heavyweight enterprise business intelligence platforms, Tableau offers an online and desktop version of its servers. Many folks I know try to figure out why to opt for online versus Tableau Desktop and Tableau Server, beyond the fact that you can access all the tools on the internet. After all, doesn't the online version lack certain features that Tableau Desktop and Tableau Server offer? My answer is yes, yes, and yes! But the online version also has capabilities that you can't get anywhere else affordably.

Let me get the obvious question out of the way: What is the significant difference? It boils down to nuances with worksheet, dashboard, and story features that are available only on Tableau Desktop and Tableau Server. With Tableau Cloud, the user experience is more fluid in that it integrates many of the applications you need to utilize on your local computer desktop in a single platform. However, Tableau Cloud requires you to take more steps to complete a straightforward activity than you have to take in both Tableau Desktop and Tableau Server, which are not browser-based. That's the big negative. The positive of being on the internet is the ability to share and collaborate with users at a highly granular level, assuming that you are licensed to do so. You get a cadre of collaboration options in the cloud that you don't get in any other environment.

In this chapter, I cover the end-user aspect of Tableau Cloud, emphasizing how to collaborate and publish worksheets, dashboards, and stories with others. Although add-on features such as Data Management, Advanced Management, and Analytics can be enabled in Tableau Cloud, those features are specifically for targeted enterprise use cases, which are well beyond the scope of this book.

Comparing the Desktop to the Cloud

You can't get away from Tableau Desktop or Prep Builder entirely if you have some sophisticated changes to complete with your data. With Tableau Cloud, you can create a worksheet, dashboard, or story using the web authoring platform. Still, the Desktop version gives you a performance boost when handling your dataset with speed and scale. Table 11-1 lists the limiting features but also, in some cases, the significant advantages to using Tableau Cloud.

TABLE 11-1 **Features Specific to Using Tableau Cloud**

Capability	Feature Difference
Web authoring	Connect directly to data sources.
	Create workbooks in the cloud without having to publish and upload data sources using Tableau Desktop.
	Edit views created directly on the web or published from Tableau Desktop.
	Administrators control site-level access to objects uploaded, which is not even a consideration with Desktop or Prep Builder.
	Explorers can create or edit workbooks.
	Explorers can also create products from existing published data sources and connect to data sources over the web without using a Desktop application.
	Creators have the same capabilities as the Explorer but can also use additional features such as Ask Desktop, leverage Dashboard Starters, and access advanced analysis tools unavailable to others.

Capability	Feature Difference
Data management	Creators get a few more added features because they can directly connect to data sources from Tableau Cloud instead of having to create connections. Users can also use prebuilt Dashboard Starter Templates built by Salesforce.
	Although the Creator can prepare data online, Tableau Cloud limits how much users can view on a data source page. The limit is 10,000 rows.
	Tableau Cloud also limits the number of accessible records per data source to 3 million, including the aggregate of data management activities such as join calculations and unioning, pivoting, and cleansing data using Tableau's data interpreter.
	Explorers can connect to published data sources but have similar limitations regarding record count aggregation. Other nuances include limits to blending published data sources online and parameter formatting limits.
Analytics	All workbook features include full editing capabilities for sheets (create, edit, rename, duplicate, and clear).
	You can use Ask Data and Explain Data to automatically create views without using embedded plug-ins.
	Viz in Tooltip (also called Views in Tooltips) works in the Web view, but it requires configuration in Tableau Desktop.
	Actions require fewer steps in the cloud with Web views.
	Only in the cloud can you use Show Me to create views.
	You can automatically select and drag fields from the Data pane to create Show Me views. This is not possible using Tableau Desktop.
	You can create sets and show set controls, but you can't create cube data sources within the web authoring environment.
	Only in Tableau Cloud can you use the Analytics pane to drag the lines and objects into a view and make direct edits, including creating and configuring reference distributions.
	Tableau Cloud supports a variety of group and hierarchy types that are not available in Tableau Desktop.
	Because map data is much richer when connected to the internet, you can pan and zoom, show map searches, and scale maps more granularly than in Desktop.
	The showing and hiding capabilities vary somewhat from their Desktop counterparts. Some analytics features are supported, while others are not. The list is long but constantly changing as Tableau keeps improving the product.

(continued)

TABLE 11-1 *(continued)*

Capability	Feature Difference
Filtering and sorting	Data highlighting is more limited in Tableau Cloud.
	Filter control layouts are limited to the number of filterable results when authoring. The data is capped to the first 100 results returned.
	You have limitations when filtering across data sources and in your ability to apply filters across multiple published data sources.
	Certain filters, including sort field filters, don't respond in Tableau Cloud in the same way as in Tableau Desktop.
	Drag-and-drop features have limitations, including with headers and customizing a sort order within a view.
Formatting	All formatting features are generally more robust across the workbook spectrum, including the formatting of headers, rows, lines, titles, axes, marks, objects, text, buttons, links, and legends.

Strolling through the Tableau Cloud Experience

The Tableau Cloud experience combines three tools: a Sharing and Collaboration platform, a Systems Administrator console for those using Tableau in the enterprise, and an online companion to Tableau Desktop and Tableau Prep Builder that enables a user to create full workbooks and flows online. The interface doesn't divide the platform components in as cut-and-dried manner as I have, though. Figure 11-1 shows the key interface elements.

>> **Personal features:** All the features to control the Tableau Cloud experience personally and for those looking to collaborate with others

>> **System administrative features:** All the features relevant to administering Tableau Cloud using automation, feeds, templates, and configurable options

>> **Features of Tableau applications in the cloud features:** All the key features available in Tableau Desktop for New Workbook, Tableau Prep Builder for New Flow, and New Data Source

REMEMBER

Tableau workbooks, and by default, worksheets are the equivalent of a spreadsheet created using Google Sheets or Microsoft Excel. Both products produce a workbook (a single file) that may or may not contain many sheets (worksheets) in which visualizations are produced.

Personal features

Tableau applications in the cloud

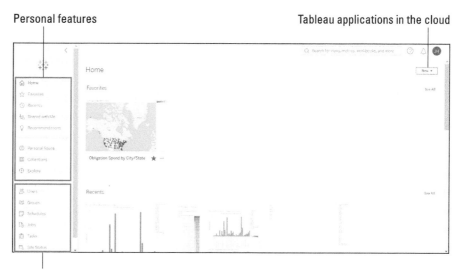

FIGURE 11-1:
The Tableau
Cloud
interface.

System administrative features

If you want to complete a universal search of all views, metrics, workbooks, collections, and data sources, or even search by Content Owner, go to the Tableau Cloud search bar (shown in Figure 11-2) and type in a relevant term. For the figure, I searched for two terms: external assets and Tableau, which could appear in any of the objects saved within the instance of Tableau Cloud across all the object types.

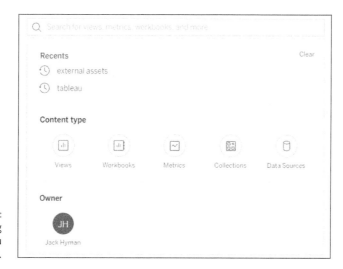

FIGURE 11-2:
Performing
a Tableau
Cloud search.

Next to the search bar, you'll find three icons: a question mark in a circle; a bell; and two letters (my initials, in Figure 11-3). Each item represents a specific function:

>> **Help:** All help functionality is available when you click the question mark icon for Tableau Cloud. Help options include Tableau Help, Support, System Status, What's New, and About Tableau.

>> **Alerts and Notifications:** Alerts and Notifications appear under the bell. For example, when you create an item to share or you receive a share notification, you see the notification under the bell.

>> **Profile:** Your profile and activity are centrally housed under your initials. Features include Personal Space, My Content, My Account Settings, Set as Start Page, and Logout.

Next, you see a button below the three icons with the word New. If you expand the arrows, you find the New menu, which contains all the features you can use as part of Tableau Cloud, just as if you were using Tableau Desktop, except for the additional capability to upload files. This option, Upload Workbook (shown in Figure 11-4), enables files to be edited in the cloud.

Although creating a project and collection is specific to Tableau Cloud, as you find out in the upcoming pages, you can select New Workbook to create a new workbook, which includes a combination of worksheets, dashboards, or stories using Tableau Cloud. The Tableau Cloud interface that allows users to manage their workbooks and data online is called the Tableau Cloud Workbook Editor. Using the Tableau Cloud Workbook Editor is similar to the native user experience in Tableau Desktop to create new worksheets. Figure 11-5 shows an example of a new workbook being created in the Tableau Cloud Workbook Editor.

FIGURE 11-5:
Creating a new workbook in the Tableau Cloud Workbook Editor.

You can also create a new flow that's like the entire user experience available in Tableau Prep Builder. Before you get to the full editor, however, you must connect to a data source so that the online Flow Editor can fully operate. (See Chapters 4 through 6 on Tableau Prep Builder for more details.)

TECHNICAL STUFF

Users often assume that data sources previously defined in Tableau Cloud are brought into a Tableau Cloud flow, but that assumption is inaccurate. Each time you want to create a new flow, you need to define your sources, just as you do in Tableau Prep Builder, and then build the flow from scratch. This process was followed in Figure 11-6 using the Tableau Cloud Flow Builder web Authoring tool. Remember, Tableau Cloud tries to replicate the experience with the Desktop companion, Tableau Prep Builder, but subtle differences should be evident across features and functionality.

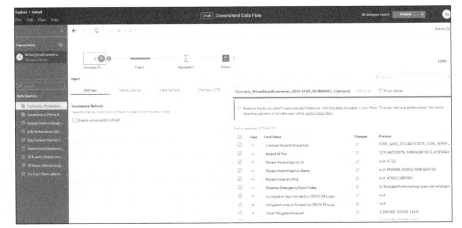

FIGURE 11-6:
Using the
Tableau Cloud
Flow Editor is
similar to using
Tableau Prep
Builder to cre-
ate a flow.

Evaluating Personal Features in Tableau Cloud

Transferring a simile of the Desktop experience to the cloud is often a tall order. Tableau has done a fine job of accomplishing just that by focusing on integrating many of the best concepts across many industry products within its product. For example, the concept of the cloud-based personal folder is mimicked by the Personal Space feature. Like other industry solutions that leverage bookmarking and recent history, Tableau has replicated those concepts with its Favorites and Recents. Collectively, users can make use of Personal Space, Favorites, and Recents to organize and find their data rapidly, often in one click if well enough organized. The following sections tell you more about each of these features.

Personal Space

If you've used Google Drive, Microsoft One Drive, SharePoint Document Libraries, Dropbox, Box, or other document collaboration solutions, you should be at ease with using the Personal Space feature. The Personal Space is just that: personal. It's a private location for the Creators and Explorers (see Chapter 3 for more about these user types) to create, edit, and save their work using Tableau Cloud. Any time you save content to a Personal Space, it can't be shared with other users until you move it to a project, which is when it's ready for others to see and explore.

You can save workbooks to a Personal Space. Workbooks may consist of worksheets, dashboards, or stories. In the example shown in Figure 11-7, two workbooks are saved. If you click the name of each workbook, you can then view the contents contained within each workbook. For example, one of the workbooks in Figure 11-7 is called "Total Obligations by City/State." Clicking that workbook reveals two worksheets, each with "Obligation Spend by City/State" in the title, as shown in Figure 11-8. A user can next click either of these worksheets to open it within the equivalent of the Tableau Desktop read-only view, but on the cloud. At this level, you can edit using Tableau Cloud's web authoring tools, as shown in Figure 11-9. To show the Tableau Workbook Editor, go to the specific workbook that requires editing and then click the Edit button within Tableau Cloud. Notice that the user experience is almost identical to that of Tableau Desktop.

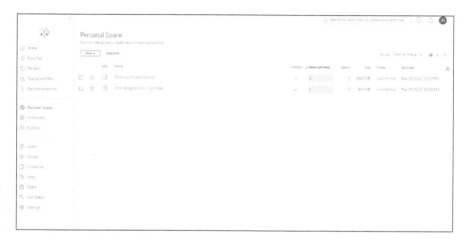

FIGURE 11-7:
The Tableau Cloud Personal Space feature.

FIGURE 11-8:
Click the workbook title to see its worksheets.

Favorites

Throughout Tableau Cloud, you see plenty of stars on your screen. The star is your way of marking something as one of your Favorites. The purpose of the Favorites page is to organize your workbooks, worksheets, dashboards, stories, and data sources that you use the most in a single location. Figure 11-10 shows the Favorites page with a list of items.

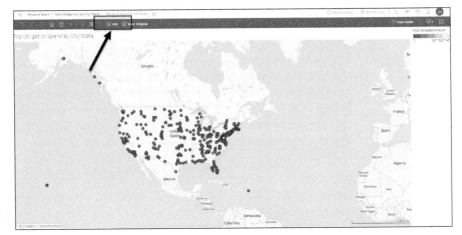

FIGURE 11-9:
Click the Edit tab to fully edit the worksheet using Tableau Cloud's web authoring tools.

FIGURE 11-10:
The Favorites page.

Several menus on the Favorites page enable users to complete additional actions, as long as you have the appropriate permissions. For example, selecting one or more Favorite items and then clicking the Actions drop-down menu allows you to complete activities such as add items to a collection, tag items in bulk, move items in bulk, apply for new permissions, change item ownership, create Tabbed views, or refresh the data extracts. You also have the option to mass delete. (Be careful!) The options you can choose on the Actions menu from the Favorites page appear in Figure 11-11.

On the right side of the Favorites screen, you can sort based on the type of content you have marked with a star. Select the down-pointing arrow to open the drop-down menu by Content Type (Figure 11-12) or Sort By (Figure 11-13). These are simple ways to review your favorites with laser focus, especially if you happen to like everything you create.

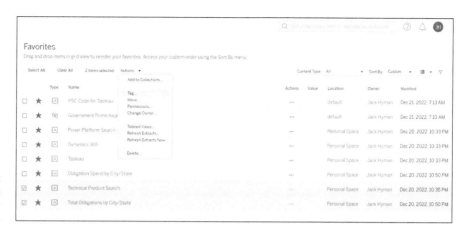

FIGURE 11-11:
The Actions menu on the Favorites page.

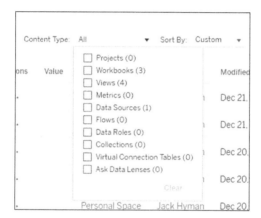

FIGURE 11-12:
The Content Type menu on the Favorites page.

FIGURE 11-13:
The Sort By menu on the Favorites page.

TIP

Be judicious in how you organize your data in Tableau Cloud. Make sure you organize your data into projects. Tag items with meaningful labels. But most important, don't put everything in Favorites; you don't want to have to sort through a very long list of items. Use Favorites for only your top picks.

FIGURE 11-14:
Recents page.

Recents

To open the Recents page, click the Recents item on the navigation pane on the left. On this page, shown in Figure 11-14, you find a list of your most accessed or recent activity. Tableau uses the combination of the two metrics to populate the page. You can slightly modify the parameters of what appears and for how long it appears on the page; see Chapter 12 for details on these settings.

When you select the check box next to an item, the Actions menu appears with the same options as those on the Favorites page Actions menu. (Notice a repetitive theme yet?) The only menu that helps you seek out information based on chronology is the Sort By menu, shown in Figure 11-15. The Sort By menu can help you sort from oldest to newest and vice versa. You can also sort by owner, location, last accessed, name, and workbook.

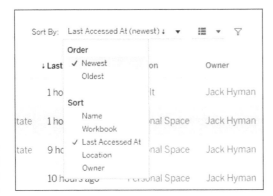

FIGURE 11-15:
The Sort By
menu on the
Recents page.

Sharing Experiences and Collaborating with Others

Tableau Cloud's shared experience is limited to users who are actively licensed in your organization as Creators, Explorers, and Viewers. Any user without an active license won't be able to view, edit, or create content unless they use the Tableau Public release. As noted elsewhere in the book, if you use Tableau Public, you are required to publish your findings to the world; you can't target your own group of users, who may have varying levels of permissiveness.

For licensed users, especially Creators or Explorers, your ability to control object-level visibility can be pretty granular, down to the data source, view, workbook, or flow level.

Sharing content

When you're ready to let your content be shared with others, follow these steps:

1. **Go to the item you want to share and then select the drop-down menu under Actions.**

   The Actions menu opens.

2. **Choose Share.**

   A pop-up asking whom you want to share the data with appears, along with a link to the document to be shared.

3. **Under Share with People, enter at least one other username (they must be licensed) to access the content.**

   As you type, the names of licensed users within your Tableau Cloud domain appear.

4. **(Optional) In the Message box, enter a message about the purpose of the shared documents.**

5. **When you're ready, click the Share button (see Figure 11-16).**

   The document is shared, and each user you decide to share the document with receives a notification about the shared document. The document also appears on the Shared with Me page.

FIGURE 11-16:
Sharing
content with
other users.

Shared with Me

In the previous section, you click the Share button to share the document with others. You should then receive an email notification with a link to the content. If, on the other hand, someone shares a document with you, open the Shared with Me page navigation and click the page to see a list of documents that have been shared.

Your ability to manipulate the file with Tableau Desktop, Tableau Prep Builder, or Tableau Cloud depends entirely on the permissions the party sharing the file has assigned to that file. In the example shown in Figure 11-17, a single item has been shared, which also triggered a received email, viewable in Figure 11-18.

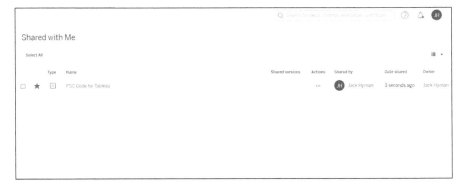

FIGURE 11-17:
The Shared
with Me page.

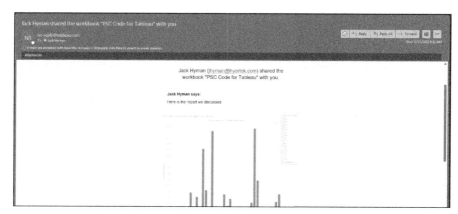

FIGURE 11-18:
An email notification that an item has been shared with you.

Click the check box within the filters pane next to the visualization to choose various options from the Actions menu that opens (see Figure 11-19). If you happen to have permission to edit the file, you can do so by downloading the file or opening the file directly in Tableau Desktop. You can then edit the workbook and publish it back to your workspace and that of the owners.

FIGURE 11-19:
The Actions menu on the Shared with Me page.

Collections

I've said it before: Organization is the key to success with Tableau Cloud. You may have a well-organized system if you've put some thought into how to organize your computer files. Most people I know, though, always have files that fall through the cracks. A *collection* is a virtual folder that lets you place related items in an easy-to-access list to organize items based on your specific topic or theme. Collections also enable you to break down items based on visibility and ownership. You can keep a project private or make it public, assigning it to a user or a group of users within your Tableau site.

TECHNICAL STUFF

Although you can give access to others for a collection, you should not worry about exposing data because collections are permission neutral. Users can see only the items to which they are given access. Furthermore, when selecting an item and heading to the Actions menu, you have limited options depending on your permissions. Those given the most permission can modify and delete a file from a collection.

In previous sections, I mention that users can select the check box and move an item to a collection. Assuming that a collection has already been created, the user selects the collection to which the item should be saved. Then it appears as part of the virtual list.

For the examples in the following figures, I've assigned items to specific collections based on the files uploaded to Personal Space. Tableau Desktop automatically loads files published to Tableau Cloud into the default folder. It is up to you to move the file to another collection. Figure 11-20 provides a representative example of two collections, and Figure 11-21 offers a glimpse of how you can organize items in a collection (in this case, the collection is named "Government Procurement Data").

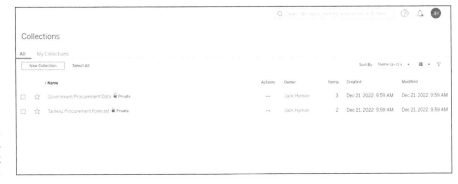

FIGURE 11-20: The Collections page listing two collections.

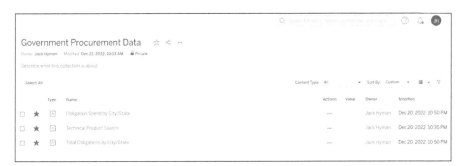

FIGURE 11-21:
Items stored
within a named
collection.

REMEMBER

You may have noticed a tab called My Collections on the Collections page. The My Collections tab houses only collections you've created, not ones that have been shared with you by others.

Explore

The Explore feature in Tableau Cloud is the equivalent of the Windows File Explorer or the Apple Finder, with a twist concerning the capability to create folders and files. Because you are in the cloud, Explore presents all your file systems on the Explore home page. Each project, represented by a new folder, can contain a combination of objects, including workbooks, flows, and published data sources.

To create a new workbook, flow, or published data source, or to upload a workbook, click the New drop-down menu in the upper-left corner of the Explore page (see Figure 11-22).

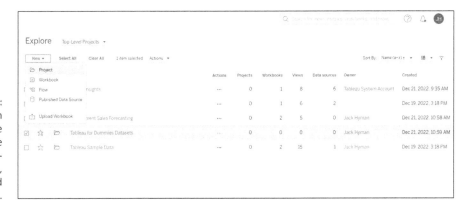

FIGURE 11-22:
Click New on
the Explore
page to create
new work-
books, flows,
or published
data sources.

What happens, though, when you've been using Tableau for months, if not years, and you've collected thousands of documents in your Explore repository, much like you do in your My Documents folder? You'll want a quick and easy way to search for the documents. That's where filters come in handy. Right next to the word *Explore* in the upper-left corner of the Explore page, the name of the default filter, Top-Level Projects, appears. When you click the down-pointing arrow next to that filter, you open a drop-down menu (see Figure 11-23) that lists all the ways you can filter and thereby organize your documents and folders.

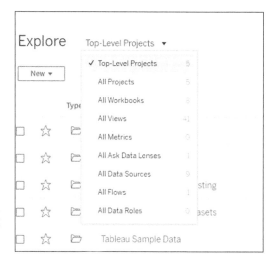

Recommendations

Tableau Cloud has a "big brother" element to it as well. But don't worry: No trackers are looking at your activities online other than in Tableau Cloud. Instead, Tableau Cloud offers recommendations that it thinks may be useful to you. Its "recommendation engine" notices what content you view the most and looks for trends of popular content on your site. It also picks out the popular content of others who share content with you. Recommendations then appear on your site that best match what you've looked at most and what has been trending for a given period, generally one week.

TIP

You may not like the recommendation. That's okay; Tableau won't take offense if you want to hide its recommendations. To do so, select the Actions menu ellipsis and then choose Hide on the menu that appears.

TECHNICAL STUFF

In the Recommendation for You section of the Recommendations page, you'll likely find the names of others, not just yours, who have looked at the content. Don't worry; no one has inappropriately accessed your Tableau instance. These users have access to view the same content as you do.

IN THIS CHAPTER

» Comparing Tableau Server key
features with Tableau Cloud

» Exploring key administrative
features

» Configuring user and group
authentication for Tableau Cloud

» Using Tableau Cloud on a mobile
device

Chapter **12**

Administration in Tableau Cloud

D epending on the number of users leveraging your Tableau Cloud instance, you may be given the incredible power of filling the system administrator role. As a single user, you automatically inherit the capability to control all features in Tableau Cloud. If, for example, you have control over several Creators, Explorers, and Viewers, you likely have system administration access. The adage "With great power comes great responsibility" applies to Tableau because an administrator controls everything from user authentication to granular access to third-party extensions and integrations. In this chapter, you find out how to configure and administer standard functionality within Tableau Cloud.

Noting How Tableau Server and Tableau Cloud Differ

Tableau Server is a web-based platform that allows users to share, organize, and automate their visualizations and dashboards. It can be hosted on-premises or in the cloud and offers extensive customization and integration options for organizations that want to have complete control over their data and how it is accessed. However, hosting Tableau Server internally also requires the organization to handle infrastructure hosting costs and maintenance, and to shoulder the responsibility of keeping the system stable, which includes troubleshooting any issues that may arise.

Tableau Cloud, formerly known as Tableau Online, is a software-as-a-service (SaaS) version of Tableau Server that provides the same functionality without needing internal infrastructure or maintenance. Organizations can use Tableau Cloud without worrying about hosting or maintenance costs, but they also lose some control and customization options. Tableau Cloud is constantly updated to the latest version. Still, organizations need help to perform a rollback in case of bugs or other issues. Additionally, Tableau Cloud may be suitable only for organizations with strict security requirements or the need to integrate with on-premises systems.

Opting for Tableau Server

Tableau Server is a popular choice for large organizations because of its flexibility in deployment and integration with internal systems and on-premises sources. This flexibility allows advanced administrators to optimize the system's performance for their specific needs and monitor the server's usage and health with administrative views in the PostgreSQL repository, the centralized database. Tableau Server allows an organization to deploy multiple sites on a single instance and license, giving the organization more control over the system and the ability to schedule maintenance and upgrades around busy times.

However, hosting Tableau Server internally also involves infrastructure hosting costs and the need to employ additional staff to support the server, which can be expensive. In 2022, the average salary for a Business Intelligence or Data Management Engineer was $110,000–125,000 per year, and infrastructure costs can add up quickly, potentially exceeding the cost of a Tableau Cloud license. Additionally, the organization is responsible for keeping the system stable and troubleshooting any issues. Overall, maintaining a dynamic infrastructure like Tableau Server can be costly.

TIP

You must ask yourself what security and customization requirements prevent you from jumping to the cloud. Tableau Cloud is often cheaper if you can't justify high-touch security requirements or significant customization, including multiple server instances and tightly integrated features.

Considering Tableau Cloud

Tableau Cloud is a popular choice for organizations looking to take advantage of the capabilities of Tableau Server without the burden of hosting and maintaining the system internally. One of the main advantages of Tableau Cloud is that it requires no internal time or resources for maintenance or upgrades because the service provider handles those tasks. Letting Tableau (through Salesforce) handle cloud infrastructure can increase system reliability and predictable downtime, as well as provide access to the latest features and functionality without requiring manual updates.

REMEMBER

Choosing to go with Tableau Cloud is a no-brainer for users with just one or two licenses. As soon your license count begins to creep up into the teens for user count, even for Viewers and Explorers, that's when you need to think twice about your system administration options, because Cloud may become cost prohibitive.

Tableau Cloud eliminates the need for infrastructure costs and hardware scaling because the system is hosted in the cloud and can easily be scaled up as needed. Not having to manage infrastructure also means that organizations using Tableau Cloud have fewer people to work with to scale the system because the service provider handles many of the maintenance and upgrading tasks. Finally, Tableau Cloud does not require back-end performance tuning; again, the service provider is responsible for optimizing the system for performance. Tableau Cloud is software-as-a-service-based, meaning that software and infrastructure are fully managed by the service provider, which, as mentioned previously, is Salesforce.

WARNING

Using Tableau Cloud does have some drawbacks. One area that needs improvement is the limited support Tableau Cloud provides for identity stores, which may make it more challenging to integrate with specific systems or data sources. Additionally, Tableau Cloud doesn't offer control over upgrade schedules or the ability to perform a rollback in the event of issues, and the user has no control over performance tuning.

TECHNICAL
STUFF

Unlike its Server counterpart, Tableau Cloud does not offer access to the PostgreSQL repository, so organizations cannot create custom administrative or governance views. To access local systems, Tableau Cloud users must use Tableau Bridge (explained later in the chapter), which may result in network latency or other issues. Finally, Tableau Cloud needs to offer greater capability for release management through development or test environments, which may be a concern for organizations with complex release processes.

Setting Up Your Tableau Cloud Site for Success

If you are the system administrator and you've chosen to take the Tableau Cloud road to data analytics and business intelligence, don't dive in by dumping data right onto the platform the second you get that license key email. Instead, you should plan the Tableau Cloud instance by setting up user accounts, assigning the users the appropriate security credentials, configuring projects against a specific site, and addressing any integration concerns.

Before configuring the site, you should familiarize yourself with the site authentication options, user roles, projects, and permissions. You're also well-advised to create a plan for your projects, groups, and overall permissions strategy and document it.

TIP

After you have all these pieces in motion, this will be your first chance at configuring the environment as the system administrator. If you create a test project, try different settings and fine-tune your strategy. Although it is possible to modify many site settings after users have started using the site, it's best to aim to minimize post-production changes.

ON THE WEB

Whether you're moving from Tableau Server to Tableau Cloud or this is your first rodeo with Tableau, I strongly suggest that you head over to Tableau's documentation on how to thoroughly plan your deployment strategy (`https://help.tableau.com/current/blueprint/en-us/bp_move_to_cloud.htm`).

Administrative Functionality in Tableau Cloud

A Tableau Cloud user has far less to worry about than a user of Tableau Server does. The most significant role of a Tableau Cloud user is that of the user and group management administrator. As this chapter explains, most features are controlled by toggle buttons that you use to switch a setting on or off. Most features require that a user or group is assigned to one or more Tableau applications, so an administrator's essential responsibility is to understand authentication and authorization management relative to the licensing model. Unlike the Tableau Server console, which has hundreds of independent settings, Tableau Cloud has consolidated the features that an administrator needs to navigate to administer the platform across a few operational areas, as indicated in Figure 12-1.

FIGURE 12-1:
Tableau Cloud
administrative
navigation.

Managing users and groups

A good portion of the functionality of a cloud-based administrator involves user and group management. As the administrator, you are responsible for setting the site roles — that is, each user's level of access. The administrator can also create user groups and assign guest access.

If you intend to use Tableau, a system administrator must assign you access, even as a guest. The system administrator has three ways to assign you access:

» Adding you through a local user account or a user account through Active Directory

» Importing your user account by adding an Active Directory account from a group

» Including you in a mass import of a list of users via CSV file

Users can be set up directly from the General Settings menu or through the Users and Groups options, a shortcut to the General Settings option.

TIP

To learn the full scope of how to manage and, even more important, simplify your role in handling security, go to `https://help.tableau.com/current/server/en-us/users.htm`.

As an administrator, to set a user's role, you go to the Users option on the Administrative pane on the left side of the interface. The example in Figure 12-2 shows you the current user in the system; it's a Creator account called "Jack Hyman." You can either create a local account by email or import an account by file.

FIGURE 12-2:
Viewing who currently has Tableau Cloud access.

After you click the Add Users button, you can create a Creator, Explorer, or Viewer account, with or without multifactor authentication. Each account is entered based on an email address, as shown in Figure 12-3, which displays two accounts being added. In this figure, both accounts are unlicensed. The administrator decides whether the user gains access as an administrator by selecting the Site Role drop-down menu, as shown in Figure 12-4.

WARNING

You can add as many users as possible (necessary?) to an environment. Still, to gain access to Tableau, they must be assigned a license. For example, if you add your entire Active Directory, all users could appear in Tableau Cloud. However, only those users you give access to are assigned the role of Viewer, Explorer, or Creator. The rest are deemed unlicensed.

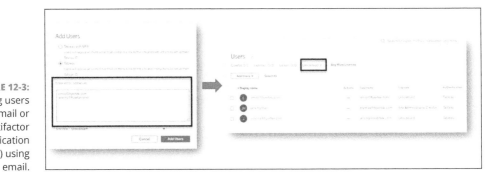

FIGURE 12-3:
Adding users by email or multifactor authentication (MFA) using email.

FIGURE 12-4:
Assigning
users as
administrators.

If you head over to the Groups link in the left pane or go to General Settings, under Authentication, you can create dedicated groups and assign users to each group. For example, Figure 12-5 shows that a user group called Tableau for Dummies Creators has been created. All those Creator users can then be assigned to this specific group when the administrator clicks the group name and then clicks the Add Users button. In this case, only one user, Jack Hyman, can be added.

REMEMBER

You can add unlicensed users to a group. That doesn't mean that they can access any Tableau features, though. After the user has obtained a Tableau license, the user will then gain access to viewing, editing, and potentially administering Tableau features. It all depends on which license type they've been assigned.

FIGURE 12-5:
Configuring a
user group in
Tableau Cloud.

Setting automated schedules

In Tableau, a schedule is a feature that allows you to regularly automate publishing or refreshing data sources, workbooks, or dashboards. You can use schedules to ensure that your Tableau Cloud content is up to date and accurate without manually publishing or refreshing it.

To create a schedule in Tableau, you first need to open the Tableau Cloud web interface and navigate to the content you want to schedule. Select the content and then choose the Schedule option by selecting one or more check boxes in the left column to set up the schedule. The Schedule dialog box appears and enables you to specify the schedule type (daily, weekly, or monthly), the frequency of the schedule, and any other relevant options, such as the time of day when the schedule should run.

You can also use schedules to send notifications or alerts when the schedule runs. For example, you can set up a schedule to send an email to your team when a dashboard has been refreshed with new data. Using the schedule can help ensure that everyone stays updated with the latest information and can take action as needed.

An example Schedules page is shown in Figure 12-6.

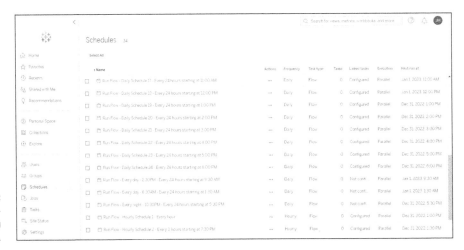

FIGURE 12-6:
Prebuilt schedules in Tableau Cloud.

Arranging jobs and tasks to run in the background

In Tableau Cloud, tasks such as extract refreshes, subscriptions, or flows are scheduled to run periodically. These tasks are initiated by a process called

Backgrounder, which creates unique instances of the tasks known as jobs. Jobs can also be manually initiated through the web interface, REST API, or tabcmd commands. For example, if you set an extract refresh task to run daily at 7 a.m., the Backgrounder creates a job every day at the set time.

Site administrators can use the Job Management feature to view and manage the jobs on their site, including acting on specific jobs to manage resource usage better. They can also use the Run Now settings on the General settings page to allow or block users from manually running jobs. By default, this option is set to allow manual job runs. Still, it can be disabled to prevent users from initiating jobs manually.

The Tasks page provides information on all job states including failed, completed, or canceled. The example in Figure 12-7 shows one failed job, a weekly extract refresh task.

Identifies the job status

FIGURE 12-7: An extract refresh task operation in Tableau Cloud.

Four task types can run in Tableau: extract refreshes, subscriptions, alerts, and accelerated views. Here are key takeaways about each task type:

» **Extract refreshes** automatically update the data in a Tableau extract, leveraging a snapshot of data from a data source that has been saved locally. Extracts are used to improve the performance of Tableau dashboards and views by allowing users to access the data faster. That's because the data is stored locally rather than having to be queried from the original data source every time the dashboard or view is accessed.

» **Subscriptions** are a way to receive updates about a view or dashboard regularly and automatically. You can subscribe to a view or dashboard to receive updates via email or other methods, such as Slack or Microsoft Teams, at a specific frequency, such as daily, weekly, or monthly.

» **Alerts** are a type of notification that's triggered when certain conditions are met within the data in a view or dashboard. For example, you can set up an alert to notify you when a specific metric exceeds a certain threshold or when there is a sudden change in the data.

>> **Acceleration view** speeds up view loading by precalculating and retrieving the data in the workbook through a background process. There are two potential obstacles when loading a view: retrieving data from the data source (called querying) and creating the visual elements (called rendering, which may include drawing shapes or rendering a map).

Figure 12-8 shows that an extract refresh is scheduled to run weekly.

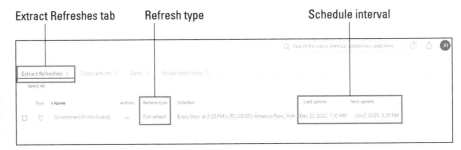

FIGURE 12-8: Running a job in Tableau Cloud.

Checking the status of your site

One of the advantages of using the Cloud versus Server version of Tableau is that you are not responsible for the infrastructure or system maintenance. You won't need to be on pins and needles monitoring operational readiness. For the techies in the organization, however, there is always a need for reassurance that things are working as intended at the project and global level. Under the Site Status tab on the left navigation in Tableau Cloud, you can find a bevy of reports to help calm those concerns.

To gain insight on a specific project and how it's being utilized, you should consider using Admin Insights, shown in Figure 12-9. Admin Insights evaluates three specific metrics:

>> Site traffic, adoption, and reach

>> User roles and sign-in activity

>> Publishing activities

ON THE WEB

Configuring your site for Admin Insights is well beyond the scope of this book. Each project has its bells and whistles to consider. To read more on the configuration process, go to https://help.tableau.com/current/online/en-us/adminview_insights_manage.htm.

With Tableau Server, the infrastructure lead is fully responsible for the health and wellness of the Tableau software and its storage. Given that Tableau Cloud is 100 percent SaaS-based, you forgo all the worries in the world about managing the hardware infrastructure required to operate Tableau Server. You simply focus on your data. That said, Tableau offers a collection of reports, mostly centered around data extracts and job/task delivery, to help mitigate system performance issues. These reports are specific to system administrators and those who are given access to system performance metrics. The reports are derived from activities completed under tabs such as Jobs and Tasks. Figure 12-10 provides a glimpse into Tableau's reports to support your cloud administrative efforts.

Seeking Tableau Cloud Settings

Under the Settings option in the System Administration pane on the left, you find seven tabs: General, Authentication, Bridge, Extensions, Integrations, Connected Apps, and Mobile. Each tab has a collection of capabilities that allow Tableau to run in an organization. Bear in mind that an organization can consist of one user or thousands. If you're a single user, some configurations may be overkill. If you've distributed licenses to Explorers and Viewers for many projects, your ability to establish fine-grain functionality is housed under the Settings link, under a single roof. In contrast to other business intelligence and data analytics platforms, configuring on Tableau Cloud is truly low-code, no-code because most, if not all, actions are controlled merely by On/Off toggle switches or drop-down menus. It's that easy to manage most of the Tableau Cloud functionality.

Configuring General settings

The General tab is where the bulk of the, you guessed it, general configurations appear for you to set up your corporate user experience as well as set limits on features based on user role. For example, you can add a site logo, set up what page in Tableau Cloud should be your start page, enable Ask Data lenses, determine whether you want Explain Data turned on or off, configure whether you want Data Stories (not Stories) turned on or off, and set a host of sharing and alert features. This tab also enables you to set subscriptions, alerts, and notifications. As an administrator, you can turn notifications on or off for all features and enable or disable users from performing specific actions in their Personal Space.

TIP

As of this writing, more than 50 settings are available in the core Tableau Cloud General tab, found under Site Settings. If you purchase add-ons like Data Management, additional features will be added under General. See Figure 12-11 for an example of items found under General.

Authenticating users

In the "Managing users and groups" section, earlier in the chapter, you find out how to add users locally. You may also want to add users by leveraging Active Directory, Google, SAML, or your enterprise Salesforce account. In that case, you can add additional authentication on the Authentication tab, shown in Figure 12-12.

Tableau allows you to select whether you prefer a single login or multifactor authentication (MFA). On this tab, you as the administrator can require users to set up an MFA login or give them the option; it's really up to the system administrator how secure they want their Tableau instance to be. To set up MFA, go to the Default Authentication Type for Embedded Views section and select the Tableau with MFA radio button.

FIGURE 12-11: Features found on the General tab in Tableau Cloud.

Within Tableau Desktop and Tableau Prep Builder, users are also given the option to connect from these applications directly. The default permission to do this from Tableau Cloud and Server is set to Yes, under the Connected Clients section. Some organizations may want something other than automatic connectivity, however. You can set the Let Clients Automatically Connect to This Tableau Cloud Site parameter to Off if your organization falls in that bucket.

Finally, you can access the management tools available under Users and Groups by selecting the Manage Users drop-down menu.

FIGURE 12-12: Authentication options for Tableau Cloud.

Bridging to your data connections with Tableau Bridge

Tableau Bridge is a feature that allows users to keep their data in a central location. All the data refreshing occurs in real time within Tableau Desktop, not Tableau Cloud or Server. Tableau Bridge works by continuously querying a data source for updates and then pushing those updates to Tableau Desktop, eliminating the need for manual data refreshes. This can be especially useful for users who work with large datasets or need to refresh their data frequently to stay up to date.

Tableau Bridge allows extracts to refresh and maintain live connections to on-premises data sources or in the cloud. Still, for that to happen, either Tableau Cloud or Server must be configured with specific parameters. Users must set up pooling parameters in Tableau Cloud under the Bridge tab.

WARNING

Users must install the Tableau Bridge software client on their desktop to connect Tableau Desktop and Tableau Cloud for pooling to work. You can access the Tableau Bridge Installer under the Server menu in Tableau Desktop.

Assuming that you've configured the Tableau Bridge Client correctly, you'll see the default pool connection in Tableau Cloud, as indicated in Figure 12-13.

TECHNICAL STUFF

You may need to loosen up or tighten access to your Tableau Cloud instance. Tableau uses an *allowlist*, which is the equivalent of a whitelist and a blacklist. With a Tableau allowlist, you specify which users gain access to trusted data sources within an organization. This list can be useful in a corporate setting to ensure that only approved data sources are used and to prevent the use of potentially malicious or unreliable sources.

FIGURE 12-13: Options to configure a Tableau Bridge.

Adding extensions to Tableau

Tableau offers various types of extensions that can be used to enhance the functionality of its platform, depending on whether you're using Tableau Cloud or Tableau Server. Here is a brief overview of the main types of extensions:

>> **Dashboard extensions** allow you to add custom functionality to Tableau dashboards. This can include visualizations, interactivity, or data manipulation.

>> **Analytics extensions** let you incorporate advanced analytics capabilities into your Tableau workflows. This can include learning algorithms, predictive modeling, or statistical analysis.

>> **Tableau Prep extensions** are designed explicitly with Tableau Prep data preparation and cleansing tooling. Prep extensions allow you to extend the functionality of Tableau Prep by adding custom steps and transformations to your data preparation flows.

Configuration must be completed by a system administrator because most extensions require an upload, the configuration of a connection string, or being pointed to a targeted URL, as shown in Figure 12-14.

FIGURE 12-14: Configuring dashboard extensions, analytics extensions, or Tableau Prep extensions.

Integrating Tableau with the Salesforce CRM and Slack

Queue the sales pitch. (Just kidding!) On the Integrations tab, you'll quickly recognize that Salesforce is the proud owner of Tableau. Given that Salesforce acquired Tableau for $15.7 billion in 2019, it isn't surprising that Salesforce immediately took advantage of the analytic features and integrated them with the highly lauded Salesforce Customer Relationship Management (CRM) and collaboration platform Slack.

CRMs are big data analytics tools consisting of many fields that can be analyzed, yielding hundreds of reports. Salesforce admitted that until the acquisition of Tableau, its analytics were not as robust as they became. Tableau was the game changer, and all Salesforce products have embedded many of Tableau's best features for user consumption.

Slack collaboration with Tableau is a unique use case. Depending on your role in the organization, you can gain access to productivity reporting, assess communication trends and patterns, or even measure content analytics embedded with unstructured datasets. Slack can't do those things, but combining Slack with Tableau gives you the extra horsepower to interpret and visualize the data without completing the manual analysis.

To gain complete visibility from an analytics perspective, users of CRM or Slack must also procure fully licensed versions of Tableau and integrate them with the platform. The integration is relatively simple. Choose Settings in the pane and then click the Integration tab (see Figure 12-15) to choose one or more options under "Sales Workbooks and Data Sources" or "Slack Connectivity."

Integrations tab

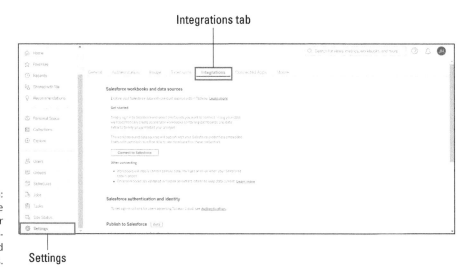

FIGURE 12-15: Integrate with other Salesforce-based products.

Settings

Connecting third-party apps with Tableau

Connected apps are third-party applications that you can use with Tableau to extend its functionality or allow it to interact with other systems through a Direct Trusted relation or OAuth-connected credentialing. Connected apps can be integrated with Tableau through application programming interfaces (APIs), webhooks, or other integration points and are often used to perform tasks such as data preparation, data enrichment, or data visualization. Access to connected apps generally takes place through one of the many Tableau marketplaces on the internet. One such marketplace is the Tableau Exchange, where you find dashboard extensions, connectors, and accelerators created by Tableau developers. Some examples of connected apps that you may want to use with Tableau include data preparation tools, data visualization tools, and cloud-based data storage platforms.

To connect to a connected app, click the Connected Apps tab. Figure 12-16 shows the Direct Trust and OAuth 2.0 Trust options.

REMEMBER

Connected apps can be developed by Tableau partners or third-party developers and are often available through the Tableau App Store or other online marketplaces. Make sure that the app is reputable and secure, especially if Salesforce does not recognize the marketplace as a trusted partner.

FIGURE 12-16:
Connect to other apps via Direct Trust or OAuth.

Going mobile

Ah, mobile! You can take your data anywhere. Well, that is partially true. If your organization gives you access, though, the sky is your limit! But first, your administrator must configure what you can access using the Tableau Mobile app and the responsible Mobile Web experience.

Tableau has its mobile app just as every other business intelligence platform does, allowing users to access and interact with their Tableau dashboards and data on the go. You connect to your targeted instance of Tableau with your specific data as if you were accessing Tableau Cloud or Tableau Server. The mobile app is available for iOS and Android devices, allowing you to view, filter, and interact with your dashboards and data using your mobile devices.

With Tableau Mobile, you can stay connected to your data and make informed decisions from anywhere, at any time. The app also allows you to share your dashboards with others, collaborate in real time, and receive alerts and notifications when your data changes.

But to possess all these capabilities, you need to be sure that an App Lock is not in place, Offline Preview is enabled, and targeted mobile security policies are set. You take care of all these settings in the Mobile Setting area, shown in Figure 12-17.

FIGURE 12-17: Configuring Tableau environments for use with mobile devices.

5
The Part of Tens

IN THIS PART . . .

Understand how to configure the ten most popular function types used in creating Tableau calculations.

Explore ten of the most useful resources beyond this book to grow your Tableau expertise.

Chapter **13**

Ten Tableau Must-Know Function Types

I don't know about you, but I am not a fan of doing extra data crunching when it's unnecessary. Most big vendors agree that such activity is not a good use of time for folks like you and me. It is common practice for business intelligence and data analysis software to include functions, which provide a way to calculate and convert complex values easily.

This chapter aims to give you a Top 10 list of crucial function areas you might want to use when crunching. Rather than using extraordinarily painful formulas and converting data slowly with a pen and paper (or some other computer application), using these functions can save you lots of time and yield data value precision.

Number Functions

The number function is among the most heavily used in Tableau. Why? Because Tableau first and foremost builds data based on quantitative results. And how do you generate quantitative output? By using numbers. Table 13-1 lists key number functions to support creating numerical output.

TABLE 13-1   **Key Number Functions**

NAME	DESCRIPTIONS
ABS	Presents the absolute value of a number.
ACOS	Presents the arc cosine of a number.
ASIN	Presents the arc sine of a number.
ATAN	Presents the arc tangent of a number.
ATAN2	Presents the arc tangent of two numbers.
CEILING	Presents a rounded number up to the nearest integer.
COS	Presents the cosine of an angle.
COT	Presents the cotangent of an angle.
DEGREES	Converts an angle from radians to degrees.
DIV	Presents the integer portion of a division of the first value by the second value.
EXP	Presents a superscripted *e* raised to the power of a number.
FLOOR	Rounds a number down to the nearest integer.
HEXBINX	Positions an x/y coordinate to the x-value of the nearest hexagonal bin.
HEXBINY	Positions an x/y coordinate to the y-value of the nearest hexagonal bin.
LN	Presents the natural logarithm of a number.
LOG	Presents the logarithm of the first number using the second number as a base. If no base exists, then a base of 10 is used by default.
MAX	Presents the maximum of two inputs.
MIN	Presents the maximum of two inputs.
PI	Presents the numeric value of the constant PI.
POWER	Raises a number to the specified power. The ^ symbol may also be used.
RADIANS	Converts an angle from degrees to radians.
ROUND	Allows for the rounding of numbers to a specified number of digits.
SIGN	Presents the sign of a number.
SIN	Presents the sine of an angle.

NAME	DESCRIPTIONS
SQRT	Presents the square root of a number.
SQUARE	Presents the square of a number.
TAN	Presents the tangent of an angle.
ZN	Presents an expression if it is not null. Otherwise, the output is zero.

String Functions

String functions are helpful when classifying, seeking, or retrieving alphanumerical data in either one or more tables. For example, the number eleven is a string, whereas the number 11 is a numerical function. Table 13-2 lists the string functions that can help you create and retrieve alphanumeric data.

TABLE 13-2   **Key String Functions**

NAME	DESCRIPTION
ASCII	Presents ASCII code for the first character of a string.
CHAR	Presents the character encoded by the ASCII code.
CONTAINS	Presents TRUE if the string contains the substring.
ENDSWITH	Presents TRUE if the string ends with the substring.
FIND	Presents the index position of a substring in a string. If the substring is not present, the output is '0.'
FINDNTH	Presents the position of the nth occurrence of a substring within a string.
LEFT	Presents the left-most number of characters in the string.
LEN	Presents the length of the string.
LOWER	Presents a string with all lowercase characters.
LTRIM	Presents a string with any leading spaces removed.
MAX	Presents a maximum of two inputs.
MID	Presents string starting and ending at specified positions.
MIN	Presents the minimum of two inputs.

(continued)

TABLE 13-2 *(continued)*

NAME	DESCRIPTION
REPLACE	Presents a user the ability to search a string. If found, the string or substring is replaced with new data.
RIGHT	Presents the right-most number of characters in a string.
RTRIM	Presents a string with any trailing spaces removed.
SPACE	Presents a string made up of a specified number of repeated spaces.
SPLIT	Presents a substring from a string, using a delimiter character to divide the string into a sequence of tokens.
STARTSWITH	Presents true if a string starts with a substring.
TRIM	Presents a string with the leading and trailing spaces removed.
UPPER	Presents string with all uppercase characters.

Date Functions

Have you ever wanted to search for a specific month, date, year, or time within a dataset? Were the results overwhelming or laser-focused? Tableau has a specific function for capturing date and time-related data. You'll be able to identify a date function because there is heavy use of the pound (#) symbol.

REMEMBER

It is not uncommon for the date function to include the use of date_part, which is a constant string argument. When you need to use a targeted date and time parameter, include date_part, which may include the functions found in Table 13-3.

TABLE 13-3 **Key Date Functions**

NAME	DESCRIPTION
YEAR	Presents the year of the given date.
QUARTER	Presents quarter of the given date.
MONTH	Presents the month of the given date.
DAY	Presents the day of the month (1-31).
WEEK	Presents the week of the given date.
DATENAME	Presents the specified portion of a given date.

Type Conversion

Unsure of your string's very best type and need the data translated to fit a model? Look no further than the Type Conversion function. With a Type Conversion, any expression in a calculation can be converted to the appropriate data type. You may find, for example, STR( ), DATE( ), INT( ), and FLOAT. Here's a hypothetical scenario: Say you want to take the value of PI (3.14) and make it an integer. In that case, you put the value of 3.14 inside the INT( ), like this: INT(3.14). The result is an integer value equal to 3. To explore the most common Type Conversion functions, check out the list in Table 13-4.

TABLE 13-4   **Key Type Conversion Function**

NAME	DESCRIPTION
DATE	Presents a date given a number, string, or date expression.
DATETIME	Presents a datetime given a number, string, or date expression.
DATEPARSE	Presents a string to a datetime in the specified format.
FLOAT	Presents an argument as a floating-point number.
INT	Presents results rounded to the integer closest to zero.
STR	Presents all its arguments as a string.

Logical Functions

When you are trying to see whether a condition is true or false, yes or no, greater than or equal, less than or equal, or one that meets or does not meet a condition, logical functions should be your go-to for comparing data. Table 13-5 explores the essential logical functions used in Tableau.

TABLE 13-5   **Key Logical Functions**

NAME	DESCRIPTION
IN	Presents TRUE if any values in the first expression match values in the second.
AND	Tests two expressions that seek a specified match.
CASE	Specifies a field upon which to perform logical tests.

(continued)

TABLE 13-5 *(continued)*

NAME	DESCRIPTION
ELSE	Executes a default instruction after all other logical tests have failed.
ELSEIF	When an initial IF fails, ELSEIF checks additional conditions.
END	Closes chain of logical functions when placed at the end of the expression.
IF	Checks for a condition to be met between two expressions.
IFNULL	Presents values in the first expression. If null, the function presents the second expression.
IIF	Presents a specified value if TRUE, a specified value if FALSE, and a third value (or NULL) if unknown.
ISDATE	Presents TRUE if a given string is a valid date.
ISNULL	Presents TRUE if an expression doesn't contain valid data.
MAX	Presents maximum value in the specified list of values.
MIN	Presents minimum value in the specified list of values.
NOT	Executes logical negation on an expression.
OR	Executes logical disjunction on two expressions.
THEN	When a logical condition is met and accurate, the THEN function executes a specified instruction.
WHEN	Finds the first known value that can match an expression and displays the corresponding return.
ZN	Presents a value if it is not null; otherwise presents a value of zero.

Aggregate Functions

Suppose you need an easy way to summarize or change the specificity of the dataset. In that case, you'll likely want an output that produces a single value, not a laundry list of additional statistics. For example, to evaluate the total revenue generated across 12 months, you can use the SUM function to establish a single value. Then you can use other functions to determine the lowest (MIN), highest (MAX), and average (AVG) revenue generated in a single dataset. Table 13-6 illustrates the special aggregate functions available in Tableau.

TABLE 13-6 **Key Aggregate Function**

NAME	DESCRIPTION
ATTR	Presents the value of the expression if it has a single value for all rows. Otherwise, it presents an asterisk (*).
AVG	Presents the average of all the values in the expression.
COLLECT	Presents an aggregate calculation combining values in the argument field. Null values are ignored.
CORR	Presents the Pearson correlation coefficient of two expressions.
COUNT	Presents the number of items in a group.
COUNTD	Presents the number of distinct items in a group.
COVAR	Presents the sample covariance of two expressions.
COVARP	Presents the population covariance of two expressions.
MAX	Presents the maximum value in the expression.
MEDIAN	Presents the median of all values.
MIN	Presents the minimum of all values.
PERCENTILE	Presents the specified percentile of all values.
STDEV	Presents the sample standard deviation of all values.
STDEVP	Presents the population standard deviation of all values.
SUM	Presents the sum of all values.
VAR	Presents the sample variance of all values.
VARP	Presents the population variance of all values.

Pass-Through Functions (RAWSQL)

Pass-through functions, also called RAWSQL, allow users to send SQL expressions directly to a database. What's different with these functions is that Tableau does not require data interpretation. For example, if you use a database and Tableau doesn't even know it exists, you can use a pass-through function to call the data using these custom functions.

TECHNICAL STUFF

With pass-through functions, the data source, usually a database, doesn't know what field names are stored in Tableau. Because Tableau is not responsible for data interpretation using the SQL expression, you may experience many errors. The fix is the substitution of such syntax by inserting the correct field name or calculation into the calculation entered in Tableau using pass-through SQL. Table 13-7 illustrates thirteen examples of RAWSQL.

TABLE 13-7   **Key Pass-Through Functions**

NAME	DESCRIPTION
RAWSQL_BOOL	Presents a Boolean result from a SQL expression.
RAWSQL_DATE	Presents a date result from a SQL expression.
RAWSQL_INT	Presents an integer result from a SQL expression.
RAWSQL_REAL	Presents a numeric result from a SQL expression.
RAWSQL_SPATIAL	Presents a spatial from a SQL expression.
RAWSQL_STR	Presents a string from a SQL expression.
RAWSQLAGG_BOOL	Presents a Boolean result from an aggregate SQL expression.
RAWSQLAGG_DATE	Presents a date result from an aggregate SQL expression.
RAWSQLAGG_DATETIME	Presents a date and time result from an aggregate SQL expression.
RAWSQLAGG_INT	Presents an integer result from an aggregate SQL expression.
RAWSQLAGG_REAL	Presents a numeric result from an aggregate SQL expression.
RAWSQLAGG_STR	Presents a string from an aggregate SQL expression.

User Functions

Securing data might be your priority when specific users should see only a report. Or perhaps you want to target data to specific users or groups within an organization. A series of user-based functions allows for such filtering, which you can even use to help support row-level security. Table 13-8 provides examples of crucial user functions.

TABLE 13-8 **Key User Functions**

NAME	DESCRIPTION
FULLNAME	Presents the full name of the current user.
ISFULLNAME	Presents TRUE if the current user's full name matches the specified full name or FALSE if it does not match.
ISMEMBEROF	Presents TRUE if the person currently using Tableau is a group member that matches the given string.
ISUSERNAME	Presents TRUE if the current user's username matches the specified username or FALSE if it does not match.
USERDOMAIN	Presents the domain for the current user when the user is signed on to Tableau Server.
USERNAME	Presents the username for the current user.

Table Calculation Functions

In previous chapters, you tinkered with creating table data. What if you needed to create calculated fields based on data in a table? For example, say you wanted to order data from smallest to largest and then calculate the final value. You'd use a combination of Table Calculation Functions to achieve these specific outputs. In Table 13-9, you find Tableau's most common Table Calculation Functions.

TABLE 13-9 **Key Table Calculation Functions**

NAME	DESCRIPTION
FIRST	Presents the number of rows from the current row to the first row.
INDEX	Presents the index of the current row in the partition.
LAST	Presents the number of rows from the current to the last row in the partition.
LOOKUP	Presents the value of the expression in a target row as a relative offset from the current row.
MODEL_ EXTENSION_BOOL	Presents the Boolean value of an expression as predicted by a named model deployed on a TabPy external service. TabPy is Tableau's Python Server, an analytics extension to support using Python scripting for table-based calculations.
MODEL_ EXTENSION_INT	Presents the integer value of an expression as predicted by a named model deployed on a TabPy external service.

(continued)

TABLE 13-9 *(continued)*

NAME	DESCRIPTION
MODEL_ EXTENSION_REAL	Presents the actual value of an expression as predicted by a named model deployed on a TabPy external service.
MODEL_EXTENSION_ STRING	Presents the string value of an expression as predicted by a named model deployed on a TabPy external service.
MODEL_PERCENTILE	Presents a specified percentile predicted value for a target expression based on a predictor expression.
MODEL_QUANTILE	Presents a specified quantile predicted value for a target expression based on a predictor expression.
PREVIOUS_VALUE	Presents the value of this calculation in the previous row.
RANK	Presents the standard competition rank for the current row in the partition.
RANK_DENSE	Presents the dense rank for the current row in the partition.
RANK_MODIFIED	Presents the modified competition rank for the current row in the partition.
RANK_PERCENTILE	Presents the percentile rank for the current row in the partition.
RANK_UNIQUE	Presents the unique rank for the current row in the partition.
RUNNING_AVG	Presents the running average of the expression, from the first to the current row.
RUNNING_COUNT	Presents the running count of the given expression, from the first row in the partition to the current row.
RUNNING_MAX	Presents the running maximum in the given expression, from the first row in the partition to the current row.
RUNNING_MIN	Presents the running minimum in the given expression, from the first row in the partition to the current row.
RUNNING_SUM	Presents the running sum of the given expression, from the first row in the partition to the current row.
SIZE()	Presents the number of rows in the partition.
SCRIPT_BOOL	Presents a Boolean output from an expression.
SCRIPT_INT	Presents an integer result from an expression.
SCRIPT_REAL	Presents the actual result from an expression.
SCRIPT_STR	Presents a string result from an expression.

NAME	DESCRIPTION
TOTAL	Presents a total for the given expression in a table calculation partition.
WINDOW_AVG	Presents the average of the values within the window.
WINDOW_CORR	Presents the correlation between expressions within the window.
WINDOW_COUNT	Presents the count of the values within the window.
WINDOW_COVAR	Presents the sample covariance of the values within the window.
WINDOW_COVARP	Presents the population covariance of the values within the window.
WINDOW_MEDIAN	Presents the median of the values within the window.
WINDOW_MAX	Presents the maximum of the values within the window.
WINDOW_MIN	Presents the minimum of the values within the window.
WINDOW_ PERCENTILE	Presents the percentile of the values within the window.
WINDOW_STDEV	Presents the sample standard deviation of the values within the window.
WINDOW_STDEVP	Presents the population standard deviation of the values within the window.
WINDOW_SUM	Presents the sum of the values within the window.
WINDOW_VAR	Presents the sample variance of the values within the window.
WINDOW_VARP	Presents the population variance of the values within the window.

Spatial Functions

Tableau is unique because it offers specific functionality to evaluate spatial data. Unsurprisingly, targeted spatial functions assist in analyzing and combining spatial files across various file formats. The list in Table 13-10 explores essential spatial functions. Keep in mind that supported unit names are: meters ("meters," "metres" "m"), kilometers ("kilometers," "kilometres," "km"), miles ("miles" or "mi"), feet ("feet," "ft").

TABLE 13-10 **Key Spatial Functions**

NAME	DESCRIPTION
AREA	Presents the total surface area of spatial polygons in a unit of measure.
BUFFER	Presents the distance between two points in a unit of measure.
DISTANCE	Presents distance measurement between two points in a specified unit of measurement.
MAKELINE	Presents a line mark between two points.
MAKEPOINT	Converts data from latitude and longitude to a spatial object.
MAKEPOINT(X, Y, SRID)	Converts data from geographic coordinates to a spatial object.

Predictive Modeling Functions

Finally, the Predictive Modeling Functions make up Tableau's newest set of functions. Predictive modeling helps users generate predictions based on data points, which can be manipulated, visualized, and exported to other applications.

In the previous versions of Tableau, you were required to use tools outside Tableau, such as R and Python, to perform statistical calculation acrobatics. After you had a reasonable dataset, you could import the data into Tableau. No longer is that the case! As of version 2020.4, you can select data targets across multiple sources and identify predictors by updating the variables. The result is your ability to visualize multiple models and datasets using predictive indicators. In Tableau, you can filter, aggregate, and transform predictive data using formulas that allow you to auto-calculate data in one or more views. The two primary functions that data scientists use most often with Tableau are MODEL_QUANTILE and MODEL_PERCENTILE. Table 13-11 describes the benefits of using both for predictive analysis.

TABLE 13-11 **Key Predictive Modeling Functions**

NAME	DESCRIPTION
MODEL_QUANTILE	Presents a specified quantile predicted value for a target expression based on a predictor expression.
MODEL_PERCENTILE	Presents a specified percentile predicted value for a target expression based on a predictor expression.

Chapter **14**

Ten Helpful Tableau Resources

I f you go to any of the major search engines and type the word *Tableau*, the search engine presents you with tens of millions of URLs resulting from a single query. If you are like me, you may review the first page or two, click a few interesting links, and then close your browser.

The truth is that most of the resources you'll need are found on the Tableau website or managed by Tableau's marketing team on social media platforms. In this final chapter, I provide a list of indispensable resources for anyone using Tableau. Let the countdown begin.

Tableau Free Trials

In the first chapter, I warn you that Tableau is pretty expensive per user. Depending on the technical need, you may not require all the bells and whistles to create, edit, and view data. Tableau allows users to take a test drive of their software for 14 days. Afterward, you can extend the trial, but some features will no longer be enabled. Free trials are a great way to get your feet wet by trying the exercises in this book. And, of course, if you have a real dataset and want to see how Tableau can handle it, the trial gives you the perfect window of opportunity.

You can find the latest Tableau trials at `https://www.tableau.com/products/trial`.

Tableau Training

Tableau is a complex product. As mentioned elsewhere, Tableau is not a single product but rather an ecosystem of products. This book is a primer on Tableau Desktop, Tableau Prep, and Tableau Online, but to get the full benefits, you'll want to learn many more facets of these products. Tableau has its training community, but I find that the courses on platforms such as Udemy, LinkedIn Learning, and Plural Insights offer great opportunities for more learning.

The training platform with the most courses available is undoubtedly Udemy. To augment your knowledge with more than 1500 courses, go to the Udemy Marketplace at `https://www.udemy.com/courses/search/?src=ukw&q=tableau`.

Tableau's official training focuses heavily on three certification paths. The training offers some free primer courses, but most Tableau training requires a subscription to gain access. To access Tableau's training catalog, go to `https://www.tableau.com/learn`.

Tableau Help Documentation

I can't stress enough that Tableau has many details that you'll need to seek help with, especially when it comes to data manipulation. Although I've covered most of the functions, which should make your life so much easier in completing complex data analysis, Tableau documentation gets into the weeds. You'll see walkthrough examples and use cases across the Tableau product stack that are not included in this book. The Help Documentation home page is categorized by product. As you drill down, you access the most relevant content for a specific product, such as Tableau Desktop or Tableau Prep.

You can find the Tableau Documentation site at `https://www.tableau.com/support/help`.

Tableau Resource Gallery

Similar to the official training website, Tableau has a centralized repository for video tutorials (which in most cases link to YouTube), introductory use cases, free e-learning resources, and on-demand webinars. Although the name implies that the Tableau Resource Gallery is a centralized location for all Tableau content, think of this as your cockpit to accessing all the free training and product assets to help you immerse yourself in Tableau.

ON THE
WEB

The Tableau Resource Gallery is accessible at `https://www.tableau.com/resources`.

Tableau Community

Every IT vendor nowadays seems to offer to communicate and collaborate with others about their product challenges. Tableau is no different. Yes, you can pay for support to walk you through your problems. But platforms such as the Tableau Community have tens of thousands of users who probably have the same issues you might be experiencing. Before you use paid support, consider checking out the Community as your first stop.

ON THE
WEB

To access the Tableau Community, go to `https://community.tableau.com/s/`.

Tableau Newsroom

Tableau is an evolving product that is constantly changing. Tableau Server, Cloud, and Desktop are updated quarterly, and Tableau Prep Builder is updated monthly. You'll want to visit the Newsroom from time to time to see posts about updates that offer a customer-centric view, not a laundry list of fixes and enhancements. In other words, Tableau humanizes product updates. The Newsroom is also a hub for learning about customers using Tableau, accessing profiles on Tableau experts, and following the activity that is part of Tableau's non-profit foundation. The content on this site is more use-case–driven than technical.

ON THE
WEB

To access the Newsroom, go to `https://www.tableau.com/about/newsroom`.

Tableau Academic Programs

At the very beginning of the book, I mentioned that Tableau offers free (you read that correctly) software to students and educators. Since its start, Tableau has shared the singular message that it wants to focus on closing the data literacy gap. Data is at the heart of almost every job in a knowledge worker economy. Using tools powered by Tableau can help folks do their jobs successfully. And where should data education start? In the classroom, of course.

Tableau licenses a gratis copy of Tableau Desktop, Tableau Prep Builder, and an online account to learners for a single year. You can renew the account with a caveat at the end of your license period. The software must be used for academic purposes only, not to complete professional endeavors.

REMEMBER

You undergo a qualification process to access the Tableau Academic license, which includes having an .edu email address. If your institution does not have a .edu address, an alternative is to provide proof of enrollment or employment at the academic institution. It takes seven to ten calendar days for Tableau to validate your credentials and issue the academic license.

ON THE WEB

The registration process is easy. You do, however, have to provide institutional information when registering. To get Tableau's academic license, go to https://www.tableau.com/community/academic.

Tableau Templates and Dashboards

Let me guess: You've got an abundance of reports and a boatload of key performance indicators (KPIs), and you require a single view of all these data points. Sound familiar? You bet! When I create dashboards, I am as concerned with the aesthetics and data placement as I am with the data output itself. That's because, like a photo, a dashboard speaks a thousand words based on what indicators you incorporate. Tableau has created prebuilt report templates and highly configurable, aesthetically pleasing dashboards to augment the standard desktop, data prep, and online experience. The range of output possibilities is extensive, as you can see if you go to https://www.tableau.com/data-insights/dashboard-showcase.

Tableau Accelerators

If you are new to Tableau, you are likely coming from business productivity applications such as Microsoft Excel or Google Sheets. Organizations often create industry-specific templates full of formulas, functions, and programmatic code. Would you be interested if you could get prebuilt application accelerators and a targeted view of data capabilities from dashboards to programmatic scenarios? Thought so!

An accelerator is a targeted application with prebuilt dashboards to solve specific department, industry, and enterprise-wide challenges. Targeted templates for the department include Sales Pipeline, Web Traffic, Financial Management, Call Center, and Project Management. Similarly, Tableau offers industry accelerators, such as Patient Records, Citizen Serve Requests, and Hospitality Management.

ON THE WEB

To access the entire Accelerator catalog, go to `https://www.tableau.com/solutions/exchange/accelerators`.

Tableau YouTube Channel

I've saved the Tableau YouTube channel as the last resource because most people don't often associate Tableau with YouTube. Tableau has a vast social media presence, however, posting several times a day on Twitter and maintaining a strong presence on other platforms such as Facebook and LinkedIn.

Of all the platforms, YouTube has the most to offer. Every time Tableau has a webinar, it is posted to the YouTube Channel. You can view hundreds of keynote speeches from Tableau conferences on YouTube. Tableau also posts new product demos there.

TIP

Make no mistake, when you go to the Tableau website, a majority of the videos are embedded directly from the Tableau YouTube channel. Instead of scouring the Tableau website for a specific video topic, go straight to the YouTube channel for fast access, because all public Tableau events seem to be located here.

ON THE WEB

If you search YouTube, you'll come up with many rogue channels claiming to be the official Tableau channel. To access the authentic Tableau software channel, go to `https://www.youtube.com/c/tableausoftware/`.

Index

C

calculated fields
  Analysis menu options, 139
  creating, 200–202
  formatting, 202–203
  overview, 200
  syntax of, 204–205
calculated value filter, 102
Calculation Field Editor, 201
calculations. *See also* functions
  calculated fields, creating, 200–202
  in crosstabs, 192–194
  in data flows, 104–105
  essential components of, 203
  formatting, 202–203
  in join clauses, 76
  syntax of, 204–205
  types of, 197–200
canvas, Tableau Desktop, 164
captions, 226–227, 232–234
cards, Tableau Desktop, 157–160
CASE function, 281
categorical legends, 226–227
categorizing fields, 118–120
CEILING function, 278
Chabot, Christian, 27
Change Parameter option, Action submenu, 152
Change Set Values option, Action submenu, 152
changes in Input pane, viewing, 89
CHAR function, 279
charts
  area, 180–182
  bar, 171–173
  bubble, 175–178
  bullet, 189–190
  dual combination, 182–184
  Gantt, 188–189
  line, 178–180
  pie, 170–171
circles, 175–178
cleaning data
  in flows, 96–97
  overview, 30
  text formatting, 103–104
cleanliness of data source, 65
Clear option, toolbar, 146
clipboard data, working with, 81–84
Cloud, Tableau. *See* Tableau Cloud
Cloud consumption license, 50
clusters, applying, 209
collaboration, 46–47, 53. *See also* dashboards; stories
COLLECT function, 283
collections, Tableau Cloud, 254–255
color coding, 76, 191–192, 225
color palette, for accessibility, 226, 228
columns
  pivoting data, 124–126
  structuring data, 117–118
Community, Tableau, 291
comparison operators, 205
condition filtering, 151
conditional operators, 205
configuring
  dashboards, 214–218
  data flows, 88–89
Connect button, 58–59
Connect panes, 61, 63
Connected Apps, Tableau Cloud, 273
connecting data sources
  data structure differences, 60
  in Desktop or Prep, 61–63, 162–163
  in flows, 86
  options, 58–61
requesting new connectors, 64
  in Server and Online, 63–64
Connections pane, Tableau Prep, 42
connectors, requesting new, 64
constant line, applying, 209
CONTAINS function, 279
Content Type menu, Favorites page, 248–249
context, adding to flows, 96
continuous area chart, 180–181
continuous data, 16, 119–120
continuous line chart, 178
copying and pasting data, 81–84
core (server-based) consumption model, 49
cores consumed, 50
CORR function, 283
COS function, 278
COT function, 278
COUNT function, 283
COUNTD function, 283
COVAR function, 283
COVARP function, 283
COVID-19 Google Search dataset, 123–124
Creator license, 2, 36–37, 49–54
CRM Analytics, 34–35, 211
crosstabs, converting visualizations to, 191–194
.csv files, 92–93, 109
Custom Calculation, 104–105
custom data roles, 107–108
custom distribution bands, applying, 209
custom reference bands, applying, 209
custom reference line, applying, 209
Customer Relationship Management (CRM), 34–35, 211, 271–272
customer satisfaction, 9

About the Author

Jack Hyman is the founder of HyerTek (www.hyertek.com), a Washington, D.C. based technology and training services firm specializing in cloud computing, business intelligence, learning management, and enterprise application advisory needs for federal, state, and private sector organizations. During his extensive IT career, Jack has led U.S. federal government agencies and global enterprises through multiyear technology transformation projects. Before founding HyerTek, Jack worked for Oracle and IBM. He has authored many books, provided peer-review guidance for scholarly journals, and developed training courseware with an emphasis on Microsoft technologies. Since 2004, he has sat on the faculty at George Washington University, American University, and the University of the Cumberlands. Jack holds a Ph.D. in Information Systems from Nova Southeastern University.

Dedication

To my children, Jeremy and Emily: I hope you always love learning as much as I do.

Author's Acknowledgments

Many folks were involved in getting the second edition of *Tableau For Dummies* into your hands. Thanks to Executive Editor Steve Hayes and Senior Managing Editor Kristie Pyles for allowing me to write this book (and so many other Dummies projects over the years). A great big thanks to Project Manager Susan Christophersen for keeping me on track throughout this project. A hearty thanks to Technical Editor Ken Hess for ensuring that the content in this edition of *Tableau For Dummies* remained accurate and technically sound. Also, thanks to Carole Jelen of Waterside Productions for bringing me yet another exciting project to share with the world. And finally, thanks to my wife, Debbie, and kids, Jeremy and Emily, for allowing me to take on yet another extensive book project.

Publisher's Acknowledgments

Executive Editor: Steven Hayes

Senior Managing Editor: Kristie Pyles

Project Manager and Copy Editor:
  Susan Christophersen

Technical Editor: Ken Hess

Production Editor: Mohammed Zafar Ali

Cover Image: © Maksim Kabakou/Shutterstock